Inventing Better Schools

Inventing Better Schools

An Action Plan for Educational Reform

Phillip C. Schlechty

JOSSEY-BASS
A Wiley Company
San Francisco

Jossey-Bass books and products are available through most bookstores. To contact Jossey-Bass directly, call (888) 378-2537, fax to (800) 605-2665, or visit our website at www.josseybass.com.

Substantial discounts on bulk quantities of Jossey-Bass books are available to corporations, professional associations, and other organizations. For details and discount information, contact the special sales department at Jossey-Bass.

TCF Manufactured in the United States of America on Lyons Falls Turin Book. This paper is acid-free and 100 percent totally chlorine-free.

Library of Congress Cataloging-in-Publication Data

Schlechty, Phillip C.
    Inventing better schools : an action plan for educational reform /
Phillip C. Schlechty. — 1st ed.
        p.   cm. — (The Jossey-Bass education series)
    Includes bibliographical references and index.
    ISBN 0–7879–0339–6 (cloth)
    ISBN 0-7879-5610-4 (paper)
    1. School management and organization—United States.
    2. Educational change—United States.   I. Title.   II. Series.
    LB2805.S35   1997
    371.2'00973—dc21   96–45876

FIRST EDITION
HB Printing   10 9 8 7 6 5
PB Printing   10 9 8 7 6 5 4 3 2 1

The Jossey-Bass Education Series

Contents

Preface

In 1989, I wrote a book entitled *Schools for the 21st Century: Leadership Imperatives for Educational Reform* (Schlechty, 1990). Many who read *Schools for the 21st Century* have said something like: "All right, we're persuaded. Now what do we do?" The present book is written partially in response to readers of that first book.

The ideas upon which this book is based are the same as those that guided my earlier work. The careful reader will, however, notice some subtle, and some not so subtle, changes in the arguments I presented in 1990. For example, in 1989 I was just beginning to appreciate the power of electronically based technologies as a condition driving school reform. In fact, I was just beginning to appreciate the power of computers as a tool to be used in the effort to reform our schools. Today, I see the presence of electronic technologies as the major reason schools must change and as a major tool to be used in bringing that change about.

What I have to say in the following pages is much more specific than was the case when I wrote *Schools for the 21st Century*. Although I still refuse to provide a list of prescriptions for "saving our schools," the pages that follow do contain specific suggestions for action and many specific questions to guide that action.

In addition to the requests of the audience of my earlier book, there is another reason for this book. My more recent work in schools and my conversations with local leaders across the nation convince me that change in schools is much more urgently needed than most teachers and school administrators seem to realize. Indeed, I believe that if schools are not changed in dramatic ways very soon, public schools will not be a vital component of America's system of education in the twenty-first century. Because of this belief, and because I believe that vital public schools are critical to the survival of American democracy, I also believe that anyone who has something to offer that may be used constructively on behalf of improving public schools should step forward. I believe I have something to offer.

Our schools are better than most critics say, but our modern school system is less able to meet the demands of contemporary society than were schools in the past. It is not true that schools have lowered their standards. The problem is that our society no longer can tolerate schools that produce so many students who meet only the lower standards schools have always had and so few who meet the higher standards schools have had as well. Many Americans, including too many educators, do not know these things, or if they do, they choose not to believe them.

In the past, high-quality academic performance was expected of only a relatively few of the students who graduated from school: usually those who were awarded the grade of A, and sometimes B. For the rest of the students, marginal academic performance was acceptable as long as they demonstrated a willingness to do the kinds of things that served the factory system well (for example, tolerating a great deal of boredom with a minimum amount of fuss). Today, both the demands of citizenship in an information-saturated environment and the demands of the emerging workplace make it essential that nearly all students perform academically at a level at which, a generation ago, it would have been assumed that only a few could and would perform.

I am not an apologist for the schools as they presently operate. Indeed, I find those inside the education establishment who believe that the schools would be just fine if only we had better parents, more well-behaved students, and smaller classes just as dangerous to the future of democratic education as are those outside the establishment who would abandon the public schools for some privatized alternative. What we need are educators who understand that our schools are not nearly as good as they must be to survive, even though they are much better than they ever were in the past.

Goals

I have written this book with the following goals in mind. First, I hope to frame the problems confronting schools so that those who live out their lives in schools and those who depend on them can see a reasonable prospect of doing something about those problems without abandoning public education and the democratic values for which the public schools stand.

Second, I hope to help the reader see the connection between what happens in district offices and the community at large and what happens between teachers and students in classrooms. Indeed, I hope to persuade the reader who is not already persuaded that one of the keys to reforming schools and classrooms is the creation of the district- and community-level capacity to support that reform.

Third, I hope to provide the reader with propositions and questions that can be used as tools to enhance the capacity of school districts to support and sustain reform at the level of schools and classrooms.

Fourth, I intend to suggest strategies for redesigning schools so that they are more clearly focused on providing quality work for students and on helping students design such work so that the students become the true focus of all decisions made in and around schools.

Finally, I hope that the arguments presented prove useful in ensuring that teachers have the tools and support they need in working with students to design and deliver the highest-quality academic work that it is possible to create.

Significant Influences

After an early career as a teacher, I pursued a career as a university professor. In 1976, after completing a book on school organization and attaining the status of professor, I realized that I had made a mistake. I liked the university, but I found life in the public schools much more exciting. About twenty years ago, I began seeking ways to work more closely with public schools. After serving as the executive director of the Metrolina Teacher Education Consortium, a special assistant to the superintendent in the Charlotte-Mecklenburg, North Carolina, Schools, and the founding executive director of the Gheens Professional Development Academy in Louisville, Kentucky, I decided it was time to create an organization focused exclusively on providing support to those who are leading school reform, that is, superintendents, principals, and classroom teachers. This organization, the Center for Leadership in School Reform, which was started with considerable support from the BellSouth Foundation, the Panasonic Foundation, and the Annie E. Casey Foundation, has made it possible for me to work with schools throughout the United States and Canada.

As a result of these experiences, I learned much about myself, something about the communication of complex ideas in understandable terms, and something about the management of change. I learned, for example, that theory could be translated into practice through the conscious use of metaphors. Theoreticians are not always going to be happy with the translations, but if ideas are to move action, then they must be made accessible to those who will be called on to use them.

I also learned that there is a difference between arguments and data intended to convince universal audiences and those intended to persuade particular audiences (see House, 1980). Researchers and theoreticians must convince universal audiences; reformers must persuade particular audiences. As an advocate of school reform, I am much more interested in persuading practicing educators that they can and should reform America's schools than I am in convincing members of the academy of the universality of my arguments. Therefore, my arguments and analysis do not purport to be universal. They are time-bound and derive as much from my own experience as from disciplined research.

This book is written for an audience of men and women of action: superintendents, principals, teachers, activist parents, civic leaders, and business leaders, for they are the reformers—if there is to be reform. Consultants, professors, and researchers are not reformers. What we should strive to be are sources of assistance to reformers. The real reformers are those who are on the firing line every day.

In my close association with these reform leaders, I have also learned that men and women of action are likely to trust people first and the ideas people advance second. If it appears likely that the person advancing an idea will abandon those who try to act on it when controversy arises and careers are at risk, then men and women of action will turn to others for ideas, even if these ideas are not quite so compelling.

From experiences in boardrooms and legislative halls, I have learned that too many people with ideas seem to lack the intestinal fortitude to engage in the degrading confrontations that must sometimes be tolerated in the real world of school reform. When the partisan forces show up in the boardroom, many people with ideas retreat to the anteroom, obfuscate the issues with jargon, or filibuster in professorial tones. Perhaps this is the reason people of action sometimes need to be convinced that men and women who make their living promulgating ideas deserve to be trusted.

Some of what I have learned is the result of failures I have had in my efforts; some is the result of the successes I have experienced. Most of what I have learned, however, comes from careful observation of others as they have attempted to bring about change in the school systems and school buildings they are called on to lead. This learning has, of course, been supplemented by books I have read about change and leadership and by research I and others have done on the subject. I hope the reader will find what I have learned useful.

Organization of the Book

The first three chapters of this book are intended to help the reader understand how I have come to the conclusions I have regarding the condition of education in America. I generally agree with Berliner and Biddle (1995), who, in their book *The Manufactured Crisis,* argue that the data do not support the assertion that America's schools have deteriorated in quality or that American public schools are inferior to private schools or schools in other nations. I do not agree, however, that the crisis in education is primarily the product of public ignorance about educational matters and ill-intended manipulation on the part of some reformers, educational critics, and the press.

Certainly there is some truth to the fact that the crisis that many Americans perceive to be present is contrived, but that is not to say that no crisis exists in American education. *There is a crisis and it is real.* Indeed, if the public really understood the problem, the public outcry for change in our schools would be more intense than is now the case. Furthermore, if educators themselves more fully understood the problems they face, they would feel a much greater sense of urgency about changing schools than many now seem to feel.

My goal in these chapters, therefore, is to frame the argument about American education in a way that is different from the way such arguments are conventionally framed. In reading these chapters, the reader will find little information or many facts with which he or she has not had some prior acquaintance. What the reader may find are new ways of thinking about and giving meaning to these facts.

Chapter Four sets forth a way of thinking about schools that is somewhat unconventional. However, those who have read some of my earlier writing (for example, Schlechty, 1990) or the work of Theodore Sizer (1984) or William Glasser (1986) will hear much that is familiar. Readers from outside the schools who are familiar with the work of W. Edwards Deming, Philip Crosby, Peter Drucker, and others who have influenced or are influencing the thinking of America's business leaders will find much that is familiar as well.

Chapter Five, "Beliefs, Vision, and Mission," clarifies and amplifies some ideas I set forth in *Schools for the 21st Century*. However, as the reader will see, I have refined my thinking regarding these matters since 1989. Because one cannot think well about inventing new schools without considering the centrality of beliefs to this invention, this chapter ensures that beliefs are placed where they belong in the educational debate: right in the center of things.

Chapters Six and Seven present the argument that the greatest barrier to school reform is the fact that most school districts do not have the capacity to support reform at the level of school buildings and classrooms. This, too, may seem unconventional, for most critics of education in America see the "bloated bureaucracy" of the central office as a part of the problem. Indeed, as happens in business, restructuring school systems has come to be synonymous with downsizing the central office or abolishing it altogether. I believe, however, that in modern society the school district, rather than the schoolhouse, is the only level at which communities (as opposed to isolated neighborhoods and selected sets of parents) can be involved in the educational argument. For that reason alone, district offices are worth preserving, unless, of course, we want to give up on the idea that the community as well as parents should have an interest in the schools and what is learned there. But there is another reason for preserving the central office.

Much that is needed to support and sustain school reform at a building level is not located, and cannot be located, at the level of the school building or the neighborhood. The most obvious illustration is the taxing authority. If schools are to be able to change, they must have the financial support they need to survive. The taxpayers of the community, not just the parents, pay for schools. If the community is to pay, it must be informed about what it is paying for and why. Few schools, especially in large urban areas, can regularly access the media to make sure that their story is told. Properly managed district offices can be a tremendous help in this regard.

Similarly, the training and development needs of schools cannot always be met by appealing to the resources available within the local school, and no amount of decentralization will change this fact. Even now, many individual schools waste a great deal of money flying in an outside guru for a one-day visit, only to have the same guru show up in the school down the street the following week. If nothing else, a little coordination of effort would help. The issue of district capacity is much more profound than either of these illustrations might indicate, even though the points made by these illustrations are not trivial ones.

Chapter Eight may be the most important chapter. Here, I try to show how the properties of school districts affect the operation of schools and classrooms. My intent is to bring greater clarity to the term *systemic reform* and to show what might be involved if systemic reform were to occur.

In Chapters Nine and Ten, I attempt to demonstrate the power of thinking systemically about schools in order to bring about changes in what is taught and what is learned. I hope the reader will become convinced that the key to answering the critics of public schools lies in the ability of teachers to quit working on students and to start working on the work students are provided and encouraged to undertake. I also hope that the reader becomes convinced that this cannot happen until and unless total systems change. Teachers often cannot do what they know they should do in the present system precisely because the present system was designed to encourage other things.

Chapter Eleven presents a general discussion of the problems and prospects of leading systemic change. In this chapter, I discuss different types of change—procedural, technical, and structural-cultural (systemic) change—and show how each of these kinds of changes places different demands on systems and on those who lead these systems. The chapter also discusses the kinds of lessons that must be taught by leaders if change is to be implemented effectively and makes a few observations about the different responses different individuals make to structural-cultural change, including some suggestions about what these responses might mean for change leaders.

Chapter Twelve is an effort to deliver on what the subtitle of this book promises: an action plan for school reform. It is not my intent here to prescribe particular programs or recommend particular reforms, but instead to demonstrate how the ideas, questions, and tools presented in the preceding eleven chapters might be used by those who must make decisions about the direction reform should take and the way it will be given direction.

Finally, the appendixes present two concrete illustrations of work being done in school districts where the idea of systemic reform is being taken seriously.

Taken as a whole, this book is intended to help the reader think through the issues that must be confronted if America's children are to have the schools they deserve. I hope I have succeeded in my effort.

January 1997

Phillip C. Schlechty
Louisville, Kentucky

Acknowledgments

This book, like most books, is the result of a great deal of lonely effort on my part along with a great deal of inspiration and support from many others. I will not endeavor to list all of those who have supported and inspired me over the years. However, I would like to acknowledge some who have provided specific help on this book.

First, I would like to thank the entire staff at the Center for Leadership in School Reform: Ron Barber, Dennis Boswell, John Campbell, Rick Campbell, Joan Cole, Jack Edwards, Marilyn Hohmann, Judythe Hummel, Tom Johnson, Robert Nolte, Darlene Settles, Linda Shelor, Barbara Smith, George Thompson, Margaret Vowels, and Joan Wimsatt. I am especially indebted to Hugh Cassell, who edits all my material, and to Tena Lutz, my assistant and a person upon whom I depend for support in nearly every professional activity I undertake.

A number of superintendents with whom I work have also been kind enough to read and react to this book in manuscript form. The book is much improved by their efforts. Those I would especially like to acknowledge are Dennis Buzzelli, Donald Dyck, Lee Eastwood, Gayle Ecton, Gerry House, Thomas Seidenberger, and Eric Smith.

I would also like to take this opportunity to acknowledge the impact on my life of three men for whom I have never found an appropriate forum in which to say "thank you." The first is Robert Jewett, my longtime adviser, mentor, and friend. Even though I am now sixty years old, I continue to value the advice of my elders. Bob Jewett was my adviser in undergraduate school and graduate school. He made graduate study possible for me and sociology inviting to me. More important, he has stuck with me over the years, up to and including helping me with questions I have had to work through to write the present book.

In the process of making the transition from the university back to the public schools, I had the opportunity to work with two other individuals who did much to shape my life and my way of thinking about the process of change. The first is William Self, whom I first met as a professor and with whom I worked when he became associate dean and then dean of the School of Education at the University of North Carolina at Chapel Hill. (Prior to being a professor, he was superintendent of schools in the Charlotte-Mecklenburg Schools, where he guided the school district through the early implementation of a court-ordered busing plan.) The second was Jay Robinson, at the time the superintendent of the Charlotte-Mecklenburg Schools, since retired after serving as a vice president of the University of North Carolina, and now the chairman of the North Carolina State Board of Education.

From Bill Self, I learned much about the importance of planning and patience. I also learned that most of the good things and the bad that happen in any major effort to bring about change happen by accident. Many, if not most, critical events in the change process are outside the control of those who are supposed to be leading the change. However, those who plan seem to have more good accidents than bad, and those who have *patience* seem to have more control than do those who try to force events beyond their limits.

From Jay Robinson, I learned that the most important attributes of a change leader are clear vision, persistence, integrity, and *impatience* with inaction. Change, at least systemic change, does not happen unless someone forces the issue. But Jay also taught me that those who are bent on forcing issues must tolerate setbacks with good humor while constantly probing for new points of attack, new approaches, and new allies. Between them, Self and Robinson taught me to be *patiently impatient,* or at least to use all of the little patience I have.

As those who know me recognize, I value very much what I have learned in my work with teachers, administrators, and school board members in the United States and Canada. I cannot name all of these people, but I am indebted to them. Sometimes I have not liked what I have been taught, but the lessons have always been valuable.

Finally, to learn what I needed to know to write this book, I have been away from home and in many schools, school districts, boardrooms, and legislative halls. My wife, Shelia, seldom complains about my absence, and she often holds up my end of our domestic agreement as well as her own. Thanks, Shelia!

The Author

Phillip C. Schlechty is founder and CEO of the Center for Leadership in School Reform and author of *Reform in Teacher Education: A Sociological View* (1989), *Schools for the 21st Century: Leadership Imperatives for Educational Reform* (1990), and *Shaking Up the Schoolhouse: How to Support and Sustain Educational Innovation* (2000), as well as numerous other publications. Formerly a professor at the University of North Carolina at Chapel Hill and executive director of the Jefferson County Public Schools/Gheens Professional Development Academy, an organization he conceived and instituted, he serves as an adviser to many school districts in the United States and Canada and conducts seminars and training sessions for superintendents, school board members, union leaders, principals, teachers, and parent groups.

Schlechty is one of the nation's most sought-after speakers on topics related to school reform. Business groups, as well as educators, find his perspective useful and understandable.

He received his B.S., M.A., and Ph.D. degrees from The Ohio State University.

Born near Rossburg, Ohio, Schlechty has two daughters. He and his wife reside in Louisville, Kentucky.

Inventing Better Schools

Chapter One

The Never-Ending Story

One need not be an alarmist to see that America's system of public education is being threatened as it never has been before. Public concern about the quality of education is at an all-time high, and public confidence in the ability of educators to address these concerns is at an all-time low. It is not, however, declining performance that threatens America's schools; rather, it is the failure of America's leaders to properly frame the problems that beset these schools. Too few leaders understand that America's schools have never performed as we would now have them perform, and of those who do understand these facts, too many behave defensively when confronted with the charge that today's schools are not meeting the needs of modern society.

Ignorance of the history of America's schools leads many to seek solutions where solutions cannot be found. Some would return to a past golden era when all parents were supportive and most children learned what it was intended that they learn. These people do not seem to know that there never was a golden era. America's schools have always been suspect as centers of academic excellence (see Hofstadter, 1963, pp. 299–322). For others, a misreading of the history of school reform leads to the conclusion that the public schools cannot be reformed and should, therefore, be abandoned in favor of privately run schools. These people do not seem to understand or appreciate the contribution America's schools have made, and continue to make, to the continuation of democracy in America as well as to the quality of life of individual men and women.

Both those who would take the schools back to the "good old days" and those who would replace public education with some

1

form of privatization are wrongheaded, and because they are wrong in their analysis, they are also wrong in the recommendations they make for improving schools.

The Danger of Denial

Unfortunately, too many of those who understand the "facts" about our schools use that understanding to justify the present performance of our schools. Teachers are especially prone to respond defensively to criticism of the schools. For example, according to a recently published report, "Teachers say that given societal pressures and a lack of parental involvement, the schools are doing as well as possible" (Farkas and Johnson, 1996, p. 11). This same study indicates that most teachers believe that for schools to improve, the changes that must occur are largely external to the schools; what is needed are better parents, better-disciplined and better-mannered students, smaller classes, and more money.

It is not surprising that so few educators show great enthusiasm for school reform and that many find great comfort in blaming forces beyond their control for what they are experiencing. Neither is it surprising that many, if not most, teachers are skeptical, if not cynical, about the need for and prospects of school reform. (For a description of the depth of this skepticism, see Farkas and Johnson, 1996.) As Richard Hofstadter has observed, the history of school reform is a "history of complaint" (1963, p. 30). Each generation discovers what the generation before it discovered: something is wrong with America's schools and someone ought to do something about it. And each time reformers try to bring about change, the reforms fail to deliver what has been promised (see, for example, Cuban, 1992).

The fact remains however, that even though critics of America's schools are often wrong in their analysis of what is wrong with these schools, they are not wrong when they assert that the performance of America's schools is inadequate to meet the needs of modern society. *Something is fundamentally wrong with America's system of education. Too few children develop the academic skills they need to develop, and too many children leave school without having developed the skills, attitudes, and habits of mind that will equip them for life in the twenty-first century.* But what is wrong with our schools has been wrong for a long time. As Hofstadter has also observed, one of the paradoxes of American life is "that in a society so passionately intent upon education, the yield of our educational system has been . . . a constant disappointment" (1963, pp. 394–395).

Today, the demands that schools be improved have reached new highs. The level of frustration with schools is so great, in fact, that increasing numbers of citizens seem willing to seriously consider solutions that if enacted would lead to the abandonment of America's commitment to public schools. If public schools are to remain a vital part of the American system of education, those who are committed to public schools need to have a clear-eyed view of the situation they confront. My intent in this chapter is to help to clarify the situation that confronts reform-minded educators today.

The Good Old Days

Anyone who believes that everything was fine in the good old days should consider statements like the following, taken from different time periods:

[1870]: They [the elementary schools] are mainly in the hands of ignorant unskilled teachers. The children are fed upon mere husks of knowledge. They leave the school for the broad theater of life without discipline; without mental power or moral stamina. . . . Poor schools and poor teachers are a majority throughout the country. Multitudes of schools are so poor that it would be as well for the country if they were closed. . . . They afford the sad spectacle of ignorance engaged in a stupendous fraud of self perpetuation at public expense. . . . Hundreds of our American schools are little less than undisciplined juvenile mobs [Phelps, 1870, pp. 13, 17].

[1892]: When we were boys, boys had to do a little work in school. They were not coaxed, they were hammered. Spelling, writing and arithmetic were not electives, and you had to learn. In these more fortunate times, elementary education has become in many places a vaudeville show. The child must be kept amused and learns what he pleases. Many sage teachers scorn the old fashioned rudiments, and it seems to be regarded as between misfortune and a crime for a child to learn to read [*New York Sun*, 1892, reported in Valentine, 1952, p. 354].

[1931]: It is unnecessary to say that we are in the midst of great educational uncertainty, one probably unparalleled at any past time. There is nothing accepted as axiomatic, nothing beyond the possibility of questioning, and few things that are not actually attacked. Conservatives who urge return to former standards and practices and radicals who criticize present conditions agree at least on one point: neither party is satisfied with things as they are. It is not merely this or that method for securing educational results that is attacked, but ideals and aims are under fire [Dewey, 1931, p. 1].

The fact is that a very good case can be made that not only are America's schools not worse than they once were but, in fact, are better than they have ever been. Consider the following:

- In 1945, only four out of ten Americans who entered school completed four years of high school. In 1993, more than eight out of ten had completed high school. And, as Figure 1.1 indicates, these gains have been reflected in increased post–high school academic attainment as well.
- Although the level of functional literacy in America is substantially less than is desirable, America is clearly among the world's leaders in terms of the number of adults who can read. The adult literacy problem in America is a *functional* literacy problem; *literal* illiteracy has virtually been eliminated. Almost all Americans can read (see Figure 1.2). Unfortunately, many (perhaps 50 percent or more) still do not read very well.
- In the not-too-distant past, many Americans could not read at all and many read poorly. This fact was clearly reflected in the way the U.S. Army went about testing recruits in World War I. The Army found so many literally illiterate inductees that it developed two intelligence tests—one for those who were literate and one for those who were illiterate.
- In 1889, 335 out of 400 colleges found the backgrounds of entering freshmen so deficient that they set up special preparatory departments to compensate for these deficiencies.
- In 1941, the Naval Officers' Training Corps reported that 62 percent of the 4,200 college freshmen tested failed a test of basic mathematical reasoning.
- In 1954, 62 percent of the nation's colleges found it necessary to teach high school algebra to freshmen.

Figure 1.1. Better Educated.

Graduation rates have been rising steadily:

Percentage of people 25 and older who
completed four years of high school or more:

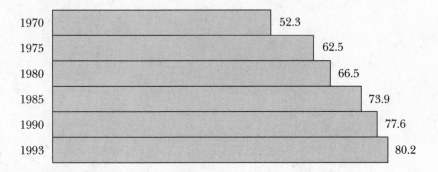

1970	52.3
1975	62.5
1980	66.5
1985	73.9
1990	77.6
1993	80.2

Percentage of people 25 and older who
completed four years of college or more:

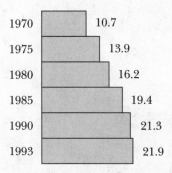

1970	10.7
1975	13.9
1980	16.2
1985	19.4
1990	21.3
1993	21.9

Source: Data from U.S. Bureau of the Census. Graphic by Suzy Parker, *USA Today,*
Feb. 7, 1995. Copyright 1995, USA Today. Reprinted with permission.

Figure 1.2. World's Adults Who Can Read.

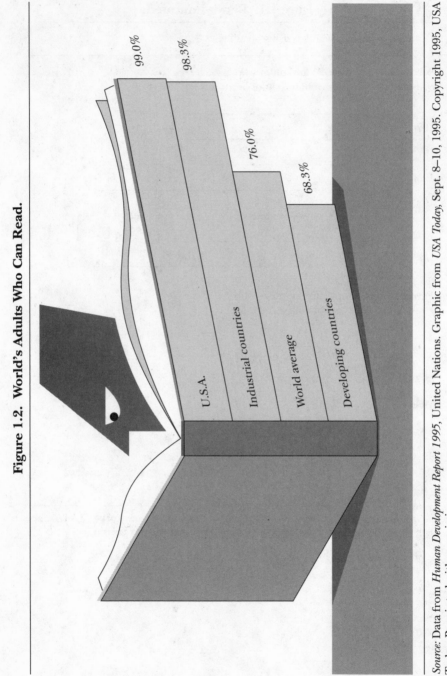

99.0%

98.3%

76.0%

68.3%

U.S.A.

Industrial countries

World average

Developing countries

Source: Data from *Human Development Report 1995*, United Nations. Graphic from *USA Today*, Sept. 8–10, 1995. Copyright 1995, USA Today. Reprinted with permission.

Anyone who needs further evidence that dissatisfaction with the American system of education has a long history only needs to read such books as Mortimer B. Smith's *And Madly Teach* (1949), Albert Lynd's *Quackery in the Public Schools* (1953), Arthur E. Bestor's *Educational Wastelands* (1953), James Koerner's *The Miseducation of American Teachers* (1963), or Ivan Illich's *Deschooling Society* (1971).

The demand that schools be changed or returned to their former good state is clearly not new. Indeed, the problems the current group of critics have identified—for example, low standards and poor discipline—have been identified in the past as well. Apparently, the good old days were not nearly as good as the people who would take us back to those days would have us believe. What has changed is the context in which these problems are manifested, for the schools themselves have changed very little—and *that* is the problem. Unless the schools can be changed to accommodate the new context in which they exist, they not only will not get better; they are almost certain to get worse.

The Present Situation

The fact that the nature of the educational debate in America has not changed much for over a century does not mean that the circumstances in which the debate is taking place have not changed or that the consequences of failure to reform the schools today will be the same as they were in the past. In the past, the consequences were more complaints, new calls for reform, and a continuing struggle between those who would change the schools to some new form and those who would take the schools back to an old form that "worked in the past." The failure of school reform in this decade may well mean the demise of public education in America. It is critical, therefore, that reform leaders understand how the present context differs from that of the past, for these are differences that make a difference. Among the more critical are the following:

• As Berliner and Biddle (1995) make clear, anti–public school propagandists have taken advantage of the tendency of Americans to be critical of their schools, the penchant of the press to prefer "bad news" and negative statistics, and a general ignorance among the populace regarding statistics and statistical analysis in order to create the impression that schools are worse than they really are. Given this fact, unless pro–public school forces can find effective means to educate the public about the condition of education, the anti–public school lobby is almost certain to be increasingly successful in persuading policy makers to abandon public education and to embrace some form of privatization as a solution to what ails our schools.

• Changes in the economy and changes in the nature of civic life, to say nothing of the revolution that is taking place in the way information is generated, used, processed, and transmitted, have created a circumstance in which the schools *must* deliver on what they have always promised but have so far failed to deliver: providing a high-quality academic education for all the children and youth of our nation, not just the children of the rich, the well born, and those from the lower classes who are extremely able or unusually motivated. Failure to deliver on this promise now, especially in a context where so many believe that a golden age existed when schools did deliver what was promised, will almost certainly lead to the abandonment of public education.

• The reservoir of goodwill and support for public schools is eroding, not simply for the reasons outlined above but for demographic and economic reasons as well. Historically, America has been a nation predominantly made up of young families who had, or anticipated having, children in school. Such people have a vested interest in believing in the public schools, or at least in the public schools their children are attending. As reported by the annual Gallup Poll sponsored by Phi Delta Kappa and published each fall in the *Phi Delta Kappan* (see, for example, Elam and Rose, 1995), parents with children in public schools generally have a more favorable impression of these schools than do those who have no children in school.

Because the proportion of the population with children in schools is now decreasing, an erosion in positive sentiment toward the public schools is likely to occur. Unfortunately, as things now stand, many senior citizens, parents with children in private schools, and nonparent taxpayers do not see much connection between what goes on in public school and other matters of real concern to them. Indeed, increasing numbers see the funding required by public schools as directly competitive with their own interests. Parents of children in private schools, for example, resent paying taxes for public schools and paying their children's tuition as well. Senior citizens see their tax dollars going to support schools that they view as worse than the schools they attended and wonder if the money would not be better spent on Medicare.

• The growing concern of taxpayers with the level of taxes and the visibility and vulnerability of education budgets to taxpayers on the local level provide an even stronger motive for growing segments of the population to abandon traditional commitments to public education. Alternatives that promise to be better, as well as cheaper, a claim often made by the advocates of vouchers, are almost certain to appeal to senior citizens on fixed incomes who fully understand that public dollars saved on education may well be used to reduce their property taxes. For different, but equally compelling reasons, other nonparent taxpayers and parents of private school students have reason to believe such arguments as well. Unless these issues are addressed head-on, vouchers and privatization will have increased appeal.

• Concern about the *academic* quality of America's schools has become much more widespread among the public than was the case in the past. For example, in the past, concern about the quality of the academic preparation of students was usually expressed by university professors, college presidents, and other members of the academic elite. Business and labor leaders frequently had concerns about the schools as well, though they were more likely to question the vocational training than the quality of academic and general education.

Today the criticisms of business leaders sound very much like those of the college professors and university presidents. It is not simply that the schools are teaching the wrong things—for example, not enough vocational or technical training. Today, business leaders, like college professors, are concerned that not enough students are meeting the academic standards they need to meet to function in a work environment where management of information and working in groups to solve problems are expected and required.

• Compounding this condition is the fact that, since the early 1950s, the debate over the quality of education has been moving from being largely a local issue to being a state and national issue as well. This, in turn, has made education much more vulnerable to the vagaries of state and national political agendas and much more susceptible to the kinds of distortions that occur when the media seek to popularize complex issues.

Prior to the 1950s, other than in North Carolina and Hawaii, where school finance has long been predominantly a state function, education was a local affair, left up to local officials. In the early 1950s, attacks on progressive education and a national back-to-the-basics movement made the education debate a national affair. Events in California rippled through Ohio and into New York, and such ripples went from east to west as well.

In 1954, the decision in *Brown* v. *Topeka Board of Education* further nationalized the debate on education, as did the National Defense Education Act of 1957, the Supreme Court's decisions relating to school prayer, and the very effective work of the special education interest groups that resulted in legislation aimed at ensuring inclusion of the handicapped into regular programs and the provision of federal funding for children with special needs. Prior to the 1970s, however, in most states, education was seldom discussed by governors as a meaningful state-level issue. In the late 1970s and early 1980s, with leadership from governors who now have places of prominence on the national scene, such as Bill Clinton, Lamar Alexander, Robert Graham, Richard Riley, William Winter, and James Hunt, the quality of education became a front-line issue for many governors and state legislatures.

The way this issue has been framed in different times is illustrative of how context affects the argument. In the early to mid-1950s, the issues of concern were largely cultural, civic, and moral. The debate began over the consequences of progressive education and the assumed impact of John Dewey on the schools. Political and religious conservatives, joined by academics from elite universities, launched all-out assaults on what they saw, sometimes rightly, as soft pedagogy and a decline in standards. Issues like desegregation and prayer in schools only served to heat up this debate.

The launching of *Sputnik I* and the aftermath of that event linked education to national defense issues as well. In the 1980s, under the leadership of a group of governors from Southeastern states where educational performance was notably low and the need for economic development notably high, school reform became an issue of economic development as well. It is ironic that the idea of "high skills or low wages," which was something of a slogan among many of these late-twentieth-century reformers, was actually first used by business leaders in the 1870s as an argument for creating the public high schools that modern reformers now want to change (see Handlin, 1959). It is little wonder that those who would resist reform sometimes suggest that nothing is really new and we have been here before. In some ways, few things are new and the ground is familiar.

The publication of *A Nation at Risk* in 1983 placed the quality of America's schools squarely in the center of the national debate and heated up debates in statehouses, in both corporate and school boardrooms, and in national publications and local newspapers (National Commission on Excellence in Education, 1983). The continuing debate over national standards and the interest of various congressional leaders in advancing the cause of privatization of public schools are certain to keep the quality of America's schools a focus of national attention—and especially media attention. This is particularly true because, as mentioned earlier, so many of the key players in the reform movement of the early 1980s are now highly visible as actors on the national political scene.

Unless those who run America's schools and those who create policy relative to these schools can invent ways to govern schools that take into account the changes in the context of the educational debate, America will almost certainly give up one of the central tenets upon which its education has been based—the idea that schools are a community affair. Notwithstanding the promises of conservatives to return control over education to local communities by giving parents vouchers, the fact is that many moves toward parental control of schools remove the community, which includes nonparent taxpayers as well as parents, from any position in which it can control the education for which it pays.

The Problem Reframed

In the preceding paragraphs, I have argued that American public schools are better at doing what they were designed to do than ever in the past. *Unfortunately, what the schools were designed to do is no longer serving the needs of American society.* The schools were designed to ensure that all citizens will be *basically* literate (able to decode words), that most will be *functionally* literate (able to read well), and that a relatively small number (20 percent or less) will be able to meet reasonably high academic standards. This goal has been achieved.

Today, being basically literate is not enough; all citizens must be functionally literate. It is not enough for individuals to be able to do arithmetic problems; they must use arithmetic to solve problems. It is no longer enough for individuals to decode words and write simple sentences; they must now be able both to summarize what others have written and to write persuasively and analytically. In a society where the ability to work with information and knowledge is the key to employability in well-paying jobs and essential to effective citizenship, it is no longer enough to have a relative few who are well educated. Today, most must be well educated.

Those who argue that all students must meet high academic standards (and I am among them) should keep in mind that in the not-too-distant past, it was assumed that such standards were relevant only to students who were likely to go to college (the A and B students). The "solid C" student may be much admired in the teachers' lounge, but colleges and universities with anything approaching selective admission standards are not usually impressed with a string of C's, no matter how solid. (There are exceptions, of course; C students with special talents in basketball and football are much sought after by selective colleges.) Yet, in the lore of education, the grade of C is the grade most students deserve. It is an average grade, signifying average performance. If this is so, the expected average *academic* performance of the American high school student is quite low and has been quite low for a long time.

The circumstance described here is compounded by additional problems attributable to contextual changes. For example, the colleges and universities of America, if they applied what are considered to be reasonably high-academic standards in the admission process, have long had a need for more students than the public schools could provide. As the data presented earlier indicate, this was as true in the 1890s, when fewer than 5 percent of eighteen-year-olds attended college, as it is today, when more than half enter college. It was in 1889, not 1989, that 335 out of 400 colleges reported feeling compelled to offer remedial courses because the preparation of entering college students was so bad.

After World War II, because of the GI Bill and its side effects—for example, the growing understanding that higher education belonged to all the people, not just the children of the elite—more and more students wanted to go to college and more and more colleges grew up, or expanded, to respond to this demand. The high schools responded to the demand by increasing "holding power" dramatically during the 1950s, to the point that by 1960 more than 65 percent of all eighteen-year-olds were graduating from high school. (In 1940, about 40 percent graduated from high school.) Today, the graduation rate is in excess of 85 percent. Furthermore, all of this was done in the face of rapidly expanding enrollments, for in 1958 and 1959 the front edge of the postwar baby boom hit the high schools. By the mid-1960s, high schools were being called on to provide a higher proportion of students who met high academic standards, usually signified by A and B grades, from an expanding population of students, the majority of whom, in a previous generation, would have been solid C students or would have dropped out altogether.

The American educational system was not, and is not, up to such a task, and educators have no reason to be defensive about the matter. The system is flawed, not the people who are in it. Neither is it surprising that the phenomenon known as grade inflation occurred. The demand for high school students who met reasonably high academic standards exceeded 15 to 20 percent, but the schools were incapable of providing them. Colleges and universities were still reluctant to admit C students, but they needed more students than the schools could provide at the then-existing A and B standard. It may be, therefore, that some schools (both public and private) simply began using the grade of B or B- to stand for what a C stood for a generation earlier.[1] No one really knows for sure. What is known is that colleges and universities have always complained about the standards of American high schools, even back in the good old days of the 1930s, or 1910, or 1890. Furthermore, whatever the case, America's schools, as they are presently organized, cannot make it possible for nearly all students to receive the kind of education that, a generation ago, only a few students were assumed to be capable of receiving.

---

[1] I usually find the idea of *student as product* distasteful and harmful. In this case, however, I cannot resist a comparison to business. The reader may recall that one of the responses of General Motors Corporation to the need to quickly produce a variety of products to compete with the Japanese was to produce automobiles made up primarily of Chevrolet parts and call them Oldsmobiles. The erosion of standards in organizations that are not designed to do what they are being asked to do is not limited to schools.

In summary, the problem educational reformers confront is that America's schools are now being asked to do things they have never done in an environment that is more hostile to supporting quality education than has ever before existed. For example:

• America's schools were designed in a time when it could be assumed that most children would come to school from a relatively stable home environment with two or more adults present in the household. No more.

• America's schools were designed in a time when schools, the libraries, the local newspaper, and the church and synagogue were the primary sources of information in the community. Further, the community had relatively strong control over the level of access the young would have to the information available. Indeed, Willard Waller ([1932] 1967, p. 34) once described the schools as "museums of virtue": places where communities communicated to the young what they wanted the young to believe that adults believed, even if the adults did not behave that way. Even in a less information-overloaded society, this was a difficult position for the schools. Today, it is impossible. I suspect that one of the reasons increasing numbers of bright and precocious youngsters are giving more of their time to the Internet and interactive video games than to homework is that they believe that these sources of information are more in touch with the realities of life than are the schools.

• With the advent of radio, television, the Internet, CD-ROMs, and interactive cable, the control that traditional institutions have over what children come to know is increasingly problematic. It is still possible to age-grade the curriculum, but the evening television news cannot be age-graded, and the evening news reports much that adults would like to keep from the young, such as accounts of rape, murder, famine, starvation, fear, and war; foul language; controversial interpretations of events; far-out ideas; and strange doings, including the doings of witches, the far left, the far right, and on and on.

To deal with these circumstances, educational leaders must be prepared to think of schools in new ways and to articulate what they envision compellingly to others. School improvement and school renewal are not enough. What is needed is a fundamental reexamination of the assumptions upon which our system of schooling is based and a willingness to modify those assumptions in ways that take into account the emerging realities of the twenty-first century. Going back to the good old days when all parents were supportive and all children learned to read is to go back to a fairy tale.

Certainly, some schools today are horrible. Some are unsafe for both children and adults; I have been in a few of them. In some schools little learning is taking place, and little learning is likely to occur unless things change dramatically. But I would remind the reader that it was 1870, not 1996, when W. F. Phelps, who eventually became president of the National Education Association, characterized many American schools as "little less than undisciplined juvenile mobs" (1870, p. 6). The movie *Blackboard Jungle* was first shown in the 1950s, not the 1990s.

It would be foolish to deny that the level of violence in America's schools today is higher than was the case fifty years ago. Furthermore, it does not make parents feel more secure to point out that the violence in schools simply reflects the increased violence in society generally or that more incidents of murder and assault take place in the nonschool workplace than in schools, though both statements are accurate. Parents do, however, have the right to expect their children to be safe in school. If public schools cannot guarantee the safety of children while they are in school, then all else is for naught. And if safe schools are not academically productive, then there is no reason for schools at all.

What educators must do, therefore, is to invent a system of education the like of which has never been seen anywhere in the world: *a system of education that provides an elite education for nearly every child.* Without a commitment to inventing such a system, not only will the American dream not be realized but we will also soon find that what we thought was a fairy tale is a nightmare.

A Systemic View

One of the reasons school reform efforts fail is that reformers do not fully appreciate the implications of the fact that schools and classrooms, which are the proper focus of change, are part of larger systems. As Robert Dreeben has observed, "There is an ironical association between our familiarity with schools and our ignorance about them" (1968, p. vii). Among the facts about which reformers seem to be most ignorant are those that have to do with the structural and systemic properties of schools and school districts.

Too few teachers and school leaders recognize that achieving substantial change in schools and classrooms requires accommodating changes in the structures and systems in which these schools and classrooms are embedded. Indeed, one of the greatest barriers to lasting change in schools is the fact that few district offices and few communities have developed the capacity to encourage, support, and sustain change in classrooms and in schools. Thus changes in school districts and communities are as critical to changes in classrooms and schools as is the behavior of teachers and students in schools.

Put differently, if public education is lost, and it may be, it will be more because of the failure to properly frame the problems that schools must confront than because of an inability to create solutions. If schools are to change, it must first be understood that it is not enough to change the behavior of individuals—what must be changed as well are the systems that encourage, support, and maintain present behavior patterns and discourage new patterns from emerging.

In the chapters that follow, many topics are discussed, but the bottom-line question being addressed is, What can be done to enhance the capacity of school districts and communities to encourage, support, and sustain fundamental reform at the level of the schoolhouse and the classroom? Unless this question can be answered, school reform is almost certainly a lost cause, and if it is lost, so is America's great and noble struggle to provide an elite education for nearly everyone.

Chapter Two

The Need for Invention

Should present efforts to reform public schools fail, the likely result will be a continuing move toward some form of privatization, which will almost certainly include the use of vouchers. It may, as well, include some type of contracted private management system or some yet-to-be-designed system or strategy. The specific shape privatization will take is not clear. What is clear is the increasing support for the idea that the present system of public education is beyond repair and that some form of privatization is the only solution to the problems that beset education in America.

Like many who will read this book, I am not persuaded that privatization will produce the results that proponents claim. Indeed, I fear that after some short-term successes, efforts at privatization will fail to meet expectations just as badly as the public schools are doing now. If this occurs, not only will we lose public education; we may well lose commitment to the idea that the public has a civic obligation to provide for the education of all children, regardless of whether the provider is public or private.

Unfortunately, too many educators seem to lack the sense of urgency it will take to bring about the kinds of reforms that are needed if public education is to be a vital force in American life into the twenty-first century. Unless this sense of urgency can be generated, the abiding vision of a great democratic educational system designed to promote a common bond among a diverse population while providing a high-quality education for every child will be replaced by an increasingly disintegrating system, where our differences will be amplified and our common heritage will be denied.

The Motivation to Change

Change is usually motivated by one of two conditions: (1) a threat so grave that change is mandatory for survival or (2) a vision so compelling and attractive that the preservation of the status quo and the security of present arrangements pale in significance. Lasting change cannot, however, be sustained by threats, though the presence of threats is sometimes essential to get change started. Threats without vision create fear, defensiveness, and a siege mentality. Real threats, coupled with a positive vision of the future, can create commitment and passion, two ingredients that must be present if change is to be sustained.

In the preceding chapter, I made an effort to create some sense of urgency by pointing out why schools must change. In this chapter, my intent is to point out what may happen if educators fail to respond to the urgent need for change. My hope is that together these two chapters will serve to increase the sense of urgency regarding the need for school reform. Proponents of privatization probably will not appreciate what I have to say here, for the scenario I present as a result of privatization is not a happy one. Some will argue that what I suggest is mere speculation because privatization has not been tried. I agree that what I present is highly speculative, but I would suggest that the idea that privatization will solve the problems that beset our schools is speculative as well. Before abandoning a system that has served this nation well, the least its critics should do is to consider seriously the possible downside of the alternatives.

Short-Run Successes of Privatization

If the forces of privatization and vouchers carry the day, public schools will not disappear. Rather, they will become increasingly pathetic reminders of the fact that the present times are the good old days for the generation that follows this one. Unfortunately, the nostalgia the next generation may have for today's schools may be based more in fact than is the case with our current idealizations of the past.

It is also likely that privatization, especially privatization by way of vouchers, will seem to be highly successful in the short run. The children who will first benefit from vouchers are likely to come from families in which adults give education some degree of priority in their lives and are willing to behave so as to support schools' demands. This fact, compounded by the probability that private schools will continue to exercise some degree of selectivity—even if based only on the requirement of significant parental involvement and support—means that the performance of private schools, on conventional measures at least, will likely be better than that of public schools. Further, as the high-performing youngsters increasingly enroll in private schools, and they will, the performance of the residual group will appear to decline. This apparent discrepancy between the performance of private schools and public schools will further erode public confidence in public schools.

The Long Run

Unfortunately, after some short-run success, a privatized system of education will prove to be no more effective, or ineffective, than the present system of education seems to be. As Berliner and Biddle (1995) make clear, we have no reason to assume that privatization alone will result in the kinds of improvement being sought. In spite of claims to the contrary, if we control for such factors as the level of parental support and involvement and the conventional measures used to identify at-risk students, there is no convincing evidence that private or parochial schools increase the likelihood of high academic performance in previously poorly performing students.[1] In fact, there is every reason to believe that the most important differences between private and public schools lie in the nature of the students served and the ability of private schools to uphold standards through exclusion.

Private schools, like public schools, do well with poor and at-risk students if they are the *right* poor and at-risk children. Indeed,

---

[1]Parents of at-risk students who, with the help of vouchers, choose private schools for their children and who agree to be involved in their children's academic life are not the same as parents who do not do these things. These differences undoubtedly affect student performance. Given the same level of commitment as that of parents of children in private schools, students in public schools will do equally well, as numerous effective big-city schools illustrate.

some of these children do well in the most horrible public schools and might do a little better if they were in better schools—either public *or* private. Also, in some public and private schools, nearly all poor and at-risk children do well, as do their more fortunate peers. Good schools exist in both the public and private sectors.

The unfortunate fact is that most private schools and most public schools are based on the same assumptions. When these assumptions are consistent with the conditions represented by the students served, both work reasonably well. For example, both private and public schools assume a consensus among adults in the community being served regarding the kind of education children should receive, and both assume that the traditional authority of the teacher should be the primary authority base from which the order of the school proceeds and that parents generally understand and support this authority.

When children come from families where these and related assumptions are upheld, they generally do well in either private or public schools. When these assumptions are violated, children do poorly in either setting. Presently these assumptions are more frequently violated in public schools than in private schools. The parents of public school children are less likely to share a common view of what education is about than are private school parents. The interest groups that support individual private schools, such as donors, boards of trustees, and church deacons, are more likely to be in agreement regarding the means and ends of education than is the case in the public schools. Thus, in the short run, private schools are likely to appear to be, and perhaps to be in fact, better than public schools. In the long run, however, as private schools become more embedded in the workaday realities of American society, they will work no better than many public schools, and some private schools, now work.

The diverse needs and interests that plague the public schools today are no more reconcilable in the private schools than in the public schools. In the short run, private schools can control diversity through exclusion. This works for a while, but eventually it leads to Balkanization and the destruction of democracy. *Unfortunately, by the time it becomes clear that the problems are systems problems, rather than a public school–private school issue, the dismantling of our educational system will be so far along that, like Humpty Dumpty, the system will not be capable of being put back together again.*

By the time we discover that our system, as it is presently designed and regardless of privatization, cannot ensure that most young people will graduate from high school having mastered algebra and the basic sciences; having developed a reasonable grasp of history, an understanding of geography, the ability to be conversant in at least two languages, an appreciation of the fine arts and music, and the ability to converse with educated adults on a mutually satisfactory plane; and having become disciplined in the approach they take to tasks (the list could go on), it may be too late to save America's public schools.

If Privatization Fails: What Then?

Suppose the scenario described above occurs. Suppose educational leaders who are in a position to inspire and direct the reinvention of America's system of education fail to do so. (Whether or not this failure is because of a lack of commitment, skill, insight, or will is of little matter. What matters is the failure itself.)

Suppose that, in frustration, policy makers and leaders pursue the privatization agenda. Whether or not that privatization occurs through the takeover of entire school systems by private corporations, the takeover of individual schools by private groups, the widespread use of vouchers, a dramatically increased number of charter schools, or a combination thereof really does not matter. What does matter is the dismantling of the system of public education and the destruction of what remains of public confidence in the part of the American dream that is based on faith in education. What might be the long-run consequences of such an occurrence?

• It seems likely that many senior citizens will come to look upon vouchers as nothing more or less than intergenerational transfers of wealth and will begin to use their support for education as a bargaining chip for support for such programs as social security and Medicare. Taxes to support schools, though not popular, are certain to be more popular than taxes to pay tuition directly for children who are not one's own. Among senior citizens (other than those who are recipients), food stamps are among the least popular components of our welfare program. Why is this so? Surely, in part, it is because many seniors do not approve of the things the poor "choose to buy" with the stamps they are given. Is it reasonable to expect that seniors will be any more pleased with the education the young choose to buy for their offspring?

It should not escape our attention that the food stamp program, introduced with great enthusiasm, is now one of the most embattled programs in America's welfare system. Thus one of the long-term consequences of privatization may be a continuing and accelerating diminution in public support for education rather than the increased and/or stable support imagined by the proponents of privatization and vouchers.

• Over time, the free market economy will lead to abuses, as has happened in Medicaid and Medicare and is clear in today's proprietary vocational schools. This, in turn, will lead to pressure for regulation at both the state and national levels. The private schools, especially those that have a religious affiliation, are almost certain to resist such regulation as an unwarranted intrusion of the state into their affairs or as an invasion of their religious freedom.

If private schools are successful in resisting regulation, abuses will continue, which, in turn, will further erode public support for education. If private schools are not successful in resisting regulation, their independence and integrity will be compromised. In either case, both public schools and private schools come out losers in the long term.

• Given advances in technology and the increasing interest of the entertainment business in entering the education market, it is likely that the elite will turn away from both private and public schools and will adapt, instead, some form of home schooling— perhaps through neighborhood or block charter schools—that relies heavily on the use of interactive television as a primary instructional tool. Lewis J. Perelman (1992) may be right: school will be out but only because educators failed to prevent it from being so. What will become clear is that education is not a monopoly of schools. Indeed, schools may become viewed as barriers to education rather than as providers. (See Chapter Three for an elaboration of this argument.)

• Eventually, and probably sooner rather than later, religious and ethnic groups will begin to see how technology can be used to support the kind of education they want for their limited group. The consequence will be that the ideal of education as a promoter of a common culture will give way to "market niche" education, where, for the price of the vouchers, each ethnic or religious group will be provided with electronic hardware and software to support whatever bias or creed it wants to support. Such is the way to Bosnia.

Financial Equity and School Reform

Historically, public education in America has been funded primarily through local taxes derived from the property tax base. Such a pattern of finance is consistent with the idea that education is a local community affair. Unfortunately, using property taxes, or any other local taxes, as a basis for funding schools leads to wide variability in the amount of money available to educate children. This disparity has long been of concern to policy makers and reformers. Over the past two decades, this concern has resulted in increased involvement of state legislatures in the funding of schools as well as in the management of local school districts. Increasingly, courts are ordering state legislatures, as the constitutionally mandated source of authority over schools, to do something to remedy what is demonstrably an inequitable situation. Apparently the courts agree with Jonathan Kozol's statement: "If money is inadequate to improve education, the residents of poor districts should at least have an equal opportunity to be disappointed by its failure" (1991, p. 169).

In response to court orders, various means have been tried to "equalize" resources and "level the playing field." One of the concerns of educators from traditionally advantaged districts (largely suburban schools) is that, for them, leveling may mean leveling down. Few have stopped to consider the possible relationship between vouchers and the effort of advantaged school districts to resist what they perceive to be the unfair burden of the so-called Robin Hood effect, where funds from the more wealthy school districts are, in effect, transferred to less affluent districts.

A case can be made that vouchers, unless they are carefully conceived, provide a way out of the problem that leveling presents to suburban schools. All that suburban communities will need to do to escape the Robin Hood effect is to create a private school system to replace their present system, lower taxes to the minimum level required by the state, accept the vouchers offered by the state, and charge tuition to offset the difference between the present level of per-pupil cost and the worth of the vouchers.

Senior citizens and other taxpayers who live in the community could, with proper marketing, be brought to see how the presence of a high-quality private school enhances the value of their own property and thus might be encouraged to volunteer in donations part of what they would have been taxed if the community had stayed with a public school system. This strategy would be especially advantageous in states that are moving away from using property taxes as a base for funding education, other than as a base for providing local supplements to core state funding. Should this scenario occur, today's most clearly successful public schools will show up on the ledger of the private school movement. In the short term, therefore, a system of vouchers for private schools is likely to appear to be highly successful. In the long run, however, the results could be devastating for public education, for private education, and perhaps for American society and the economy.

It seems to me that two systems are likely to emerge, both funded by increasingly shrinking tax dollars. One set of privately operated independent schools will be subsidized by vouchers, and another system of schools will be run by the state as charter schools or perhaps as state schools, managed something like the way the U.S. Department of Defense manages its schools. Community control of schools and school districts will disappear.

The Long Run Starts Today

To accomplish the task that must be accomplished if education in America is to improve the way it should, educators must first inform the community about the nature of the problems to be addressed. Simultaneously, they must prepare themselves to totally reinvent the American system of education, both public and private, for neither the public schools nor the private schools are up to the task that will confront them. Unfortunately, failure to understand this fact is leading to competition between groups that must cooperate if the future of our children and our society is to be assured.

It is up to informed educators to ensure that the community is educated about what ails America's system of schooling. Whether they do this or not, it will eventually be recognized that the issue of quality in American schools is not a question of private schools versus public schools but of the assumptions upon which the schools are based and the effects of the social, political, and economic context in which these assumptions are played out. If this recognition comes soon enough, systemic reform will begin in earnest. If it comes too late, at some time in the future complaints will again break out about America's schools, only this time there will be much that is real to complain about and nothing to build on or with. Of equal concern is the prospect that at precisely the time in the American experience when we most need community-building organizations that uplift and promote what is good and common to all Americans, our leaders may dismantle the one agency that holds the greatest promise for promoting these ends—the public schools.

The remainder of this book is dedicated to the proposition that this dismantling should not and need not occur. I hope that what I write will help to prevent calamities and will contribute to the common good.

| The Technological Imperative

Nowadays it is commonplace to use the word *technology* as a synonym for electronic information processing and/or information transmitting technology. It is equally common to speak of the changes occurring as a result of these technologies as *the* technological revolution. To use the word *technology* in this way is to speak and think without reference to history. Technological revolutions have often occurred in the history of humankind. The invention of the printing press changed fundamentally the way information was stored and communicated. The invention of the steam engine altered the way manufacturing was done and goods were produced.

Technology is nothing more or less than "the means of getting a job done, whatever the means and the job happen to be" (Dreeben, 1970, p. 83). The creation of electronic means of processing, storing, and communicating information does constitute a change in information technology. Information technology, however, is only one of many types of technology.

A Historical Perspective

If we view technological change in a historical context, it is clear that most such changes are incremental improvements on prior technologies rather than fundamental changes in the core assumptions upon which the technologies are based. For example, the change from the quill pen to the ballpoint pen was gradual and incremental, moving first to the metal-pointed pen, then to the fountain pen, and finally to the ballpoint pen. The advent of the overhead projector represents a similar evolution from the slate board.

With gradual change, those who are affected have, within limits, some choice as to when, how, or whether they will participate in and adopt the new technology. Furthermore, when technological change is incremental, the organizations and institutions whose technology is affected have the time to gradually modify the rules, roles, and relationships (or structure) that govern the way work is done, so that the system can take advantage of the benefits of the new technology without totally disrupting the system. Individuals can even refuse to use the new technology or can insist that it be used in ways that compromise its benefits, in an attempt to avoid seriously affecting the short-term health of the systems of which they are a part.

Many teachers continue to rely on the chalkboard in preference to the overhead projector. John Marshall, chief justice of the U.S. Supreme Court from 1801 to 1835, refused to use a metal-pointed pen up through the writing of his last opinion, even though the new technology was available. So far as I can tell, the reluctance of teachers to use overhead projectors has not done serious harm to schools. Those who should know say that Marshall's last opinions were as impressive and precedent-setting as they might have been had he used a word processor. However, another type of technological change goes to the very core of the way a given enterprise conducts its business, because that change is based on assumptions radically different from those of prior technologies.

The industrial revolution that dominated the scene in Europe and America in the not-too-distant past is an illustration of such technological change. The new technologies assumed a power source other than human beings and animals. This assumption revolutionized the way the business of manufacturing was conducted. It also revolutionized the way lives were lived and political power and authority were distributed and used.

When a radical technological change occurs, choice regarding the use of the new technology is limited. Organizations that refuse to use the new technology, that cannot afford it, or that cannot adapt to it will be replaced by organizations that can. The invention of the power loom is an example of such a revolutionary change. Even the Luddites could not stop the introduction and effective use of machines powered by something other than muscles and brawn, hands, feet, and hooves. Textile manufacturers were forced to come to terms with this invention whether they chose to or not. Some did not and they went out of business. I hope to persuade the reader who is not already convinced that a similar fate may await both the public and private schools. (Lewis J. Perelman, in his book *School's Out* [1992], arrives at a similar conclusion, but he does not see the matter as distressing. I do.)

Unlike incremental improvements in technology, fundamental changes in technology force dramatic supportive changes in other parts of the system as well. Where such supportive structural changes do not occur, serious dislocations can be anticipated. When technological change goes to the core of an enterprise, the entire system of rules, roles, and relationships that governs the way work is done and business is conducted (that is, its structure) must be altered in fundamental ways. What is more, the changes required must occur quickly (usually within a generation or less).

When a core technology changes, massive structural mutations occur rather than small and incremental changes. The way work is done and the way lives are lived will change in ways that make them nearly unrecognizable to those raised in another era. These transitions are painful, but they cannot be avoided. Educators can refuse to use the overhead projector with little consequence, but the Pony Express disappeared when the transcontinental telegraph was connected.

Lessons from History

As a study of the history of technological change would show, individuals, groups, and organizations often respond to revolutionary technological changes as though they are dealing with mere incremental change. Some refuse to acknowledge the significance of a technological change and go about business as usual. Or, as the case of the Luddites' efforts to destroy power machinery illustrates, individuals, groups, and organizations may acknowledge the significance of the new technology to their lives and actively resist its incorporation into their work.

Others, because they either cannot afford the new technology or are ignorant of it, continue to do what they have always done and suffer the relative deprivation that results. Thus many farmers in underdeveloped countries continue to this day to harvest crops with a mowing scythe and cradle and to thresh their harvest by stamping on it with their feet rather than using a steam-driven thresher, to say nothing of a combine.

When technological change goes to the core of the way work is done in an enterprise, resistance to the change will only lead to extinction. In the face of resistance or the inability of existing organizations to adapt, new enterprises will arise that will redefine the business so that the systems in which the new technologies are embedded are congruent with and responsive to the requirements of the technologies. Eventually, the new businesses will replace the old.

Understanding One's Business

It is apparent that for leaders to understand when the core technology of their enterprise is under threat, they must understand the nature of the business they are in. Many, unfortunately, do not; as a consequence, they are overwhelmed by events. Peter Drucker (1974) suggests three questions that organizational leaders must constantly ask of themselves and of those they lead:

1. What business are we in, and what business do we want to be in?
2. Who are our customers, and what needs do they have that our business can respond to?
3. What product or products do we have with which to respond to the needs of our customers, and what additional products might we produce, given the business we are in?

Though the answer to all three of these questions is critical to the continuing health of any organization, the answer to the first is especially critical in a time when the core technology of an enterprise is changing. When the technology of an enterprise—especially the core technology—shifts, its leaders must be prepared to comprehend that the shift is occurring so that they can take advantage of the opportunities provided or consciously decide not to go into the new business that the new technology makes available and will require of them. Unless leaders fully understand the nature of the enterprise they are leading, they will not know how to respond to an emerging technology and may see that new technology as a threat rather than a resource.

For example, the early railroad magnates defined their business as hauling people and freight by rail. As Peter Drucker (1974, p. 89) has observed, had they understood their business better and differently, they would not have behaved as they did when buses, trucks, and airplanes came along. If they had defined their business as the transportation business, rather than as the railroad business, when new technologies like buses came along, they would have bought them. Instead, they fought them as they fought the emerging truck lines.

The technologies the founders of railroads thought to be of concern were those related to locomotives, rail cars, routing, and scheduling. When automobiles, buses, trucks, and later airplanes became available, they were thought of as a threat; this flaw in the thinking of the railroads' leaders had devastating effects on the industry. Railroaders, who had for so long resisted governmental reglation of their own business, suddenly found themselves sympathetic to governmental regulation of the trucking industry. Though they had built their own system in part by using governmental land subsidies, they resented the fact that a public highway system was subsidizing truckers. Rather than seeing that the transportation industry was undergoing a fundamental technological shift, they saw buses and trucks as optional technologies and competitors. As this case illustrates, the question What business are we in? is not a trivial one, and the answer to the question is not as obvious as it may sometimes appear to be.

The Business of the Schools

In America, as in most other nations, the schools have been and continue to be the leading provider of educational experiences for children and even for adults. Education as an institution is, however, much more than schools and schooling. The family, the church, the print media, and increasingly, the electronic media are a part of the educational institution as well. Though educators have defined their business in various ways—for example, as "the business of educating children," "the business of developing each child's potential," "the enlightenment business," or "the cultural transmission business"—the fact is that the primary business of schools is the transmission, preservation, and processing of knowledge and information and the development in others of the skills needed to carry out such tasks. *The aim of schooling is an educated citizenry, but the core business of schooling is engaging students in work that results in their learning what they need to learn to be viewed as well educated in American society.*

Given this definition of the core business of schooling, it becomes clear that the core technologies of schooling are those associated with the means of doing the job of transmitting, preserving, and processing knowledge and information. In the past fifty years, many incremental changes have taken place in this technology, but until the past twenty years, they did not go to the core of the enterprise. The invention of the overhead projector, the record player, and later the audiocassette player and the invention of radio and then television are but a few examples of incremental changes.

Schools have not been notably quick in adopting even these technologies, and when they have, they have often used them merely to do old things in new ways. Thus the overhead projector, which David Thornburg says took twenty years to move from the bowling alley to the classroom, is used as a substitute chalkboard. The talking-head teacher lectures to thousands via television rather than only to the relatively few who can fit into a single classroom. Of course, some schools and some teachers have taken full advantage of these technological advances, and when they have, their capacity to do their job has improved. But for those who have refused to use the new technology or who have failed to master it, the losses have not been notable nor the effects profound. Teachers who do not use overhead projectors are seldom censored by their peers. Teachers who misuse and abuse movies, using them as time fillers, may be talked about by their peers, but for such teachers the movies are simply a new way of doing what they have always done: finding something to fill up the time when they are with students.

What seems to escape many educators and policy makers is the fact that the advent of electronically based technologies for transmitting, storing, retrieving, and processing information is a change that is different in kind from such modest improvements as the overhead projector or even the tape recorder. All of these technologies made more efficient the transmission of knowledge—information that has already been processed, summarized, and given meaning—but they did little to make information, raw facts, and idiosyncratic experiences more generally available. The technologies that have emerged in the past twenty years permit random access to information as well as to knowledge. The linear storage represented by a book is also represented by an audiotape of the book, but the audiotape is more constraining, because we can leaf through the book. To "leaf through" a tape recording requires relatively sophisticated equipment and a great deal of patience. However, we can "leaf through" a CD-ROM with the touch of a button.

These new technologies go to the core of the educational enterprise. Whether schools can be organized to accommodate the new technologies is yet to be seen. If they cannot, schools will not be at the core of the educational enterprise, though the new technologies will remain, to be exploited by new organizations that will provide the education America needs. Such a profound change in the core technology of education has not occurred since the invention of the printing press. And just as the printing press created the need for and possibility of public education, the new technologies make schools—in their present form—obsolete.[1]

Just as the railroads were limited because they had to follow the established tracks, schools that assume that print and teachers are the preferred or only sources of information are limited in their power to educate. Furthermore, the linear assumptions upon which schools are based—the graded school, the lack of flexibility of schedules, the compartmentalization of knowledge into isolated disciplines, the physical separation of older students from younger ones, and the isolation of schools from the larger community— make it difficult and indeed impossible to take advantage of these emerging technologies. *The linear assumptions of the world of print undergird our system of schooling. The random assumptions of electronic information processing technology dominate the emerging reality within which education occurs.*

---

[1]As my 1976 book, *Teaching and Social Behavior,* demonstrates, I have a long-standing interest in the relationship between structure and technology. Most of what I have written here I arrived at independently; footnotes indicate where I believe the thinking of such authors as Lewis J. Perelman and David Thornburg has preceded or shaped mine.

Reaction to Technological Change

A study of the history of technological change would support a number of propositions that if properly understood, could serve as a source of guidance to educators confronted with the present assault on the core technology of schooling. Among them are the following:

- To avoid extinction, existing organizations have no choice but to adapt to the new technologies. To do this, the rules, roles, and relationships (the structure) that govern the way work is done in the system must be modified to incorporate the new technology. Such changes will lead to new forms of work within the system as well as new relationships with the larger environment from which the new technology emerges, in this case the world of computers, interactive television, and so on.
- When leaders cannot bring about changes in the old system of rules, roles, and relationships, the advantages of the technology are lost or foregone. Rather than creating new forms of work within the system, the technology will be used, if it is used at all, to do old forms of work in new ways. The dust created by the old-fashioned slate board may disappear, but the computer used as an electronic slate board is only a slate board without the dust.
- When technological changes are gradual and modest, an established enterprise can relatively safely look at the adoption and use of a new technology as a matter of choice, at least in the short run. However, when a technological change goes to the very core of the operation of an enterprise or an industry, failure to incorporate the new technology and use it in optimal ways almost ensures the failure of the existing enterprise and the rise of new systems to replace it.
- The adoption of new core technologies requires the adoption of new ways of life, new organizational forms, and the modification or abandonment of cherished values, meanings, and beliefs. *Technological change that goes to the core of an enterprise requires not only changes in the means of doing the job; it also requires changes in the culture in which work is embedded and in the structures that govern the way work is done and life is conducted. In such cases, the progressive nature of*

technology directly confronts the conservative nature of organizational culture. For example, the preservation of a culture and a way of life led the Amish to resist mechanized farming; theirs was not a calculated economic decision.

• It is, therefore, impossible to think clearly about changes in technology without thinking about both structural and cultural changes. Any organization that endeavors to adopt a new technology without being willing to change the organizational structure in ways that accommodate and provide support for the new means of doing the job is doomed to failure. The introduction of a new technology and the restructuring of the systems into which the technology is to be introduced are inextricably connected.[2]

Schools, Education, and Information

In the Western world, during medieval times and up to the invention of the printing press, the Roman Catholic Church dominated education and schooling. Usually, though not always, schools were run by members of religious orders; furthermore, they were sometimes organized around the meaning that information was to be given—thus the origin of the idea of schools of thought. Those who ran the schools decided the nature of the knowledge to be transmitted just as monks and scribes decided what information was worth preserving. These schools also determined to whom the knowledge would be made available and who would have access to the information from which the knowledge was derived.

Schooling organized in this way was limited in scope. The information from which knowledge was derived was scarce, because it was stored in hand-copied manuscripts that were usually single copies. Even books that contained the wisdom and knowledge produced by those who had access to the needed information were in low supply; books were rare and libraries meager. (A large private library contained thirty to forty books, not even enough to accommodate the Great Books of University of Chicago fame.) The means of doing the job in education—the core technologies—were

---

[2]The reader who is interested in exploring further the arguments related to the linkage between structure and technology should consult Perrow (1972).

largely individual and highly personalized. The way information was stored and retrieved depended on the penmanship of scribes and monks. The way information was processed and transmitted depended on the intellectual and communication skills of individual scholars and teachers.

Most efforts to educate the young, prior to the printing press, were up close and personal. Long-distance communication of information was exceedingly difficult. Letters had to be transcribed by hand and carried by courier. Diaries, logs, journals, and individual observations and opinions were difficult to share beyond one's intimate circles. Thus the raw information with which scholars worked was generally limited to scholars who clustered together in such places as monasteries, universities, and royal courts, pooled information, and transformed the pooled information into knowledge. Once they had done this, the knowledge was likely to be protected and distributed to only a relative few. As Francis Bacon observed: "Knowledge is power."

The invention of the printing press changed the nature of schooling dramatically, precisely because it altered the core technology by which men (and a few women) were educated. Information and the knowledge that scholars produced from it could be quickly and easily duplicated. Libraries became relatively commonplace. Schools—especially schools for the elite and for older students—were organized around libraries as well as around collections of scholars. Even in lower schools and schools for common folk, students had access to books like the Bible as well as to teachers.

Clearly, as long as there are illiterates in the world, the effects of the printing press will not be uniformly distributed and felt. This limitation aside, the printing press did make knowledge available to the masses, even though some lacked, and some still lack, the skills needed to access it. The printing press did not, however, make the information from which this knowledge is derived available to the masses. Raw data, primary sources, and unprocessed facts are simply too cumbersome to store in books, and their potential uses are too varied to submit them to the linear order necessary to produce a book. Books, as I observed earlier, are based on linear assumptions. Raw information is randomly—or at least unpredictably—distributed. Though cross-indexing helps, the problems linear filing causes when we retrieve facts stored in books can never be fully overcome. Even the encyclopedia begins with A and ends with Z.

So, although schools were always based on information and the processing of information, limitations in the technology by which information can be stored, retrieved, and processed meant that for the most part, education, especially for the masses, was limited to the transmission of received wisdom. The textbook, which would not have been possible without the printing press, became the basic medium through which received wisdom was transmitted. Schools, therefore, were organized primarily as transmitters of knowledge. The processing of information and the act of giving meaning, order, and form to facts and producing products based on this work (Peter Drucker [1974] calls this "knowledge work" and those who perform it "knowledge workers") was left to the elite, the authors of books, scientists, inventors, lawyers, journalists, and so on. Such work was not expected of the masses and certainly not of children. Indeed, schools became so stratified that they sorted children on the basis of the likelihood that they would become knowledge workers. Those who were college-bound, for example, were more likely to end up in occupations where they were expected to think, reason, and use their minds well. For these students, the curriculum (for example, the curriculum for the gifted and talented) recognized, within limits, that working on and with knowledge requires a different type of educational experience than does the uncritical transmission of received wisdom.

The invention of random access technology that stores, retrieves, processes, and transmits information makes information readily available to the masses, just as the printing press made knowledge available to the masses. And just as the printing press made it possible for every person to see himself or herself as an interpreter of the Bible and a legitimate critic of the views of other interpreters (including the Pope), the new technology makes it possible for every person to see himself or herself as a pundit and opinion maker and as a transformer and meaning giver. (Anyone who doubts this needs to watch television talk shows, listen to talk radio, or read the chat lines on America Online.) What the facts are and what they mean are now as much the purview of the ordinary citizen as of the pundit, the editor, or the teacher.

In the past, among the loftier goals of education was the development of citizens who were informed about the opinions and beliefs that shaped their lives and were able to evaluate them critically through logic and tests of facts. Even in this regard, formal education has too often failed. Now the requirement is that education prepare ordinary citizens to construct knowledge and products based on knowledge. It is no longer enough that they be informed and critical consumers of knowledge constructed by others.

Furthermore, just as the invention of the printing press threatened the established order of the day and deposed the Church as the prime source of education, modern information processing threatens to depose schools. In the same way that access to the Bible made it possible for some men and women to view their own interpretation of the "Word" as being as valid as that of the priest and the Pope, access to the raw data with which scholars, journalists, and lawyers work makes it possible for ordinary citizens to see the possibility that their views of what events mean could be equally authoritative.

Such a view can create anarchy and result in the destruction of the existing social order, but responded to appropriately, it can lead to a new reformation. The Roman Catholic Church was reformed by the Reformation, just as the Protestant sects were made possible and created by the Reformation. Furthermore, the invention of the printing press and the availability of the Bible to an increasingly schooled audience was a driving force behind the Reformation. Similarly, modern information technology is a driving force behind the current effort to reform education in America. Whether the schools will be a part of this reformation or will be bypassed by it remains to be seen.

The Need for Knowledge Workers

A knowledge worker is a person who puts to use facts, ideas, theories, beliefs, and supposed forms of knowledge to produce a product. The work I am presently engaged in as I write this chapter is knowledge work. Similarly, when the members of a team of workers on an automobile assembly line get together to analyze a problem that is interfering with product quality, they also are engaged in knowledge work.

The dominant form of work done by people in the United States, at least until after World War II, was manual work. Manual work requires physical skill, manual dexterity, strength, bone, and sinew. Knowledge work requires thought, analysis, articulation, insight, brain power, and reasoning. Many students of America's economy, Peter Drucker among them, argue that if the citizenry of America is not generally able to engage in knowledge work, our economy cannot be globally competitive, unless we are prepared to accept the consequences of a dramatic decline in wages for unskilled American workers. Manual work in America, even when the minimum wage is only $5.25, simply costs too much when compared to the cost of such work in other economies.

If, therefore, America is to be competitive and maintain its standard of living, our industries must be restructured in ways that improve productivity through mental rather than physical effort. Industries that cannot or will not restructure in this way will move offshore, as many are now doing, or die. If our industries are to restructure in ways that exploit the power of knowledge and knowledge work, we must have a strong and broad supply of knowledge workers—people who are capable of using their minds well. Thus the economic case for school reform can be made, as it has often been (see for example, Secretary's Commission on Achieving Necessary Skills, 1992).

But the need to redesign our schools to increase the ability of the citizenry to work with and on knowledge and to produce quality knowledge-work products goes far beyond the needs of the economy. It goes to the heart of our civic life and of civil society in a democracy. In the past, when the need to do knowledge work was limited to occupational elites, such as physicians, lawyers, teachers, professors, authors, and journalists, the requirements of democratic education properly gave emphasis to ensuring that children had the skills needed to access knowledge (that is, the ability to read) and the skill to understand and critically evaluate the various forms of knowledge presented to them by *the* knowledge workers. *Literacy,* cultural and otherwise, meant the ability to read and write and familiarity with the received wisdom contained in books and other knowledge-work products produced by cultural elites. As critics are quick to point out, our schools have been only marginally successful at this difficult task. Therefore, many believe that the goal of school reform and school redesign should simply be to improve the capacity of the schools in these "basic" areas. I do not totally disagree.

Indeed, the failure of the schools to meet the challenge of producing a culturally literate citizenry is now making the problem of school reform more difficult than it might otherwise have been. If the ordinary citizen understood how our schools evolved and what they did in the past, some citizens who are now yielding to the anti–public school, back-to-the-basics reformers' misleading arguments might not be so gullible and pliable. (Maybe seniors in high school, as a condition of graduation, should be expected to demonstrate an understanding of the history of education in America and the basic facts that history would reveal.)

The Democratization of Information

Until recently, church, family, and school were the primary sources of knowledge and information, especially for children. Newspapers, books, and magazines were available, but for the most part, what the legitimate press offered was limited to what the traditional values of the family, church, and school would endorse and support. "All the news that's fit to print" had a different meaning in 1950 than it has today, and what was called tabloid journalism in 1950 is now commonplace in the mainstream press. Today's radio talk shows are a far cry from the man-in-the-street interviews of yesterday, and HBO now shows movies that would have been banned in Boston in 1930. Little children sitting on an airplane are exposed to movies much more suggestive than *The Outlaw* was in 1943. The airlines may advise parents to exercise discretion, but few parents are prepared to blindfold their children, though some, wisely, refuse to buy headsets.

But these are minor changes compared to those that are coming. With the advent of CD-ROM technology, on-line computer networking, and what is being called the information highway, all citizens, from preschoolers to seniors, will be called on to handle more information each day than was available to the average citizen in a lifetime only a century ago. If our educational system does not prepare the citizenry to give meaning to this information, to create knowledge as well as to use and evaluate knowledge created by others, citizens will feel overwhelmed by the information they are receiving. And if they become overwhelmed, they are likely to turn to great simplifiers to tell them what the information means. All we need to do to see the danger of such a development is to tune in to talk radio in any local community where the great simplifiers tend to rule supreme. The meanings these simplifiers sometimes give to events are not always those that will ensure the survival of a healthy, democratic social order. Censorship and sponsor boycotts are not the answer to this problem; quality education is the only answer available in a democratic society.

Conclusion

In *Schools for the 21st Century,* I made the case that there is an economic imperative to drive school reform. I continue to make that case here because I continue to believe that it is true. I am also convinced of the civic and cultural imperatives for school reform. These imperatives are even more important for those who value democracy and want to avoid the further disintegration of the moral order of American society. Knowledge work is not only essential to the economy. It is quickly becoming a civic and cultural necessity for all of us to have the ability to work on and with information, to transform the information into usable knowledge, and to use that knowledge to solve problems, produce aesthetic enjoyment and artistic appreciation, enrich civic dialogue and discourse, and enhance the quality of our inner lives as well as the lives of those with whom we interact on a daily basis, whether on the Internet or face to face.

Processing information and transforming it into knowledge can no longer be left to the cultural elite and those who aspire to move among this elite. *The democratization of information requires that schools—or some alternative form of educational institution—provide an elite education for nearly everybody.* For this reason, I argue that the technological imperative is as important as the economic, civic, and cultural imperatives. The hope of American democracy and the economy resides in understanding the uses and abuses of technology. Without such understanding, new technologies may well become wedges that drive even deeper the fissures that are threatening to tear American society and polity asunder.

Chapter Four

Producing Knowledge Work

Students learn from what they do and from what they experience as a result of what they do. However, saying that students learn by doing and that students learn through experience and experiencing is not the same thing as saying that personal experience is the best teacher. Human beings also learn from the experiences of people other than themselves, including the experiences of people who lived so far in the past that their names have been forgotten. The term *culture,* properly understood, embodies what has been learned from those people and from the meanings they gave to what they learned.

Human beings—so far as is known—are, in fact, the only beings that have the ability to intellectualize and to translate what they intellectualize into meanings that can be shared with others through vocal and physical signs and symbols. It is through these symbolic expressions that experiences can be shared. Therefore, people can learn from the experiences of others. However, they cannot do this until those experiences become their own through the shared meanings of symbolic expressions, for example, through language, art, and music. Therefore, some way must be found to ensure that each child is provided with the means of making the experiences of others his or her own, for only in this way will the wisdom contained in the culture be transmitted from one generation to the next.

This is where the ideas that learning is an active process and that students learn by doing become important. Getting students to do things that bring them into interaction with the experiences of others and that create novel experiences for them ensures that students learn what adults want them to. And make no mistake about it, schools are not designed simply to let students learn what students want to learn. Émile Durkheim (1956, p. 123) observed that "education, far from having as its unique or principal object the individual and his interests, is above all the means by which society perpetually recreates the conditions of its very existence."

Active Learning

Philosophers, learning theorists, and experts in pedagogy spend much time thinking about and discussing the connection between learning and doing. I doubt that I really have much to add to this discussion, but I would like the reader to understand the following assumptions I make about the connection between learning and activity:

- Learning involves action (thought is a form of action), and it requires experience. This is not to say that the so-called hands-on curriculum should be preferred or that we do not learn through observation and sedentary activity. Reflection is certainly active, though it is usually not observable; it is often solitary and sedentary as well.
- Most of what students learn comes from what they do, which includes imitating, listening, creating, muddling around, and talking.
- Regardless of the mode or style of learning, it is what students do and the meaning they give to what they do that determines what they learn.
- What teachers do is much less important than what they are able to get students to do.

"Student Doings" Are Central Concerns

The observation that what students do is central to what they learn suggests that what they do and what teachers and schools try to get them to do ought to be at the heart of educational inquiry and discussion. These same matters ought to be of central concern to those seeking organizing principles for schools.

This is not so. More accurately, in current discussions about school reform, it is only so in limited cases. Educators and reformers like Howard Gardner and Theodore Sizer obviously take what students do and are expected to do as a central concern, as does William Glasser. Those who refer to themselves as constructivists also seem to have more than the usual amount of concern about what students do. For the most part, however, discussions about schools, especially those concerning school reform, have centered more on what adults do than on what students do. Furthermore, the aim of most school reform efforts, implicitly if not explicitly, has been to change what adults do, apparently on the assumption that if adult behavior in schools is changed, those changes will translate almost automatically into changes in what students learn.

Schools and much of the educational thought that guides them are organized around the assumption that teachers and what they do are and should be the key determinants of what students learn. Take, for example, the teacher evaluation process. The instruments used usually emphasize what the teacher does as a performer. Indeed, it is commonplace to refer to these instruments as "teacher performance appraisal instruments." When these instruments do give attention to what students do, they tend to focus on specified student behaviors, such as the amount of time students spend on task. It is much less common to examine the degree to which students are truly engaged in tasks, as opposed to simply being compliant and docile. The richness and texture of the content that is provided are almost never examined, and the extent to which students voluntarily persist with tasks they find difficult is seldom observed or commented on.

Similarly, when schedules are developed, it is not common to ask, What do we want students to do? Rather, the principal and others in charge of scheduling are likely to ask, How many periods is the day broken into? How many teachers do we have and how many students? What do the law and union contracts say about class size and contact hours? How many rooms do we have, and how many students will they accommodate given the state's formula for the number of students per square foot of space? How many subjects must be taught? What is the typical style of the teachers assigned to various rooms? Do they lecture, use small groups, or use some combination of techniques? What are the implications of the answer to the last question for assigning rooms to particular teachers? Only after these questions have been answered can teachers begin to figure out what they can get the students to do.

The way time, people, space, knowledge, and technology are organized clearly determines what students will be likely to do. If schools were centered on the work of students, these factors would be organized to support what teachers want them to do. Unfortunately, schedules are more often designed with the doings of adults as the focal point. It is small wonder, therefore, that teachers often feel obliged to perform for students and that, for many students, the primary task is to watch their teachers work and perform and to take careful notes so that impressions can be reported later on a test. Thus the idea that great teachers are also great performers, even actors, is usually well received by many teachers, for acting is so much of what they are required to do. It will always be so, at least until schools are organized around the performances of students rather than the performances of teachers.

Teachers as Leaders and Inventors

I do not intend to disparage teachers or teaching, to diminish the importance of teachers, or to start once again the quest for the "teacher-proof curriculum" when I argue that *not much in the way of improving our schools will occur until we abandon the assumption that the work of adults, particularly teachers and other educational personnel, is the key determinant of the quality of student learning.* The basis for reorganizing America's schools is to be found in understanding the implications of the fact that what students learn is determined by what the schools are able to get them to work at and with.

One of the most basic implications of organizing the schools around the work of students is that the role of the teacher will need to change in dramatic ways. Rather than being performers on the stage or psychiatrists "treating" the young, teachers will need to be viewed as leaders and inventors. The focus of leaders is on what they can get others to do, and their effectiveness is realized through others. The focus of inventors is to create products, systems, and services that solve problems and meet needs.

The concern of teachers as leaders is properly on what they are attempting to get the students to do: to engage in purposeful activity (work) that leads to the desired learning. Teachers invent intellectually engaging work for students and then lead them to do it. This simple idea, which has profound implications, will guide the remainder of this book.

Knowledge Work as the Product of Schools

Knowledge work involves transforming information into usable propositions, organizing information in ways that inform decisions and actions, producing products that require others to apply knowledge or use information, or arranging and rearranging concepts and ideas in useful ways. Writing a theme or an essay is a form of knowledge work, as is preparing a lesson and presenting it to students. Writing plays and skits is a form of knowledge work, and essays are products of knowledge work, as are all academic and artistic exhibitions.

Knowledge work has always been central to education. Students who are motivated to produce the kind of knowledge-work products that are valued in schools are also those who learn the most in schools. Students whose living rooms and dining room tables are places of lively debate and discussion, where they are expected to perform and where their performances are taken into account by parents and siblings, are likely to find well-conducted classroom discussions exciting and inviting. Those who come from families where such activities do not occur or are devalued as a waste of time are less likely to find the production of such performances attractive. Until the advent of the computer, the videocassette, the audiocassette, the CD-ROM, and other electronic imaging and communication systems, the range of knowledge-work products that schools could expect students to produce was very limited. Students who found the creation of this limited range of knowledge-based products compelling learned much that the schools were designed to teach. Those who were less enthusiastic about producing such products learned less. Consequently, the correlation between social class and academic achievement should not be surprising. The culture of poverty generally does not place great emphasis on producing the kind of knowledge-work products that are available in the traditional school.

Today, the range of knowledge-work products students can be called on, encouraged, and permitted to produce has expanded tremendously. Furthermore, these products are now easily transportable to sites beyond the classroom. The simple act of taping a student's speech and making that tape a part of the student's portfolio gives the classroom product (the speech) potential meaning beyond the classroom, for example, as a product for parents, siblings, or a potential employer. Using the computer to prepare a report or make a presentation opens up possibilities to the ordinary student that were once only available to the extremely talented.

It is time, therefore, for educators to give new meaning to the old adage that children learn by doing. But it is equally important to understand that schools need to have students produce knowledge-work products and performances that call on them to think, reason, and use their minds well. Furthermore, if learning is to be significant, the products students produce must require them to organize culturally significant information in ways that have meaning and then to use this information to solve problems and to invent products that communicate to others what they have learned.

Retreat and Ritual Compliance

Because school attendance is compulsory and most students have little choice about the school they will attend, it is sometimes mistakenly supposed that they have no choice. That is not so. Each day, in every school in America, students exercise choice. Some choose to do, with enthusiasm and commitment, what their teachers ask; others refuse. Students who choose not to do what their teachers ask are not necessarily in active rebellion. Some are, but most are not. They simply are not attentive to the tasks they are assigned or committed to them. They choose to attend to other matters and to give their commitment and loyalties to other things.

Most students are docile, complying in some ritual way with their teachers' commands and directions, even though they may not find what the teachers provide them with to be either engaging or compelling. As a consequence, many students refuse to give their teachers what those teachers need: attention and commitment.

The Erosion of Traditional Authority

Perhaps the most fundamental shift in American schooling is in the ability of the teacher to command the attention and commitment of the student. As long as the traditional authority of teachers can be upheld, the attention and commitment of students can be commanded, within limits. In traditional society, children do what adults say because the adults tell them to, and they are expected to do so enthusiastically. It is assumed that no adult would ask children to do things that are not good for them. In the past, when traditional authority—the authority that elders have to command the attention and commitment of youngsters—still held some sway in American society, teachers could call on it to ensure some level of attention and commitment. Traditional authority needs no justification beyond itself.

Even in the "good old days," the ability of teachers to gain attention and ensure commitment through the exercise of traditional authority was suspect, as was the idea that all or most parents supported the teachers and schools. Years ago, Willard Waller ([1932] 1967, p. 68) suggested that, in many instances, teachers and parents appeared to be "natural enemies." Today, most teachers know that traditional authority is no longer a basis for gaining commitment and attention, and many yearn for a return to the days when teachers were respected and parents supportive. We have good reason to be concerned about the breakdown of traditional authority and the disengagement of youth from the moral order. Indeed, I am convinced that unless some means can be found to reengage youth, we will suffer not only a lost generation but a lost society.

However, the maintenance of traditional authority requires general consensus among adults regarding the moral order to be advanced and sufficient trust that the actions of adults toward the young are motivated by an interest in that moral order. Much less consensus exists today than in the past on the nature of the moral order that should be advanced, and parents certainly have less trust in the motives of teachers. In most states, laws still exist that define the status of teachers vis-à-vis children as in loco parentis. Nowadays, it is quite common for parents to sue teachers and schools.

Indeed, the idea of educational malpractice has gained some currency in recent years, and malpractice is not a concept that fits easily into a traditional authority structure.[1]

Much more could and perhaps should be said about the collapse of traditional authority, the erosion of family values, the violence of youth, and a variety of other social ills that make it difficult for teachers to teach and schools to function. Important though these matters are, they are outside the control of schools. What I am concerned with here are the matters over which schools do have control. Two of these matters are the way students are defined and the kind of authority that will be used to uphold that definition.

Students as Voluntary Customers

At least two approaches can be taken to the erosion of traditional authority. The first is the "Rodney Dangerfield approach," which involves complaining about the lack of respect that teachers suffer nowadays and insisting that nothing can be done until families become more supportive. The second approach accepts the fact that students are volunteers; thus, they are more like customers in our adult world than like neophytes being inducted into the ways of the tribe.

The idea of the student as a customer acknowledges the voluntary nature of the relationship between the student and the school. Certainly, the bureaucratic authority of the state can deliver the child to the schoolhouse door, but to gain the child's attention and commitment, the teacher must become an expert in inventing work and activities that earn this response. Therefore, expert rather than traditional authority must undergird the teacher's role, and this expertise must be most clearly reflected in the act of inventing work for students and leading them to do it.

It will not be possible, however, to engage children and young people in an educational system where the quality of the experi-

---

[1]There has always been a great deal more myth than substance regarding the respect Americans have had for teachers. For every Miss Dove (Patton, 1954), an example of America's pantheon of educational heroes and heroines, there is at least one Ichabod Crane. Waller described the relationship of the teacher to the community as that of a polite stranger ([1932] 1967, p. 62).

ences the school provides is not as inviting as the quality of the experiences they get outside of school, for example, through computer games, teen magazines, and interactive TV as well as through peer groups and gangs. To reengage students who are disengaged, to continue to engage those who are now engaged, and to increase the commitment of those who are at least sufficiently compliant to hang around, it is essential to accept the fact that the school must redefine the role of the student as that of a customer. Schools and teachers must accept the fact that the attention and commitment of students must be earned; they cannot be commanded. Further, it must be understood that the authority of the schools and of teachers must increasingly be the authority of experts in the design and delivery of knowledge work for students. Appeals to traditional authority never worked well for most students in our schools. They work even less well today.

Learning as an Intended Consequence

Learning is an intended result of schooling, just as profit is an intended result of a commercial enterprise, but learning is no more a dependable short-term measure of the quality of a school than profit is of the quality of products produced by a manufacturing concern. Fortuitous circumstances (for example, a war) can make even a poorly run business profitable, just as fortuitous circumstances (for example, serving students who aspire to get into selective colleges) can result in the presence of many high-performing students even when programs are of poor quality. The view I take of the place of learning in school is similar to my view of the role of profit in business. Profit is essential to business, but it is not what business is about. Profit is what happens when a business meets customer requirements. The purpose of business is to provide products and services that have the capacity to get and keep customers. Without customers, profit is impossible.

Learning in schools, like profit in business, is what happens when schools do their business right. Learning is not, however, the business of schools. *The business of schools is to design, create, and invent high-quality, intellectually demanding work for students: schoolwork that calls on students to think, to reason, and to use their minds well and that calls on them to engage ideas, facts, and understandings whose perpetuation is essential to the survival of the common culture and relevant to the particular culture, group, and milieu from which students come and in which they are likely to function.*

Sales Versus Marketing

Sales begins with products; marketing begins with customers.[2] Those with products to sell try through persuasion, incentives, bargaining, and trading to induce others to "buy" what they have to offer. The question for the salesperson is: How do I get the customer to need—or believe that he or she needs—what I have to offer? Marketers approach the problem differently. They ask, What does the customer need? How does what I have to offer relate to those needs? If it does not, what new product or service might I create to respond to the needs that have been identified?

The approach typically taken in schools is a sales approach. The range of products (that is, the type of schoolwork available) is assumed to be limited, not quite one-size-fits-all but very nearly so. The task is to motivate students to want to do what the school and the teacher have for them to do. But if students are to be engaged in school, what is needed is a marketing approach. Educators should ask, What needs do students have that can be satisfied by the work we have to offer? What new work might we invent or create that would meet these needs better? Rather than asking, How can I motivate students? educators should ask, What motivates this particular student, and how can I present or design work that responds to these motivations? In brief, schools need to be designed so that students are viewed as customers, the work they are provided is viewed as the product of schooling, and marketing—as opposed to sales—is viewed as the organizing framework.

The Potentials of a Marketing Approach

When students are thought of as customers and knowledge work is thought of as the product of school, issues are reframed. For ex-

---

[2]Some of the discussion here will be familiar to those who have read *Schools for the 21st Century* (Schlechty, 1990) or any of a number of Peter Drucker's books.

ample, it is now commonplace for educators to speak of the school as a service delivery system in which the student is a client to be served and the teacher is a service delivery professional, something like a nurse or a social worker. Such a view assumes that the job of the teacher is to do to or for students things these students are unable to do for themselves. When students are thought of as customers and knowledge work is thought of as the product, the roles and expectations of both teachers and students change. The teachers' role is no longer to provide services for students, but to invent knowledge work for them that they can and will do. It is also the teachers' role to lead students to do the work that is provided. Thus the teachers become leaders and inventors.

This view has equally important effects on the roles and expectations schools assign to students. First, it forces the recognition that even now students have more choice in what they do than many critics and educators realize. Students in the most oppressive environment can refuse to do what they are expected to do, or they may do what they are expected to do with so little enthusiasm and attention that no benefits result.

Viewing the student as a customer places the school and the teachers in the position of accepting the proposition that it is the school's obligation to invent work sufficiently attractive that students engage in it voluntarily. (Coercion may gain compliance, but it does not produce engagement and commitment.) Furthermore, this view encourages educators to be as attentive to the quality (and qualities) of the work given to students as they are to the quality of the students' performance once the work assigned has been undertaken. This view also compels educators to embrace the notion that learning is an active process. Students learn from work they do, work to which they commit energy, time, and attention. *It is the obligation of the school and the teacher to invent work that attracts the attention and compels the energy of students, for it is in inventing products that customers will buy that a customer-focused business creates the conditions of its own survival.*

Finally, this view almost compels schools to be student-centered and child-focused. To excel at marketing, one must know customers well, even better than they know themselves, for often customers do not know what needs are motivating them. Customers usually only know what they want and the price they are willing to pay for it at a particular point in time. The marketer must understand the needs that lie behind wants and desires and translate these needs into products that are wanted by the customer. Sometimes, by knowing existing products well, it is possible to link them to needs even though the customer might not have made the linkage independently. Thus the English teacher who presents *Romeo and Juliet* as a story of young romance is likely to find a more receptive audience among adolescents than is the teacher who presents it as an illustration of Shakespearean drama.

Knowing customers well, getting close to them, and listening to them can also lead to the invention of new products that might not have been thought of without sensitivity to the customers' needs and desires. Indeed, I would argue that most of the creative and inventive teachers presently operating in schools intuitively (and sometimes consciously) view students as customers. Unfortunately, many teachers seem reluctant to acknowledge that students have the power all customers have: the power of choice.

The Issue of Quality

Just as American business has, some educators are beginning to rediscover quality. This rediscovery has reached such proportions that many now refer to what is going on in the name of quality as "the quality movement." Total Quality Management has become a buzzword in both business and education. The name most commonly associated with the quality movement is W. Edwards Deming (1986), though others, such as Philip Crosby (1979), are associated with it as well. Of course, differences exist between the various quality experts. Deming is certainly not the only person who has had something original to say on the subject of quality, but what he has said is sufficiently significant so that any discussion of quality must certainly begin with some discussion of his ideas.

The American Quality Movement

During the 1960s and 1970s, America's automobile manufacturers began to realize that the condition of the industry was becoming unhealthy. Competition from abroad, especially from Japan, was beginning to cut deeply into what had been, up to 1960, a virtual monopoly for American business. In searching for the causes of this distress, all of the usual suspects were addressed. Some of these explanations were as follows:

- Foreign labor costs were less because of lower wages.
- American workers, influenced by a "union mentality," were unwilling to work as hard as foreign workers. In addition, Americans had lost the work ethic and pride in their work.
- Unfair trade barriers placed American goods at a price disadvantage.
- Because the Japanese had lost most of their industrial base during World War II, they were in a position to modernize, whereas American automobile makers had to live with obsolete equipment and obsolete factories.
- Collusion between the government and business in Japan led to unfair practices.
- Japanese unions were really company unions, so management had more control than is possible in America.

When some management gurus began to suggest that perhaps the problem with American business rested with the way the typical American business was structured and led, business leaders, like some educational leaders today, tried to blunt the criticism with various rationalizations. For example, some business leaders found considerable comfort in saying, "The Japanese culture is different from American culture. The Japanese are more communal and less individualistic in nature than are Americans. Japanese management techniques may work in Japan, but they certainly will not work in America." Such rationalizations should have a familiar ring to those who attribute the problems with America's schools to forces beyond the control of school leaders.

In the early 1980s, two events occurred that caused some of America's business leaders to reconsider such explanations, comforting though they may have seemed. First, a series of books was published, growing primarily out of the experiences of consultants for McKinsey & Company (a prominent management consulting firm), that challenged much conventional thought about the relationship between quality and management practices and the importance of customers in the business equation. Among these books were Deal and Kennedy's *Corporate Cultures* (1982), Pascale and Athos's *The Art of Japanese Management* (1981), Ouchi's *Theory Z* (1981), and most important, Peters and Waterman's *In Search of Excellence* (1982). The second critical event was the airing of the now-famous—at least within business circles—1980 NBC documentary on the success of Japan's automobile industry, "If Japan Can . . . Why Can't We?"

The line of argument presented by McKinsey & Company consultants began to suggest that quality is, perhaps, best thought of as a result of the culture of corporations and the way corporations are led and managed rather than as an attribute of the larger society or the particular qualities of a given workforce. (Peter Drucker, who is certainly not without influence in business circles, had been making similar points for many years, but the work of the consultants associated with McKinsey & Company popularized many of the ideas that he had been advancing, while advancing some new ideas as well.)

The NBC documentary made some American business leaders aware that behind the quality revolution in Japan was a very American personage, in the form of W. Edwards Deming, who had a long history of concern about the relationship between management practices, leadership, and quality (he was eighty years old in 1981) but who had not received much of a hearing in America. The Japanese had listened. Indeed, Deming had even then become a venerated figure in Japan.

W. Edwards Deming

By 1983, many American business leaders seemed prepared to hear Deming's stern lectures on the importance of leadership and the significance of the customer and his radical views regarding the way quality is produced and maintained in the life of an organization. We can gain some appreciation of how radical his views were in the context of American business if we only consider three points he made again and again:

1. Workers want to do well. If they do not do well, the responsibility for their failure is more likely to be located in the way the systems in which they participate are structured and led than in the qualities that the workers bring to the task.

2. Quality is a result of processes. Rather than controlling quality, we should constantly endeavor to improve processes, to bring them under control, and, once they are under control, to keep them under control.
3. Eighty-five percent of the errors that occur in any process are systemic in origin. Only 15 percent can be attributed to individual variation in performance.

Much of American business thinking assumes that workers are not well motivated or even well intended and, given the opportunity, will do as little as possible. Individual interests and competition are seen as the chief sources of motivation to do work. It is also assumed that the world of quality is randomly distributed. Misfits, bad parts, and failures are simply natural by-products of a system. Quality control, therefore, is an end-of-the-line issue. The key is to prevent poor-quality products from reaching the customer or, if they do, to ensure that rework is done. For Deming, however, the key was to guarantee that the processes prevented poor-quality products from being produced, rather than to "inspect them out" at the end of the line.

Many American business leaders have begun to take Deming's teachings seriously, though some find them hard to embrace. For example, General Motors Corporation has given much attention to Deming and his work, yet, in spite of his denunciation of competition as a means of improving quality and his admonishment that one of the prime roles of management is to drive out fear and ensure that there will be a tomorrow, General Motors' management, when faced with a crisis, pitted a GM plant in Michigan against one in Texas and gave the jobs to the "winner." Deming taught that it is possible to create systems that are managed through commitments rather than through commandments. To accomplish this end, those who have authority must learn to lead rather than to manage, to direct rather than to control (Drucker, 1974).

Customers Define Quality

In a customer-focused enterprise, what the customer wants and needs determines quality. To say that a product or a service is high-quality means that it possesses qualities that are desired and valued by the customer and is lacking in qualities that are not desired or

that are devalued. The sum of these desired and undesired qualities leads to statements about the relative quality of a product or
service and thus to the commonsense assumption that quality is
best described as a continuous variable. It is not defined by a con-
tinuum going from high to low or good to bad; it either exists or
does not. Quality is categorical, existing when the product or service conforms to the customer's requirements (Crosby, 1979). This
is a simple notion, but one that seems difficult to grasp and even
more difficult to accept. Engineers often design products that have
qualities that satisfy their sense of what should be present, only to
find that the products do not satisfy their customers. Many start-up
computer companies have failed because of this error.

Designers, whether of computers, automobiles, or curricula,
sometimes forget that the customer may not bring the same needs
and values to the product that they do. In a customer-oriented
school district, where knowledge work rather than the student is
the product, the first measure of the quality of the schools is that
the students are provided with work, tasks, and intellectual activities that engage them. Regardless of the other attributes of the
work, if the students are unwilling or unable to do what they are
expected or encouraged to do, the school is not a quality school,
and the curriculum is not a quality curriculum. In making this assertion, I recognize that some readers will immediately jump to the
conclusion that I am suggesting that the school become so child-
centered that children and children alone decide what is worth
doing and learning. This is not my view, and if it were, it should be
labeled what it would be—pure nonsense. Schools should be student-focused, but this does not mean that they should be led by
students any more than a customer-focused business is led by the
customers whose needs it tries to meet.

A second and equally important measure of quality is what happens to students as a result of doing the work the school provides.
Quality schoolwork is work through which the student develops
skills, attitudes, understandings, and habits of mind that are valued by adult members of the society. Children are not adults, but
the quality of the experiences they have in school will go far in determining the kinds of adults they will be. They do not know what
they need to learn, but they know what they are ready, able, and
willing to do. Children, and adults, learn best when they want to

achieve some end that is not possible without developing new skills, new understandings, new attitudes, and new habits of mind.

Needs and Quality

Glasser (1990) asserts that five basic needs underlie all systems of human motivation: survival, power, love, fun, and freedom. Quality in schools is, in part at least, defined by the schools' ability to respond to and satisfy these needs. He writes: "But for students to do quality work, it is crucial that they see that it is for their benefit, not the benefit of their teachers, the school system, or parents" (p. 96). Taken literally, Glasser's assertion overstates the case. Schools are not only about meeting the needs of children; they must meet the needs of society as well. Those who would make schools child-focused would do well to remember this. Otherwise, focusing the school on students will degenerate into the sloppy sentimentality that has destroyed numerous past efforts to make schools more responsive to the needs of children and youth. (Glasser's phrase would satisfy me more if it read, ". . . it is for their benefit *as well as* the benefit of their teachers, the school system, and parents.")

If quality is to be built into the life of schools, those who lead school reform must know a great deal about what students value and what students believe will meet their needs. Leaders, and I include teachers as leaders, must know *as well* what kind of people the adults who provide and support the schools want children to become and what they will need to be able to do to participate fully in and contribute to the society of which they are becoming a part. Schools are about children and their needs but also about society and its future. The link between children and society is to be found in the qualities of the knowledge work the children are provided in school. And a quality school is one that best makes and sustains this link.

The Quality of Schoolwork

Up to this point little has been said about the quality of student performance. Rather, the emphasis has been on what the school, its teachers, and its administrators provide for students to do. This is not an oversight. Those who insist on using measures of student performance as the primary way to determine a school's quality implicitly assume that the student is a product of the school. To be sure, many recognize that students are not simply products of the school. They are products of their total environment, including the family, the community, and the larger social order. But students are nonetheless usually viewed as products in talk about schools; when they are not, they are thought of as patients to be treated or clients to be served. Whether students are products, patients, or clients, their role is a passive one. Someone else, usually the teacher, is doing something to or for them.

The idea that the work students are provided or encouraged to undertake in school is the product of the school is a basic assumption on which this book is based. Students are not products. They are people with motives, wills, capacities, needs to be satisfied, longings, and desires. They are not clay to be molded or widgets on an assembly line, though sometimes they must feel as though they are, given the way many schools are organized. For schools to be successful, the work students are provided must be engaging. More than that, it must be compelling, so compelling that students persist with it even when they find it difficult and demanding. The work and the products the work is intended to produce must, as well, result in satisfaction and a sense of delight. When a student successfully completes a task, he or she should say, "I'm glad I did that," rather than, "I'm glad that's done." Finally, what the student learns in the process of completing the associated tasks should be valued by his or her parents and the larger community as well as by the student.

In sum, *the business of schools is to produce work that engages students, that is so compelling that students persist when they experience difficulties, and that is so challenging that students have a sense of accomplishment, of satisfaction—indeed, of delight—when they successfully accomplish the tasks assigned.* I would use the following five descriptors to define quality knowledge work within the context of schools:

1. It is intellectual activity associated with the production of a product or performance that is sufficiently attractive to the students for whom it is intended to engage them without coercion.
2. It is sufficiently attractive and compelling to ensure that, once students are engaged, they persist with the work until the intended product meets the required standards.

3. It is sufficiently challenging to ensure that students experience a sense of delight and accomplishment as they complete the task.
4. It results in the students' learning what teachers and the students themselves intend that they should learn.
5. It results in the students' learning things that are judged by parents, other adult members of the community, and the society at large as being of social and cultural value.

Conclusion

Almost certainly, some who read this chapter will say, "It is not the schools' job to entertain students but to educate them. Some things are simply hard work and boring, but the work and the boredom are necessary parts of the task. We should not cater to students; they must learn to do some things just because they are told to. Schools are not obliged to make students happy. Their obligation is to provide students with the opportunity for a quality education."

I agree. At least, I agree that all work—including knowledge work—has its moments of boredom, routine, and disciplined drudgery. But *excitement* and *entertainment* are not synonyms for a sense of accomplishment and the satisfaction that results from it. *Schools are, or should be, about accomplishment.* I also agree that students do not know what they need to learn. If they did, they would not need to learn it; they would already know it.

But students do know what they are willing to do. Further, they are unlikely to learn anything of positive value from tasks they do not do or assignments they do not complete. Moreover, if they are to learn what teachers, parents, and the larger community want them to learn, they must be motivated to do work and engage in activities that will result in that learning. If the work the schools provide does not engage the students for whom it is intended, the schools will not produce learning any more than a manufacturing concern that creates a product customers will not buy will make a profit.

| **Beliefs, Vision, and Mission**

Actions are taken. Goals are pursued. Missions are accomplished. Visions are realized. Beliefs are to be complied with. Of course, this is not a description of reality. Sometimes inaction rather than action is the dominant mode of operation. Goals are displaced and set aside. Missions are not accomplished or are declared "impossible." Visions are not realized or are transformed into nightmares. And beliefs become nothing more than hollow rhetoric, recognized more in the breach than in any relevance to action.

In addition to failure to take action, pursue goals, and accomplish missions, another problem is confronted when we take seriously the idea that words like *beliefs, vision,* and *mission* have meaning in the context of the lives of organizations as complex as schools and school systems. That problem has to do with the connections between actions, goals, missions, visions, and beliefs. Often, failure to take these connections into account results in failure to act, to pursue, to accomplish, to realize, and to comply.

Strategic Planning: Tool, Weapon, or Distraction?

Strategic planning, which is in vogue in many schools and corporations, gives rise to considerable attention being paid to beliefs, visions, missions, goals, and action plans. It is, in fact, difficult to find a school district that does not have a strategic plan shelved away somewhere. Sometimes it will have two or three such plans, because plans often seem to have a half-life about as long as the tenure of superintendents and the stability of the composition of school boards. On rare occasions, such strategic plans actually serve as a blueprint for action over time, but their payoff in schools, at least as they are now typically conducted and as schools are currently organized, probably is not worth the energy expended on them.

But strategic planning does not only serve as a potential spur for action; it can serve other functions as well. Whether or not these functions are intended and recognized, I will leave to the reader to decide. In addition to being a spur for action and a source of direction into the future, strategic planning can serve the following purposes:

- It gives the appearance of doing something important to change the schools while teachers and principals wait for the next change in administration to occur.
- It demonstrates that state departments of education and school district offices do have the power to gain compliance with planning directives. At a minimum, these agencies can ensure that everyone has a plan, a common planning format is used, and the plans arrive in the right office on time.

It does not seem likely, therefore, that strategic planning will go out of style in schools any time soon. Furthermore, properly done, strategic plans are useful, and in the hands of leaders who are able and willing to be persistent, they are powerful tools. Even when it is done or used improperly, strategic planning can serve important functions for those who want to maintain the status quo.

I do not make these comments lightly or in order to disparage the importance of beliefs, visions, missions, and strategic planning (though I am much more partial to thinking and acting strategically than to planning strategically). In my view, too many educators have turned very powerful tools into just one more fad. Everyone did the Charleston in the 1920s and played with hula hoops in the 1950s; today every school must have a vision statement or a mission statement or a belief statement, and "everybody's got to have a plan."

Beliefs: Conditions of Willingness to Act

In the literature of business and of education, the terms *beliefs* (sometimes expressed as *corporate values*), *vision*, and *mission* are commonplace terms. Mission statements, vision statements, and statements of corporate goals are ubiquitous. One can hardly enter an airport, department store, fast-food restaurant, schoolhouse, or school board office complex without encountering a statement that is—or purports to be—a mission statement, vision statement, or statement of beliefs and values.

Beliefs are important, but they are meaningless if they are nothing more than statements hung on a wall. Furthermore, it makes little difference whether or not such wall hangings were developed by a "committee representing all the stakeholders in the community" or created by the superintendent one evening over a dry martini. Until these beliefs, whatever they are, are viewed as "conditions of willingness to act *as though* . . ."[1] and until this willingness is embedded bone deep in the culture of the schools and the hearts of the men and women who live out their occupational biographies there, belief statements will make little difference. As important as it is to develop belief statements to guide strategy development, it is even more important to develop strategies to ensure that these beliefs, whatever they are, command the attention and commitment of all those whose support is needed if the beliefs are ever to result in visions that are realized.

Vision

Vision is another of those tricky words. Sometimes people talk about vision when they mean missions, and sometimes they talk

---

[1]The idea of beliefs as the condition of willingness to act was suggested to me years ago in Hullfish and Smith, *Reflective Thinking: The Method of Education* (1961). The statement "all men are created equal" is a belief statement. It commands us to act as though it is true, accepting it on faith and totally without empirical evidence. It is a statement of the way the world is supposed to be, not the way the world is. Similarly, the statement "All children can learn and can learn more than they are now learning" is a belief statement that commands those who subscribe to it to "act as though" the belief is so, in spite of the lack of evidence to support the assertion, and sometimes when the evidence is to the contrary. *Belief statements,* as I am using the term here, are statements of hope and aspiration and the basis for dreams and visions.

about vision when they are describing beliefs. To understand the power of vision, we must first understand that visions have to do with images, with pictures in our mind. To have vision is to see. Sometimes visions are unclear ("we see through a glass, darkly"), but with enough vision-oriented missions (described in the next section), visions become increasingly clear.

We do not create visions; they happen because of what we believe. Vision statements are meaningless, for we cannot state a vision. All we can do is to make statements *about or concerning* a vision. These statements should draw pictures in the reader's or the listener's mind regarding the thing that is being envisioned. Visions derive from beliefs, so they are less basic and more subject to change than beliefs. Indeed, vision is nothing more or less than contemporary interpretations of the meaning and implications of beliefs. Our vision cannot be clear unless our beliefs are.

Because beliefs are more basic than visions, they must precede visions in the order of things (see Figure 5.1 for an example). Statements about vision answer such questions as what would the world or our school look like if our beliefs were realized? and how would we feel if they were manifested in our behavior and in the systems we have created to support them?

Statements about vision incorporate the values and commitments that guide the system as well as beliefs about structure. These statements appeal to hearts as well as to minds; they command loyalty and emotional attachments and provide orientation for specific action. Vision statements, if they are important, are not intended to be realistic but to be inspiring. They describe conditions to be realized and give a basis for determining the merit and worth of particular missions, the desirability of particular goals, and the morality of particular actions. Vision is important, but without deeply held and well-articulated beliefs, it is "as sounding brass, or a tinkling cymbal."

Missions

Missions can be accomplished and need to be stated in accomplishable terms. Mission statements are, in fact, a bundle of goals that will need to be unbundled for action to proceed. (In my view,

Figure 5.1. From Beliefs to Action: An Example.

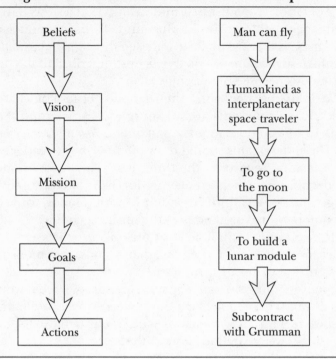

strategic planning is best thought of as a way to select high-leverage missions intended to help realize a vision, unbundle the goals inherent in these missions, and connect them to necessary and possible actions.) Mission statements made without reference to a compelling vision are unlikely to have the moral authority to command action, especially when the mission becomes difficult or risky. Take, for example, the American experience in rocketry. At the end of World War II and with the help of many German rocket scientists, America, like the USSR, conducted substantial research in rocketry and worked hard to develop missiles that could carry meaningful payloads. The Russian launching of *Sputnik I* marked the beginning of the "space race."

Recognizing that part of the problem was structural, President Dwight Eisenhower "restructured" the American rocket program, changing it from a rocket program to a space program; he thereby positioned it to be associated with positive visions as well as nuclear nightmares. The name of the new organization, the National Aeronautics and Space Administration (NASA), reflected this change of position as did the fact that it was a civilian rather than a military organization. It was not, however, until President John F. Kennedy gave NASA a clear mission (to get a man on the moon in a decade and return him safely) that the vision driving NASA began to be articulated in ways that were compelling to the nation. By insisting that a man—rather than a dog or a monkey—go to the moon, President Kennedy brought together the abiding belief that man can fly and a Buck Rogers fantasy of humankind as interplanetary space traveler. By turning this fantasy into a belief-based vision and connecting it to the moon mission rather than to military efforts to get payloads into outer space, the enterprise became a morally compelling effort to realize what, until the twentieth century, was not even a well-developed dream, to say nothing of a vision.

The preferences of scientists notwithstanding, a commitment to get a rocket on the moon, a robot on the moon, or even a monkey on the moon would not have had the compelling authority that a mission connected to the vision of humankind as space traveler was certain to have. Furthermore, America's values were expressed in the mission statement and implicit in the vision that guided this mission, for Kennedy felt obliged to emphasize that the moon traveler should return safely.

At least two additional lessons regarding the linkage between vision and mission can be learned from the NASA experience:

1. The effective pursuit and accomplishment of missions help to clarify visions and, thus, to make it more likely that the visions will be realized.
2. When missions become "unhitched" from the guiding vision, it is likely that the organization will get into the wrong business and that the business it gets into will not inspire the loyalty or commitment that were present when the mission and vision were linked together.

We only need to study some of the old Buck Rogers cartoons and Captain Video episodes and compare them to the *Star Trek* series and *Star Wars* to see that, as a result of the effort to get to the moon, the popular image of the technology that is needed for interplanetary travel and the systems required to support that technology have changed dramatically. Buck Rogers was driven by a dream. The moon mission was oriented toward a vision. Dreams stir the imagination, but dreams turned into realizable visions direct and compel action. Furthermore, the pursuit of missions that are vision-driven (as opposed to visionless) helps to clarify the vision itself.

After the successful moon landing, NASA had, and continues to have, an identity crisis. Many factors were involved in creating this crisis, including the Vietnam War, economic difficulties, and changes in national leadership. Among the most important of these factors must surely be the fact that the missions NASA undertook subsequent to Neil Armstrong's "small step" somehow became unhitched from the vision of conquering interplanetary space. As the movie *Apollo 13* depicts so clearly, few people are especially inspired by—or even interested in—routine space flights, even flights to the moon. It is the image of human beings going where they have never gone before and doing what they have never done before that inspires attention and supports action. When NASA became a hauler of freight—no matter how exotic the freight may be—the inspiring qualities of the NASA program were, for many people, simply lost.[2] The consequences of this loss of visionary focus have been a loss of confidence within NASA's structure and a loss of confidence and commitment to NASA by policy makers and funding sources.

There is a certain irony about the fact that a governmental agency was responsible for one of the proudest human achievements of this century, if not of all time. Yet, when the system fails to respond to new realities, we hear the cry to turn the space program over to the private sector, for the private sector always does things better. What nonsense! NASA, in its visionary stage, was a

---

[2]The *Challenger* disaster makes my point even more clearly. Though it was not aimed at the moon, *Challenger* did stir special interest. Why? Because it was aimed at doing something that had never before been done—putting a teacher into outer space—and this stirred the hearts of young and old alike.

model of effective operation, innovation, creative problem solving, and a commitment to results produced on rigorous time lines. Would that the Ford Motor Company, General Motors Corporation, and Chrysler Corporation—to say nothing of American Motors Corporation and Eastern Airlines—had worked as well.

Vision without beliefs is nothing more or less than dreams and fictions. Beliefs without a commitment to act are hollow rhetoric. Missions that are unattached to visions are without focus and are meaningless in the long run, for they will fail to inspire action or will get "lost in space." This is the lesson we can learn from NASA. It is also the lesson that can be learned from many failed businesses and many failed efforts at school reform.

Beliefs About Purpose, Customers, and Products

What teachers, principals, superintendents, board members, and students believe about the purpose of schools and the kinds of products the schools should produce—indeed, what they believe about what these products are, who the schools' customers are, and what kind of customers they want these customers to be—goes far toward explaining how and why schools come to be organized and managed the way they are.

Beliefs about purpose answer the question, What business do we want to be in? This is more than a question about goals and missions. To answer it, we must deal with the system's reason for being, what Pascale and Athos (1981) refer to as the superordinate goals of the system. In school terms, we want to know what the school should be designed to do, which means identifying its priority concerns and articulating the basic values toward which the school is oriented. For example, looking at the current design of many schools, we would assume that the business of schools is to select and sort students on the basis of their willingness and ability to do particular forms of schoolwork. Is that really the business we intend our schools to be in or would we prefer that they be in the business of designing activities (knowledge work) that students find engaging and from which they learn things that are of social and cultural value?

Beliefs about customers answer the question, Whom are we trying to serve, and whose loyalties and commitment are we trying to gain? In school terms, we want to know whom the schools intend to serve directly as well as for whom they provide indirect services and products, for these are the school's customers. In my view, the students are the direct customers of the school; they should be the immediate focus of all school activity. All others, including parents, the business community, teachers, and the society at large, are downstream customers, indirect customers, or sometimes the school's customers' customers.

Beliefs about products answer such questions as What do we really endeavor to provide to our customers? What need or needs are we trying to satisfy, and how do we know that our customers have the needs we assume they have? What new products might we invent that would better satisfy our customers' needs? What needs of our customers that we are not now satisfying might we satisfy with new, different, or qualitatively different products or services? If we produce these new and different products or services, will this be in keeping with our view of the business we want to be in and the purposes we want to serve? In school terms, these questions ask, What are we providing to students? My answer, of course, is that schools are, or should be, attempting to provide students with tasks, assignments, and meaningful activities that they find engaging and from which they learn what they need in order to be recognized as well educated by those who know them.

When, in school terms, we ask the question, What needs are we endeavoring to satisfy? we are asking, What do students need, want, and desire that, if it is present in the work the school offers, will lead them to engage that work? and What do parents, the business community, and other taxpayers want and need from the schools, and how can we ensure that we are meeting both their needs and the needs of students?

When schoolteachers and others ask, What new products might we invent? they are asking, Are there alternative means of doing the tasks assigned? Are there alternative tasks, which students might find more exciting and inviting, that would result in more students' learning or some students' learning more? If so, what are they and how should they be designed?

Finally, when teachers ask, If we produce these new products or provide these new services, will we be doing the business we should be doing or not? they are asking, What should be the focus of the school? For example, should the focus of the school play be on providing high-quality drama for the community or should the play be oriented toward providing high-quality experiences for students? Can it do both? If not, which value should be sacrificed and why?

Again, my answer to this question has been foreshadowed. For me, the highest value pursued in schools is providing high-quality experiences for students: experiences that they find engaging, that encourage persistence, and that produce products and performances that the students themselves find to be of value. Furthermore, if these experiences, these tasks, and this work are truly quality work, then students who engage the work will learn things that are of value to others as well as to themselves. Schools are not simply about students and their needs after all; they are the means by which society perpetuates the condition of its own existence and progress.

Beliefs About Structure

The structure of an organization consists of the relatively permanent and predictable relationships that exist between and among the people who interact in the context of the organization, the roles that define those interactions, and the rules that prescribe and proscribe what those roles and relationships will be.[3] Therefore, to know what is believed about the structure of schools we must ask what is believed about:

- *The rules that govern behavior in schools.* These include everything from law and policy to tacit agreements and customary practices.
- *The roles that shape behavior.* These include the expected and sometimes required behavior of those who occupy positions in the

---

[3]For this reason I have defined *restructuring* as "altering the rules, roles, and relationships that shape, direct, and govern behavior in groups and organizations." Unfortunately, the word restructuring has come to mean so many things in education, such as empowering teachers, decentralizing, downsizing, and privatizing, that it has lost all meaning. I have, therefore, nearly stopped using this word. In the Humpty-Dumpty world of education, it seems that anyone can appropriate perfectly good words and make them mean whatever they want.

schools. What, for example, is and should be expected of students, parents, teachers, principals, support staff, central office personnel, custodians, cooks, bus drivers, superintendents, and boards of education, to mention a few? Sometimes the outlines of these roles can be found in documents such as job descriptions, union contracts, and board policies, but equally important is an understanding of actual practice: what people really do, what is approved of, what is tolerated, what is punished, how strong are the punishments, what is rewarded, and how significant are the rewards.

• *Relationships.* These include the relative positioning of one role and another role (for example, which roles are superordinate and which are subordinate, which carry honor and status and which are stigmatized) and the fit and antagonisms between and among roles and the rules that define them as well as the fit and antagonisms between and among the rules themselves. For example, one of the more critical questions facing those who would decentralize schools through charters is that of the relationship between the charter school and the board or agency that charters and/or funds it. Such relationships are sometimes defined by rules such as laws or board policies, but they are also defined by practice and informal agreements.

When we ask questions about structure, we are also asking how the major components of the system are envisioned and enacted. The way we answer questions associated with purposes, products, and customers will go far in determining how the structure of the school will be envisioned, and the extent to which leaders uphold the beliefs upon which the vision is based will go far in determining whether the vision that derives from these beliefs will be realized.

Envisioning a New School System

What kind of structure might we envision if we believe that students are the primary customers of the school, that the work the schools provide students is the primary product of the schools, and that the business of schools is to invent work that is engaging to students and results in the students' learning the things that are of most value to themselves, their parents, their teachers, and the society at large?

1. In such a school, all who make or participate in making decisions in and for the schools will discipline what they do through asking the following questions:

- Is this decision likely to increase the number of students engaged in the work provided by the schools or, at least, increase the level of engagement of some of the students?
- If so, is the work in which students will be engaged likely to result in their learning more things of value or things of more value?

In sum, whatever system of rules, roles, and relationships emerges, the focus of all activity will be on students and the needs of students.

2. However such schools come to be organized, the role of the teacher will be defined so that teachers have the authority needed to lead and the time required to invent. This necessarily means that they will have tremendous influence over the way time, people, space, and information are organized, deployed, and used. They will also have considerable influence over the kinds of technologies that will be employed and discretion in their use. In short, the system will be decentralized and teachers empowered. Site-based decision making will be a reality; however, it will take place within the context of a common district-level vision derived from commitments to common beliefs endorsed and supported by the community at large. Rather than expecting each building to have its own vision, district- and building-level versions of that vision will be created. The particulars of the versions will vary with the circumstances confronted at the building in recognition of the fact that different customers have different needs. However, no version will be immune to discipline from the larger vision that governs the district and all that occurs therein.

3. The roles of the principal and the superintendent will change. Both will function as leaders of leaders. They will manage by results rather than by programs and inspire others to manage by results as well. Values and vision, rather than programs and

rules, will drive the system. Those who lead will do so by those values and will communicate those visions.

4. The relationship between the school board and the superintendent will differ substantially from the relationship we typically find today. Boards of education will function more like well-running corporate boards and less like political commissions representing the interests of electoral constituencies. The function of the board will be to develop policies that ensure that the system is responsive to customers and accountable to the community, just as corporate boards must ensure that the companies they run get and keep customers and are accountable to their communities of reference, such as stockholders and regulatory agencies. The tendency of board members to see themselves as political functionaries who are expected to respond to the community—as opposed to being expected to create a responsive system—will be changed. Rather than representing the disagreements reflected in the community, the board will build community consensus regarding the schools and ensure that this consensus moves the school district.

The superintendent will be viewed as the chief executive officer (CEO) of one of the largest knowledge-work organizations in the community.[4] The board and the community will understand the difference between being a CEO and being an administrator. They will understand that administrators carry out directives, whereas executives give direction, and that administrators manage programs, whereas executives lead people and teach them to lead. They will expect their superintendent to be an executive. As the chief executive and leader of the school system, the superintendent will spend most of his or her time identifying problems to be

---

[4]At present, public schools employ between 8 and 10 percent of all adult Americans who hold college degrees. Indeed, in relatively isolated rural communities, the vast majority of college-educated people are likely to be teachers. The primary products these people produce are products of the mind, such as lessons and lesson plans and assignments for others. This is knowledge work—or it should be. In almost every community, the public schools are likely to be among the largest employers of college-educated people who spend most of their time working on and with knowledge.

solved and getting others to solve these problems. It is not the function of executives to solve problems; they cause others to solve problems. Executives are not problem solvers, they are problem definers.[5]

5. The relationship between schools, the school district, and the community will change as will the relationship between schools and parents. Those who lead schools will come to understand that the schools are community agencies as well as educational institutions. As leaders of educational organizations, they have the obligation to ensure that schools stay focused on students and on providing students with high-quality work. This is the only business of the schools. As leaders of community agencies—and therefore as community leaders—school leaders will have a different role: they will be the chief advocates for children in the community. Their obligation will be to ensure that the community provides each child with the support he or she needs to be successful in the life of the community.

Values and Commitments

Beliefs about purposes, products, customers, and structure are essential components out of which a vision of schools can emerge. But such beliefs must be embedded in clearly articulated and deeply held values and supported by clear and compelling commitments if they are to be realized in action. Thus it behooves those who work in schools and those who are in positions of leadership to ask and find answers to such fundamental questions as these:

---

[5]There is just a tad of rhetorical flourish in some of these statements, especially those relating to the role of the superintendent. Executives certainly administer as well as lead; they solve problems as well as cause problems to be solved. But the important point is that problems—rather than solutions, uncertainties, or routines—are the concern of executives and of leaders. The superintendent, as CEO, finds his or her most powerful expression of the office he or she occupies in identifying, framing, and communicating problems, and the superintendent finds his or her most powerful expression as a leader in inspiring others to solve these problems and by ensuring the support necessary to do so.

• What do we believe about children's ability to learn? Do we really believe that all children can learn and that every child can learn more than he or she is now learning in school? If so, what is our obligation when children fail to learn or when their learning fails to improve on a continual basis? If not, why change?

• What do we believe about the *primary* sources of variance in learning? Do we believe that most of these sources are under the control of the schools, and do we act as if the quality of the experiences provided students is what makes the difference, or do we prefer to believe that most of the important differences are beyond the control of the schools, for example, the child's family background, level of parental support, and measured intelligence?

• What do we believe about the relationship between schools and parents, families, and other community agencies? Do we really believe that parents should be partners, or are they partners only when they do what we want? What do we believe our relationship should be to parents who are abusive to their children or those who want forms of education for their children that we believe are inappropriate or potentially harmful to the children or to the larger society? What kind of relationships should the school have with other agencies that serve children and youth and how should the relationships be governed? What rules are needed and should other systems such as collaboratives be created?

• What do we believe about the obligation of the system to its employees? Do we believe, for example, that continuing nurturance, training, and development are critical? If so, do we believe that the district ought to provide resources to support this belief or is this largely a matter left up to the individual to obtain at her or his expense?

• Finally, if we believe everything we say we believe, how are present programs, practices, policies, and procedures serving us? Are they really congruent with our beliefs, or do discrepancies exist? If so, what must we stop doing, and what must we do that we are not doing, to remove these discrepancies? Are we really willing to do these things, and do we believe that we can learn to do them?

Many additional questions could and should be asked and answered, but the most important questions are the last ones, for they have to do with commitment. Without commitment, without faith that we can do what has never been done, real change will not occur. As Adam Urbanski, president of the Rochester, New York, Teachers' Union, has said, "Real change is real hard" (Urbanski, 1993). Reinventing schools is not for the timid and those who are afraid to cause trouble and create tension, for trouble and tension come with the territory. The question is whether or not school districts have or can develop the capacity to support such change.

Conclusion

The schools America needs and the schools America has are quite different. Whether or not the reader agrees with the details of the vision I have suggested, I hope that he or she will agree that the focus of schools should be on students and their needs and that the primary determinant of what students learn is the quality of the work the school provides for the student.

The environment from which children come does makes a tremendous difference in the way they respond to school and how they behave there. Confronted with this awesome fact, some educators seem near to giving up in despair. Others, recognizing that they can do little unless students receive more support than many now have, give in to the temptation to take up the slack and endeavor to provide what the child needs that the family and the community cannot or will not provide. In my view, this is wrongheaded. It puts schools in a business they were not designed for and focuses attention on matters that distract the schools from their proper business. Schools are not welfare agencies, hospitals, juvenile detention centers, or psychological treatment centers. They are educational institutions with the singular purpose of ensuring that all children have schoolwork they can and will do and from which they develop the understandings, skills, insights, and control over facts that are considered important to them and to the culture and society in which they will live. *On the other hand, schools cannot do the business they are designed to do unless the needs children have for such things as personal safety, food, adult nurturance, health services, and psychological support are somehow provided. Left to chance, many children do not and will not receive the support they need.*

Perhaps it is time for school leaders to understand that they are also community leaders and that their role in the community is to provide leadership that ensures that the community and the agencies the community has provided for such purposes work together to guarantee each child the support needed to be successful in school and in the life of the community. Of course, much more could be said about each of the areas touched on above, and much more should be said about roles that were not touched on or were only alluded to, such as the relationship between schools and families and the role of central office personnel, counselors, school secretaries, and others.

Some of these topics will be discussed in subsequent chapters of this book, and a few will be covered in detail. For example, the role of parents and the role of the community as a guarantor of support for children will be reintroduced in Chapter Seven. Enough has been said here, however, to provide the reader with some notion of where and how the local conversation about schools might be structured. The specific details of the conversation will vary, because schools are, after all, properly local inventions. The important thing is for leaders to cause the conversation to occur and to act upon what emerges. Only in this manner can the schools that America needs be invented.

Chapter Six

Assessing District Capacity

In spite of the fact that there are numerous examples of "schools that work," few examples can be found of school *districts* where all the schools work as well as the community would like. As much variability seems to exist among schools within school districts as across district lines. Exemplary school districts are harder to find than exemplary schools within school districts that seem to be failing. Further, when exemplary districts do appear, they tend to be relatively small or to consist of clusters of schools in larger school districts such as East Harlem District 4 in New York City, which includes the highly praised Central Park East Secondary School. Indeed, much of the early research on effective schools was based on locating schools that worked inside school districts that did not.

Observations such as these have led some to the conclusion that the large size of some districts and the complexity introduced by the existence of a central office are major barriers to improving schools. The argument is often heard that because so few school districts exist in which schools are uniformly good and because the real action occurs in schools and classrooms, school district offices should be eliminated or at least made irrelevant to the operation of schools. Clearly, the assumption underlying vouchers, some of the more extreme forms of charter schools, and decentralization is that school districts and their functionaries (sometimes called central office bureaucrats) have little to contribute to the improvement of education in America and may be impediments.

Schools and Communities

Like many others, I am sometimes amazed and appalled at the bureaucratic red tape, duplication of effort, and self-serving activity

I find in the central offices of some large school districts (and some small school districts as well). Along with many others, I believe that the changes that really count are those that directly affect students. If a change does not hold the promise of increasing the number of students who learn what the schools are designed to teach them or the amount of learning of all students, then it is of dubious value. However, in spite of these observations, I do not believe that school districts should be abolished or that changes in the way they operate are irrelevant to what happens in schools and classrooms. *I am persuaded, in fact, that only through revitalizing and redirecting the action of district-level operations can the kind of widespread and radical change that must occur become possible.*

One of the reasons I feel as I do is that school districts—those agencies that correspond with locally identifiable political entities such as independent taxing authorities, municipalities, counties, and towns—are the only organizational units that can genuinely serve the interests of the entire community. Schoolhouse units, if they function as they should, necessarily center on the interests and needs of the children presently in attendance and their parents. Long-term community interests, the interests of nonparent taxpayers, and the interests of the larger civic and business community—indeed, the interests of many of the diverse groups that constitute the community from which support for schools must be derived—seldom get played out in individual schoolhouses. It is at the district level rather than the building level that the drama of community life is enacted.

As numerous commentators have observed, however, the fragmentation and the polarization of communities are major problems of our time. This fragmentation and polarization clearly have an impact on schools. Some see this impact as so great that they do not believe that school reform will be possible until schools are taken away from the control of governmental agencies and from the communities these agencies represent and are turned over to parents and perhaps to teachers and local administrators as well (see, for example, Chubb and Moe, 1990). Framing school reform issues as matters that can be resolved by reducing size and complexity and returning once again to the "little red schoolhouse" of a bygone year is attractive both aesthetically and politically. It stirs up warm reveries in the hearts and minds of many Americans, and it reduces the issues of school reform to manageable and understandable proportions. All that has to be done, the argument goes, is to dethrone the downtown bureaucrats and return control where it belongs, to the parents.

Schools that serve like-minded parents and that are staffed by teachers who are selected because they are kindred spirits also have a great deal of appeal and certainly ease problems for reform-minded educators. Finding a community to serve is clearly much easier than serving the fragmented community that exists or inventing a community. This is one of the reasons the charter school movement is intuitively attractive to so many politicians and parents; it is also the reason many educators find the idea so appealing. Yet the American experiment in education proceeds from the assumption that diversity of interests and backgrounds is healthy and can be productive. The challenge to the public schools has always been to take children from all sorts of families and all types of situations and provide them with a high-quality academic education that will simultaneously develop in them the sensibilities and civic virtues required to live in a pluralistic democracy.

To abandon school districts as a useful tool for promoting this end is an irresponsible and cavalier denial of the values that have guided American public education for over one hundred years. To abandon the idea of having schools serve as instruments for promoting a common culture—a common culture so strong that all who participate in it can benefit from and appreciate the diversity of the many cultures it contains—is to invite the kind of culture-based wars we see in Bosnia-Herzegovina. As John Dewey (1899, p. 7) observed:

> What the best and wisest parent wants for his own child, that must the community want for all of its children. Any other ideal for our schools is narrow and unlovely; acted upon it destroys our democracy. All that society has accomplished for itself is put, through the agency of the school, at the disposal of its future members. All its better thoughts of itself it hopes to realize through the new possibilities thus opened to its future self. . . . Only by being true to the full growth of all the individuals who make it up, can society by any chance be true to itself.

Public schools are about and for parents and children, and the proper focus of school activity is on the needs and interests of students. But as Durkheim observed (see Chapter Four), schools are about much more than the interests of children and the preferences of parents. They are also concerned with the interests of the community, with posterity as well as the present generation, and with ensuring that the education received by the vast majority of Americans will promote democracy in an age of information overload, cultural fragmentation, and community disintegration. Only a system that operates beyond the interests of the parents and students who attend a particular school at a particular time has the potential to ensure that these long-term cultural interests are satisfied at the same time that each child is receiving the high-quality education that he or she deserves and that parents have the right to demand.

In the short term, what individual parents want for their children may not be in the general interest or promote the common good. For example, in 1945, few white parents in the South were demanding that schools be desegregated. Today, few Americans, including those from the South, would publicly defend separate but equal as anything other than separate and evil.

The primary aim of every school district should be to ensure that each child receives a high-quality education that is responsive to the child's needs and the parents' aspirations and that at the same time is one that the wisest of parents—and grandparents—would want for their children. This is not a small task, but neither is the maintenance and growth of democracy. The task will be impossible if school districts are destroyed and schoolhouses are enshrined as the only meaningful source of direction for the American system of education.

School Districts: Barrier or Resource?

After over thirty years of working at the problem of change in schools, I have come to the conclusion that change is peculiarly difficult in schools because the schools, and the school districts of which they are typically a part, lack the capacities needed to support and sustain change efforts. Even in private corporations, where these capacities are often present, change is difficult; in public school systems, where they are usually absent, real change is nearly impossible. Regardless of this observation, I have not given up on the idea that schools can be, and should be, changed in fundamental ways. If changes are to occur, however, those who lead must come to understand that to change schools and what occurs in classrooms, reformers must first introduce the changes needed to enhance the capacity of the educational system to support and sustain change in the schools. Destroying school districts and creating schools that simply serve the short-term interests of a particular group of parents (and perhaps teachers) will weaken, rather than strengthen, both education and democracy.[1] Furthermore, as I will try to demonstrate in Chapter Eight, such a strategy may foreshadow the demise of America's commitment to a publicly supported system of education (note that I did not say "to a public school system") and perhaps sound the death knell of American-style democracy.

One of the primary reasons school reform has generally failed is that individual schools, no matter how vital and responsive their present programs are, do not have the capacity to support and sustain change independent of the support of larger political and social units. School buildings, because of the way they are located in the political and social milieu of communities, cannot develop these capacities. For example, the hundreds and sometimes thousands of schools in a given state have little ability to interact in a meaningful way with the needs and demands of the larger business community. Local school faculties can form partnerships with local neighborhood businesses, and many do so. Some particularly aggressive or well-led faculties may even form alliances and partnerships with a local representative of a national business that has offices in the vicinity. However, these interactions, vital though they are, do little to create the conditions that will cause all schools in the community to address issues raised by business leaders, religious leaders, and civil rights groups.

---

[1]The reader should not infer from this statement that I am necessarily opposed to in-district choice or charter schools, for I am not. What I do oppose is granting autonomy to such schools. Schools should operate within the context of the corporate belief system that guides the district. They should not be autonomous units operating outside of this context. Within it, however, schools can be granted a great deal of independence of action.

Local schools, no matter how decent and committed the faculty might be, cannot deal in isolation with issues of equity. Equity is a community issue that gets played out in schools and classrooms, but solutions to problems of equity must occur where they originate, in the larger community. The way money is allocated, staff members are recruited and assigned, and access to knowledge is distributed cannot be judged in the context of individual schools. Such judgments must be made in the context of the larger systems of which the schools are a part, and the solutions to these problems must occur at the system level as well. Unfortunately as things now stand, few school districts have the capacities they need to assist at the building level. Unlike schools, however, school districts can develop these capacities *if* district-level leaders and community leaders commit themselves to the task.

School districts operate at a community level rather than simply at the level of parents and students. Thus the school district, unlike the school, is capable of commanding the attention and support of total communities, not just of parents who happen to have children in a particular school at a particular time.[2] First, however, school district functions must be redesigned and reoriented so that the district office becomes a resource for local school reform rather than a barrier to the development of effective local schools.

Going to Scale and Maintaining Momentum

Interesting, useful, and provocative models, exemplars, successful experimental schools, and prototype programs are not in short

[2]Some will suggest that individual schools could operate at the community level as well, if only their leaders wanted them to. True enough, as long as the number of individual schools operating at the community level is relatively small. Even now, one of the complaints of some leaders of nationally and internationally focused businesses is that the requests from individual schools for partnerships and other support in some communities is overwhelming their capacity to respond. As an example, I have worked with many businesses that are willing to make their executive training programs available to educators if they can find a way to do so. They find it much less inviting, however, to provide these programs to a small cadre of leaders from a single school than to cohorts of leaders from a school district.

supply in American public education. The difficulty comes, it seems, in transporting these practices from the sites where they are invented and demonstrated to other sites. The history of education is replete with examples of successful experiments that were abandoned after they had proved their worth. In business this is referred to as the problem of "going to scale."

Schools have the further difficulty of ensuring that sound practices, once they have been demonstrated, are maintained over the long term or until more effective programs and practices come along to replace them. This problem even exists in schools where the innovative ideas were first created or tried. Quite often a school that develops a national reputation as a leader in a particular type of initiative will have abandoned it and embraced a new reform by the time word of the first initiative has encouraged visitors to come and see what is happening. This is especially the case if the initiating principal leaves or a substantial number of the trailblazing faculty go on to different jobs. Why are these things so? Why is it so difficult to take demonstrably sound ideas to scale in educational settings? Why is the maintenance of the momentum of change so dependent on the presence of particular personalities? The answer to these questions lies, in part, in understanding what capacities are needed to support and sustain school reform initiatives.

Critical Capacities

If substantial, purposeful change is to occur and be sustained over time, the organization that is the subject of the change must possess three critical capacities:

1. The capacity to establish and maintain a focus on the future
2. The capacity to maintain a constant direction
3. The capacity to act strategically

The Capacity to Establish and Maintain a Focus on the Future

All organizations must deal with the daily, the routine, and the immediate. In this regard schools are like other organizations. But unlike many other systems, schools and those who lead them often find it difficult and often impossible to get beyond the immediate and seriously to contemplate the future. In many schools "vision-ing" becomes an exercise people engage in as part of a strategic planning process. But once the exercise is done, they must return to reality, or so it is often argued. Thus, in school settings, strate-gic planning often becomes nothing more than a process for iden-tifying tactics to deal with the immediate problems that are tearing at the system.

In organizations where the capacity to focus on the future is present, vision is a process of imagining a preferred future, and strategic planning is a process of identifying the ways and means of attaining that future. The maintenance needs of the organization, although very real, are not permitted to overwhelm developmental needs. This is not so in most school systems. Maintenance needs al-most always overwhelm developmental needs (see Schlechty and Whitford, 1983).

The Capacity to Maintain a Constant Direction

Substantial change calls for changes in culture as well as structure. It requires changes in habits and traditions as well as in practices and procedures, in values and commitments as well as in rules, roles, and relationships. It requires time and persistence of effort. When resistance is encountered, strategies must be developed to overcome or bypass it. When enthusiasms temporarily wane, strate-gies must be developed to reinvigorate the process.

In schools, when substantial resistance occurs, the likely result will be that the chief proponents of the change will be replaced by proponents of a return to the status quo or to some other preferred past condition, such as "back to the basics." When a change begins to affect powerful interest groups, as always happens when change is real, the disaffection of these groups is too often viewed by school and community leaders as a signal that the change is ineffective, rather than as evidence that it is having predictable effects.

The Capacity to Act Strategically

Strategic action requires the ability to make choices and act on them. Because these choices are future-oriented, they are some-times necessarily antagonistic to present short-term interests. The school superintendent or school board confronted with the need to close schools or to redistrict fully understands how difficult strategic action is in the context of schools.

Because of these difficulties, school leaders are under constant pressure to abandon strategic decisions in favor of immediate accommodation to present interests. The school that should be closed is left open and budget cuts are made elsewhere, probably in staff development and training. For example, in schools it is common to assume that funds must be equally distributed and cuts equally endured, rather than that cuts could be made strategically, with an eye toward actions that are optimally supportive of long-term missions and goals. New programs almost always require new money because abandoning old programs to free up resources will almost always bring a special-interest contingent to the next board meeting.

Essential Questions

Over the past thirty years, I have had the opportunity to observe a wide range of efforts to bring about change in schools. I have led some of these efforts, and I have watched others lead. I have talked with many who are leading change efforts in schools, and I have read widely in the literature on change as well as in the literature on organizational behavior and the sociology of complex social organizations.[3] Based on these experiences, I have identified ten organizational goals that I believe school district leaders must attend to, or cause others to attend to, if the districts they lead are to have the capacities needed to support and sustain reform at the building level. I have listed the goals as well as questions that might be asked in an effort to assess just how well a district is doing in achieving these goals.

---

[3]There was a time in my life when I styled myself a sociologist who was interested in the study of organizations and occupations. I taught courses on these subjects as well as on the sociology of education generally. I even wrote a book entitled *Teaching and Social Behavior: Toward an Organizational Theory of Instruction* (1976), which was a rather ham-fisted and jargon-laden effort to apply what sociologists think they know to the problems of educators. I am still influenced by my sociological origins; however, I use less jargon than I once did.

Goal 1. To develop, among those who will be called on to lead the reform effort and those whose support must be garnered if the reform is to be sustained, a shared understanding of the nature of the problems that give rise to the need for fundamental reform in our schools

1. Do educational leaders and those whose support is needed to sustain a reform effort share a common understanding of the reasons why the school district and schools in the district need to be changed?

2. Does the district engage in practices that are intended to educate community members and staff about the reasons reform is needed?

3. Do the policies, practices, programs, and procedures employed within the district reflect an understanding of the importance of educating the community about the need for reform and of providing this education on a continuing basis using a variety of media and approaches?

4. Does the district engage in market research? Does it regularly assess students' perceptions of the quality of the work they are being asked to do and the interest this work has for them? Are the needs and satisfactions of parents and other community members regularly assessed? If so, are the data generated by this research made available to teachers and principals? Is it expected and intended that problems be identified and acted on and that opportunities to improve be seized upon?

Goal 2. To develop within the local context a compelling vision of what schools can be and how they should be related to the community—a vision capable of earning wide support in the school district and the community and consistent with a set of well-articulated beliefs regarding the nature of schools and the schooling enterprise

1. Does the school district have a well-articulated set of beliefs about
   • The purpose of schools?
   • The ability of students to learn?
   • The factors that determine the opportunity to learn?
   • The role of the family and community in relation to students and schools?

- The kind of society for which students are being prepared?
- The focus of school activity?
- The rules, roles, and relationships that should govern behavior within schools, between schools and the district-level office, and between schools and the community?
- The obligation of the system to employees and the role of the system in encouraging and supporting innovation?

2. Have these beliefs been translated into a clear vision of the way the school system should operate, and is the present operation of the school district and the schools consistent with this vision?
   - Are the beliefs, values, and operating styles of teachers, administrators, and other community members consistent with the vision?
   - Are the rules, roles, and relationships encouraged by the school district consistent with the vision?
3. Does the district have a means of communicating the vision to new employees or new members of the community?
4. Does the district regularly celebrate and affirm the vision?

Goal 3. To develop throughout the system a clear focus on the student as the primary customer of the work of the school and on the needs and expectations of those whose support is needed if students are to be served effectively

1. Is the student viewed as the primary customer for the work of the school district?
2. Is the product of the schools viewed as knowledge work designed for students?
3. Do the schools have policies, procedures, programs, and practices focused on
   - Identifying student needs?
   - Determining how to respond to those needs?
   - Modifying the initial response to better meet those needs?
4. Do teachers and administrators have a clear understanding of whose support is needed if students are to be served effectively, and have they developed strategies for getting and sustaining that support?
5. Do teachers and administrators have a clear understanding of the needs and expectations of those whose support is needed, and do they act on these understandings?

Goal 4. To develop a results-oriented management system and a quality-focused decision-making process that are consistent with the beliefs that guide the system and that ensure that the measures of quality conform to the requirements of those who provide support to the school's customers

1. Does the school district focus its efforts on enhancing the qualities of schoolwork provided to students to accomplish the purpose of the school, rather than simply focusing on the secondary measurements of that schoolwork, such as annual test scores?
2. Are policies, procedures, programs, and practices assessed in terms of their impact on the achievement of the strategic goals of the school district?
3. Does the community contribute to and support the measures of quality used by the school district?
4. Are the school district's goals and mission consistent with the vision of schooling?
5. Are goals evaluated on the degree to which they promote the realization of this vision?

Goal 5. To develop a pattern of leadership and decision making within the school district and between the school district and other youth-serving agencies that is consistent with the assumption that teachers are leaders, principals are leaders of leaders, and the community must guarantee each child the support needed to ensure success in school

1. Do those who are affected by a decision understand how it was made, feel responsible for it, and feel committed to it?
2. Are decisions evaluated on the extent to which they increase the likelihood of student success?
3. Are school district personnel and community members involved in the current decision making and strategic planning that affect the youth of the community?
4. Are school district personnel encouraged to make decisions based on their expertise and the best available information?
5. Do school district personnel have easy access to the best available information when they are called on to make decisions?
6. Do school district personnel clearly identify the anticipated results before making a decision, determine whether the

anticipated results occurred, and if necessary, modify the original decision in order to achieve the desired results?

Goal 6. To develop a policy environment and a management system that foster flexibility and rapid response; encourage innovative use of time, technology, and space; encourage novel and improved staffing patterns; and create forms of curriculum organization that are responsive to the needs of children and youth
1. Do individuals who are called on to implement policies, procedures, and programs have the capacity to respond rapidly and flexibly?
2. Are time, people, space, knowledge, and technology used as variables to create conditions that enhance student success?

Goal 7. To develop and maintain systems and programs that encourage systematic innovation and the assessment of innovations within the context of a Total Quality Management framework
1. Are school district personnel encouraged to initiate and implement new ideas?
2. Are innovations systematically evaluated for the results they produce?
3. Are policies, procedures, programs, and practices in place to ensure that innovations that are not achieving desired results are modified or discontinued?
4. Is a system in place designed to ensure that innovations are consistent with the beliefs and vision that guide the district?

Goal 8. To encourage and support the creation of new relationships between and among agencies and groups that provide services to children and youth, in order to ensure that each child has the support needed to succeed in the school and the community
1. Are opportunities to work collaboratively provided for personnel from the school district and from other youth-serving agencies?
2. Does agreement exist on the support students need in order to succeed?

3. Do formal and informal agreements between the school district and youth-serving agencies outline avenues for mutual support?
4. Do the results of these agreements produce the support needed for students to succeed?

Goal 9. To ensure continued support for innovative efforts after initial enthusiasms wane, as long as the efforts continue to produce the desired results
1. Are innovations evaluated by their contribution toward increasing the capacity of the system to realize the district's vision?
2. Are means available to ensure that successful policies, procedures, programs, and practices are continued beyond the tenure of the original leaders, developers, or implementers?

Goal 10. To provide systems of training, incentives, and social and political support for those who are committed to the objectives outlined herein and to widen support for the pursuit of these objectives among all members of the community
1. Is there a means of identifying the training, incentives, and social and political support needed by those who are committed to the vision of the school district?
2. Does the school district provide the necessary resources to provide that system of support?
3. Is the system of support designed to widen commitment to student success among all members of the community?

An Assessment Strategy

Beliefs, visions, and missions indicate where we are going. Road maps are useless, however, unless we know where we are as well as where we are headed. Assessment is a process of figuring out where we are at the present time; it consists of taking stock. Conceptually, it should be possible to develop a profile of a school district using the ten goals listed above as the basis of the profile and assessing the school district according to the extent to which these goals have been and are being realized in the district. The answers to the questions, assuming that they were disciplined with data, could indicate the extent to which goals are being achieved and where more work might be needed.

Obviously, much work would need to be done to make it possible to systematically collect and analyze data related to the goals outlined above. Indeed, much work would need to be done to ensure that the questions asked under each of the goals are the right ones to ask. The questions presented here give direction to the kinds of questions that must be asked when developing data upon which to base answers, but they are not adequate in themselves. Take, for example, the first question under Goal 1: Do educational leaders and those whose support is needed to sustain a reform effort share a common understanding of the reasons why the school district and schools in the district need to be changed?

To answer this question, we would first need to identify the relevant leaders and those whose support is needed and then design some set of questions to elicit from them their views on whether or not and why change is needed. Armed with such data, we would need to develop a means of assessing the extent of the agreement and consensus among the respondents; then we would need some way to evaluate and give meaning to what has been assessed, for example, by asking how much agreement is enough.

Clearly, undertaking such a task requires a heavy investment in time and personnel, an investment that few school districts can or should make. It is possible, however, to use this framework in ways that are useful without being as precise as a researcher might want. As Willard Waller ([1932] 1967) observed, educational research should never get too far in front of common sense, and researchers and theoreticians should be careful not to fall behind common sense.

The following situation illustrates one such process:

Key central office staff meet in seminar settings to review goal statements and make whatever modifications seem appropriate in the local context. This process might be facilitated by a knowledgeable outsider; as an alternative, the superintendent and key central office staff, including perhaps some principals and teacher leaders, might form a study group, using as core materials this book plus other materials judged to be needed and appropriate, such as video-tapes, other books, field research materials, and action research techniques.

Regardless of the approach taken, what is important is that key leaders in the district be knowledgeable about the goals, understand their significance, and also understand and believe (be willing to act on) the assumptions underlying the assertion that one of the reasons for the failure of school reform is that districts lack the capacity to support and sustain reform.

Having established among key leaders an awareness and understanding regarding the nature of the organizational goals that must be pursued to develop the capacity to support change, this leadership group, perhaps with support from outside consultants, should identify a cadre of key individuals who are judged to be positive and influential among such stakeholder groups as parents, teachers, principals, support staff, business leaders, and civic and community leaders, including school board members.[4]

A training program should be developed and implemented for the group described above, aimed at achieving the following objectives:

To develop an awareness of the need to create district capacity and an under-standing of the basic dimensions along which such capacities might be described

To develop a rudimentary understanding of basic concepts and data collection processes associated with action research techniques, along with an un-

---

[4]It is assumed that the superintendent will keep the board informed of this process and that some conversation has taken place regarding intentions from the beginning of the discussions. Indeed, it is probably advisable to have board members as a part of the initial study group. However, I have been in situations where board members, because of other obligations, felt that they did not have the personal time to give to such an undertaking. And in some cases, board members who do have the time use it to interfere in the management of schools rather than to become informed so that they can formulate better policies for managing schools. The superintendent who has a board that functions the way it should will have little difficulty in keeping the board informed and involved. If the board is dysfunctional, as too many boards seem to be, it is doubtful that this process can go too far before the superintendent is dismissed or political hassles accelerate.

derstanding of how these techniques can be employed in assessing the capacity of the school district to pursue the goals outlined above.[5]

Teams of teachers, principals, parents, and others who have undergone the training outlined above should then be organized to collect and analyze data that will support an assessment of the district's capacity to support change. The point here is a simple one. What the teams are expected to do is to collect all the information, facts, and opinions that are judged to be relevant and useful to answer the question: What is the case here with regard to the essential questions that have been outlined? Assuming that this task is carried out with diligence and care, district leaders should have available to them a useful basis for answering such questions as, Does the district have the capacity to support change? and, In what areas is the district strong and in what areas is it weak? Based on the answers to these questions, leaders should be able to decide where work is needed and what kind of work is needed if the necessary capacities are to be put in place.[6]

Strategic Thinking

It is likely that the creation of a profile such as the one suggested above will reveal that the capacities of the school district are unevenly developed. For example, it has been my experience that few school districts have much capacity in the area of marketing and community education (Goal 1), though some do have considerable capacity in the area of staff training.

---

[5]It is likely that the design and delivery of this program will require some outside assistance. Typically, local teacher education institutions will have faculty members who are knowledgeable about field research and action research techniques. Assuming that such people are available and will accept the agenda that is outlined, as opposed to bringing their own research agenda and theoretical frameworks to the table, this provides a great opportunity for local school districts and local universities to work together. Failing that, local businesses with well-developed market research capabilities are another possible source of support. Independent consultants and consulting firms are also available.

[6]The two reports contained in the Appendixes illustrate ways in which this framework has been used. Neither is completely satisfactory, but both have proved useful to those who developed them. And both have produced, and are producing, action in the districts that are the subject of these reports.

One of the most critical questions leaders must confront, even after a relatively clear understanding of district capacity is in hand, is where to start. Starting everywhere at once is ill advised. An old adage says, "One goal is a goal, two goals are half a goal, and three goals are no goal at all." Like all such adages, this one has its limitations, but it reminds us that focus is important, especially when we are trying to bring about change in complex social systems such as schools. There are no hard-and-fast rules for making such decisions. It has been my observation, however, that leaders who move systems think strategically as well as act strategically and that among the most powerful concepts in the repertoire of these change leaders are the concepts of *sequence, linkage,* and *leverage.*

Sequence

At any point in time, and under given conditions, movement toward one goal is necessary before movement toward another goal is possible—as in the game of chess, in which some pieces simply cannot be moved until others have been moved. It is nearly impossible to move very far in improving the capacity of a school district to manage by results unless the capacity of the district to provide needed training is first put into place. Making decisions about the *sequence* in which different goals should be pursued requires strategic thinking.

Linkage

Some goals can be pursued relatively independently of others. Like the knight in chess, some goals can be moved forward without much concern about blockage from other pieces. The difficulty, of course, is that when the knight gets too far out in front, it cannot be protected and may be lost to hostile forces. The same is true of some goals.

I had occasion to observe a superintendent who became concerned that the community did not understand how poorly the system he headed was performing, so he set about developing a program to inform the community about the problems that had not been revealed by past administrations. At first, he was seen as a breath of fresh air, but as time went on, people began to say, "We didn't have these problems before Dr. X arrived. Maybe it's time we got rid of him."

Strategically, before moving the ability to communicate problems too far down the road, Dr. X should have enhanced the capacity of school leaders to imagine and envision solutions to the problems this newly created capacity revealed. Without development of the capacity to envision and implement solutions, the enhanced capacity to communicate problems may bring the entire effort to a halt—or at least lead to the search for a new leader, which is what happened in this case. This is *linkage;* some goals are linked in their effects even though initial inspection may lead us to think of them as relatively independent.

Leverage

Some goals are so tightly linked to other goals that when action is taken to enhance capacity in the area suggested by them, other capacities are improved as well. If such goals can be identified and acted on, high-leverage activity results. For example, school districts that lack the capacity to manage by results can use a focus on results to almost force changes in several other areas as well. A truly results-focused district cannot emerge until and unless beliefs are relatively well articulated and agreed upon because beliefs provide the standards for determining what results are worth pursuing. Similarly, a results-focused district will not become a reality unless the capacity to identify and market problems and solutions is in place. Under the right circumstances, therefore, focusing on improving the district's capacity to manage by results will increase the capacity of the district in other areas as well. This is *leverage.*

Two Examples

Presenting arguments like those set forth above almost always raises the question, Can you show me someplace that is doing what you recommend here and, if so, what are the results? My answer at this point is that I cannot tell you of any school districts that I believe have developed, to the point I think necessary, the capacities I have suggested here. Neither am I in a position to speak of results, because nothing has produced the kinds of results I believe would be produced if such capacities were present. However, I can point to a number of districts that are worth watching, though they are not yet developed to the point where I might hold them up as finished products.

The first district is the Memphis City Schools in Memphis, Tennessee. Under the leadership of Gerry House, the superintendent, the concepts set forth here have been used to give shape to a very elaborate strategic planning process that has brought together a wide range of community actors in support of a common agenda. Since that plan was developed, the school district has been increasingly successful in procuring funding to support various innovative efforts aimed at realizing the vision suggested by the plan. In addition to receiving a very large National Science Foundation grant to promote systemic reform in urban schools, the district has also procured considerable support from local businesses and a local foundation (the Plough Foundation) that is intended to enhance the capacity of the district to provide needed and relevant training and support to teachers and administrators.

Perhaps the most significant aspect of this example is that the designers of a number of nationally recognized school reform projects who are concerned about taking their projects to scale selected Memphis as one of their exemplary implementation sites, at least in part because of the emphasis the superintendent and her staff have given and are giving to the development of the infrastructure needed to support and sustain building-level reform. (A summary of the Memphis strategic plan is included in Appendix A.)

A second example, described in detail in Appendix B, is of a process currently under way in Phillipsburg, New Jersey, where Tom Seidenberger is the superintendent. Unlike Memphis, where a systematic assessment of capacities was never formally conducted, Phillipsburg has found that the key to its effort has been an assessment process that resulted in a series of recommendations for action within the school district. Two comments about the Phillipsburg project seem in order here.

First, because the assessment and the resulting document were produced by people who were not experts in either assessment or planning, those experts who read the document will probably find many flaws. So be it. The purpose of strategic plans is to motivate and direct action. As many visitors to Phillipsburg have reported, this process is doing just that. This outcome seems preferable to the outcome for those relatively flawless and professionally done plans one often sees filed in offices and never referred to again.

Second, as indicated by the report in Appendix B, data were collected by teams made up of educators, school board members, parents, students, and concerned citizens, including senior citizens. Ten data collection teams were each assigned the task of collecting and analyzing data relevant to one of the ten goals set forth above. The report in Appendix B does not include either the data, which were rich and plentiful, or the productive discussions that occurred in the process of analyzing and giving meaning to these data. Therefore, those who are used to preparing reports aimed at convincing universal audiences of the merit and worth of conclusions are likely to find the Phillipsburg report lacking. What the reader needs to remember is that the people who collected and analyzed these data were citizens in the community who—in the process of following relatively conventional research procedures— became persuaded themselves of the validity of their conclusions, and their reputations persuaded others. This may not be satisfying to the research community, but in the world of human action, people are executed on the basis of less evidence than this "grand jury" had available to it.

The Issue of Time

In his now-classic book *Schoolteacher* (1975), Dan Lortie defines *commitment* as the willingness to allocate scarce resources. Time is one of the scarcest resources in any organization, but the way schools are currently structured, it is even scarcer in schools. An assessment process and a planning process like those described and illustrated above require a considerable commitment of time, from the superintendent's office on down. Indeed, I would argue that unless the superintendent is prepared to give strong and visible leadership to this process, it is probably not worth undertaking. (In both Memphis and Phillipsburg, the superintendent was a key and central actor in the process.) This kind of work, if properly conducted, brings into focus the moral order of the district. And as I have argued elsewhere (see Schlechty, 1990), the superintendent can delegate almost every kind of authority he or she has except the moral authority that is embodied in the office of the superintendent. This process requires the visible and continuous presence of that authority.

This does not mean that the superintendent is required to conduct all the meetings needed to move such processes along or to plan or deliver the training, though it is symbolically very powerful when he or she does such things. What is required is that the superintendent be present and attentive at key events and take every occasion to symbolize the importance attached to the process.[7]

It is equally important that processes such as those illustrated or proposed here have strong and continual leadership from some person who sees the management of the process as her or his primary responsibility. Thus, unless a district is prepared to commit a substantial amount of a relatively senior-level person's time to coordinating this effort and unless the superintendent is prepared to protect that time, it is doubtful that the process I have outlined will produce the best results.

In addition, the people on the assessment teams need to be provided with time and staff support to conduct their work. Those who are unable or unwilling to make such time commitments should not be brought into this process early, for the early work is critical and requires substantial effort.

---

[7]I have had occasion to conduct seminars for business executives as well as for educators, and I am constantly struck by the fact that school administrators give participation in such meetings much lower priority than do most business executives. The pagers of business executives go off less frequently than those of educators, emergency phone calls are less obtrusive and distracting, and crisis-oriented interactions are less frequent. One explanation for this is that the context of schools generates more crises than that of business. Another is that business leaders have learned to delegate and have developed systems of training and accountability that make it possible for them to trust that crises will be managed whether or not they are there. The paternalistic structures upon which our schools were founded continue to play themselves out in the lives of teachers and administrators.

Finally, unless the superintendent and the board of education are prepared to develop and implement strategies for communicating the results of this effort to the community, and plans for bringing about improvements in capacity where they are needed, it is doubtful that this process will yield much more than a few people who get excited for a little while.[8]

---

[8]One of the problems school boards will confront is the likelihood that some of the remedial work needed will be relatively expensive and not linked to improvement in student performance directly enough to inspire widespread and immediate community support. For example, most schools lack the ability to provide training and support to teachers and administrators, which is critical to the success of change efforts. Yet the first budget line to be reduced in the face of budget cuts is likely to be the budget for staff development and for supporting staff travel to conferences. Properly presented, the business community and philanthropic organizations can help to offset this problem. The Gheens Academy in Louisville, Kentucky, the Mayerson Academy in Cincinnati, Ohio, and the Teaching Learning Academy in Memphis, Tennessee, are illustrations of ways in which businesses, local philanthropic foundations, and other community organizations can work to enhance the capacity of a district to provide needed training and support and be somewhat protected from budgetary fluctuations.

Chapter Seven

Creating the Capacity to Support Change

In education, the changes that count most are those that directly affect students and what they learn. To produce such changes, school districts, communities, and state agencies must be changed in ways that will support and sustain the changes needed in classrooms and in schools. Enhancing the capacity of the school district to support change at the building and classroom levels is the most critical work of the superintendent and those who work in the district office and should be the central concern of boards of education as well. In the preceding chapter, I discussed issues related to describing and assessing the district's capacity to support change. Here I will discuss ways to increase this capacity where it is found to be lacking.

Developing a Focus on the Future

Three conditions must be present if schools are to maintain a focus on the future:

1. Local leaders (board members, superintendents, principals, and teacher leaders) must be in general agreement regarding the problems that give rise to the need for the change and must have a common commitment to the idea that the best and perhaps the only way to address the problem is to change the way the organization goes about doing business.
2. Local leaders must be in general agreement regarding what they believe about the purpose of the schools they lead. They must also be in agreement regarding the system of rules, roles,

and relationships they will support to pursue this purpose, and they must agree on the values that will guide their work and the commitments they will make in support of these values.

3. Local leaders must be in a position to market their framing of the problems and issues and their view of the future to those whose support will be needed if that future is to be realized.

If they are carefully designed, the assessment processes discussed in the preceding chapter can do much to lay the groundwork for enhancing the capacity to focus on the future. More can be done as well.

Creating a Common View

If real change is to occur, top-level leaders, including board members, the superintendent, principals, key central office leaders, and union leaders must be willing and able to spend enough time together and engage in enough dialogue and analysis that they come to share a general understanding about the educational landscape, both locally and nationally. They must also share a common understanding of the problems they face, and they must learn to frame these problems in common ways: for example, top-level leaders need to have a clear understanding of how the present performance of schools in general and the schools in their district in particular compares to the performance of schools in the past. Is the dropout rate really higher today than in the past? Has student performance deteriorated? Or is the source of dissatisfaction with schools a result of a change in expectations? Such serious matters cannot be addressed as an afterthought or an add-on.

Educational leaders must also come to a common understanding of what they believe about school and life in schools, and this activity, too, requires commitment and resources. At a minimum, these leaders must develop a consensus around answers to questions such as the following:

• What is the purpose of education? For example, is it to select and sort students on the basis of their capacity to do particular forms of schoolwork, or is it to develop the capacity of students to do high-quality work?

- Do all students have the ability to learn more than they are now learning in school? Is it realistic to expect all students to meet high academic standards, or are many students incapable of learning enough to meet high academic standards?

- What are the primary determinants of opportunities to learn? For example, when variance in student learning is observed, how is it explained? Does the preferred explanation—the one most commonly advanced in the group—have to do with qualities beyond the control of the schools, such as family background or inherent ability, or does it fasten on factors under the control of schools, such as the quality and characteristics of the academic work students are provided?

- What assumptions are made about the kind of society students should be prepared to live in, and what assumptions are made about the life chances of students presently in the schools? Is it assumed, for example, that schools have some obligation to prepare students to live in a democratic, multiethnic society, or are such matters not of concern to the schools? Is it assumed that schools should encourage students to aspire to high-status positions, or is it assumed that such an orientation will simply lead to disappointment for most students?

- What is the role of the family and the community in relation to students and schools? For example, is the family viewed as a true partner in the education of children, or is it seen more as a supporter of whatever the school prescribes? Is the focus of the community and community agencies on providing support for schools, or does it also focus on providing support for all children? Should the school be viewed simply as an educational agency and school leaders as primarily educational leaders, or is it assumed that schools should also be positioned as community agencies and that educational leaders should be both community leaders and educational leaders?

- What should be the primary focus of schools? For example, should the focus be on students and their needs or on the needs of business and the larger community? If the answer is "both" or "all," how should priorities be determined?

- How should schools be structured? For example, should the rules, roles, and relationships that shape behavior in schools be designed on the assumption that what teachers do and how they perform is the critical determinant of the quality of school life, or is it more appropriate to focus on what students do and how they perform? Should teachers be viewed as leaders, facilitators, and coaches, or should they be perceived primarily as organizers and transmitters of information and evaluators of student performance? How should the schools be governed and by whom?

• What obligations does the system have to employees, and what obligations does it expect employees to assume? For example, when changes require training, who is responsible for providing the training and under what conditions?

In Chapter Five, I suggested the direction in which I would push debates to determine beliefs about schools and a vision of schools if I were involved in those discussions. Whether or not the reader agrees with the substance of the belief structure I would create is not important. What is important is that those who would lead a reform effort in schools need to have some fairly well worked out answers to the questions listed above, answers they can articulate and defend.

A contrary view holds that such beliefs should bubble up from the bottom and that group processes should be employed to ensure that this happens. My experience has been less than satisfying when I have participated in, and sometimes led, such processes. Too often, if we seek consensus on beliefs from the group without someone setting forth in clear terms a set of beliefs to focus on or beginning the argument with discussions, the process yields little more than a set of pious statements and platitudes. What is needed from these discussions are statements that can be used to evaluate and direct action.

I hope that those who think it is top-down and nonparticipatory to focus initially on top-level leaders and leaders who are largely within the system, will consider the following points before judging too harshly:

• Arguments comparing bottom-up to top-down management are no more valid than arguments about centralization versus decentralization. The latter argument is not usefully discussed as an either/or question; it is a both/and question, concerning what should be centralized, what should be decentralized, and what should be left alone. Similarly, the top-down/bottom-up argument is not an either/or question. Legitimate roles exist for both the "top" and the "bottom."

• One of the obligations of people in top-level positions is to lead. They are required by their roles to do so, and if they do not, the group may have no leadership. People in positions of less authority are not required to lead, though they may do so, and thoughtful people with authority may encourage them to do so.

• Discussions about matters as important as the beliefs that will guide the direction of schools require all the leadership that can be mustered in any group. It makes little difference if the leadership comes from the top, the bottom, the middle, or the side, but it must come from somewhere. If those at the top are not prepared to provide leadership or to respond in a constructive and inviting manner to leadership by others when it is offered, the needed discussions may have little prospect of occurring.

• Top-level leaders prepare themselves to offer such leadership by thinking through and rehearsing the answers they will offer or nominate should the group not be prepared to do so. Further, they must be in agreement among themselves regarding what they believe; otherwise, they are in a poor position to lead others to a consensus on any set of beliefs.

• Democratic leaders are not without ideas and commitments of their own that they are prepared to advance, defend, and argue for, but when they are in positions of authority, they renounce the right to exercise that authority unless they are empowered by the group to use it on behalf of beliefs endorsed by the group. Those who use authority to impose their will regardless of the sentiment of their followers are authoritarians; those who use positions of authority to insert their beliefs and proposals into the dialogue are strong leaders.

The important point is that someone, somewhere, must frame the initial argument. In the Constitutional Convention of 1787, for example, the original focus for the discussion was provided by a set of nine propositions advanced by one set of delegates. Later, as the focused discussion became more heated and less civil, other groups formulated alternative resolutions and alternative plans. It was out of this dialogue, which started in someone's head, that the greatest consensus document known in human history was created. It would not have happened without the presence of leaders who knew what they believed, who were willing to articulate those beliefs, and who were also willing to listen to others who disagreed with them.

Leaders must ensure that everyone participating in the discussion understands what it is about and what its intended result is to be. The result in the case of the discussion of beliefs that should guide schools must be *a well-articulated belief structure, that is, a publicly communicated (and communicable) set of statements and propositions that is complete, comprehensible, and compelling and that if endorsed by parents and other relevant constituencies could serve as a guide for all district operations.*

Beliefs That Compel Action

To be complete, the beliefs that guide the system must address at least the areas suggested in Chapter Five: beliefs about purpose, beliefs about the capacity of children to learn, and so on. Without answers to the questions associated with these areas, the organization will have an inadequate moral compass and structural map. To be comprehensible, the statements and propositions must be available in documents, videotapes, recordings, and handbooks that, taken as a whole, serve to communicate and illuminate the set of beliefs and to enlighten effectively all who are concerned with their meaning and implications.

Many consultants argue that the key documents that communicate beliefs can and should be stated in brief and simple form. I do not disagree with this view; however, it sometimes leads to the mistaken notion that the beliefs themselves should be simple and that what is said about them should not take much time in the life of the organization. The key principles that guide the school, or any other organization, should be capable of being summarized in brief statements, perhaps so brief that their content can be brought to mind with reference to the key words or elements of these basic propositions. But the beliefs stated will not have the power to give direction to the system if all that is meant, contained, or implied by them can be understood by reading a single-page memo or the back of a business card. The first ten amendments to the U.S. Constitution are illustrative of what I mean here, as is the Constitution itself.

The first ten amendments, which are statements of belief about liberty, justice, and the relationship between individuals and government, are simply stated, so simply stated that it is commonplace to have schoolchildren memorize key words that refer to each of them. Indeed, some individuals suggest that to be culturally literate, an individual should be able to call to memory the substance of each of these amendments, and the other sixteen as well. Yet innumerable additional documents guide our nation's government, including many complex, cumbersome, and sometimes contradictory Supreme Court decisions intended to illuminate these statements and make their meaning more comprehensible to those who are called on to adhere to their principles.

The content of the Constitution, excluding the first ten amendments, has much more to say about rules, roles, and relationships than about the core values that will guide the government (that is why the radicals insisted that the first ten amendments be added). But the Constitution is certainly not a simple document; its ratification required that what was intended be clearly communicated and explained. As a consequence, numerous documents and pamphlets—not the least of which were *The Federalist Papers* ([1787–1788] 1981)—were created to make the meaning of the Constitution more comprehensible to those who were not in on the original drafting of this profound statement of national belief and intention, which is as well a profound statement of values and commitments.

If belief and believing are to be central to the reinvention of America's schools, then those who lead the schools must do much more than is now being done about the beliefs that guide—or purport to guide—these systems. An occasional weekend retreat where individuals go to "get a vision" will simply not do. Neither will an occasional goal-setting conference nor a spasm of strategic planning. *Beliefs must be constant, and they must constantly be attended to in the literature of the organization and in the symbols of the system as well as in the public expressions of those who occupy leadership positions therein.*

For beliefs to be compelling, they must be articulated in language that stirs the heart as well as engages the mind. Unfortunately, throughout history, scoundrels and demagogues who understand the power of symbols to compel action have persuaded men and women to do horrible things by employing such symbols. This has caused many to distrust the purposeful use of symbols to compel action. Yet the fact remains that humans are a symbol-making lot, and most of what binds people together and causes them to act in concert is somehow related to the symbols they use to compel action. ("Compel" does not mean "coerce." Rather, it means creating an urge toward action. The means that are used to compel are separate from the condition itself. Here, I am suggesting that words and symbols are a source of compulsion.)

For belief statements to be compelling, they must be communicated in terms that create positive meanings and images in the local context; they certainly should not stir up negative images. For example, many school statements of belief contain references to "critical thought," through which students learn to make comparisons, check sources, evaluate logic and intent, and generally try to verify that what they are being told or sold has merit and worth. Most parents would not object to their children learning to check sources and so on, but some do object to having them learn to think critically. Why? Because to many parents, the word *critical* symbolizes a lack of respect for tradition and an additional assault on the authority of the home and the family.

Why, then, do we insist on loading educational documents with the words "to think critically"? Surely it is possible to convey what is meant without alienating others, using terms that would be more compelling to parents who place a high value on tradition. Thomas Jefferson certainly understood that some words have more (and less) compelling power in different contexts when he substituted the words "pursuit of happiness" for the word "property" in the French phrase "life, liberty, and property."

Negotiating Beliefs

Given the general consensus among school leaders regarding issues like those outlined above, and given a statement of beliefs that is moving toward being complete, capable of being comprehended by local constituencies, and potentially compelling to those constituencies, attention must be given to communicating the views leaders have come to with others who are affected by the schools. The goal of these communications is not simply to tell and inform, though that should happen. Rather, it is to find ways to elicit support for the views that are proposed by leaders and, conversely, to discover which elements of the proposed beliefs key constituencies find objectionable or less than desirable, and then to find ways to modify the beliefs so that they can be endorsed and supported by those whose support is required to move forward.

If schools are to maintain a focus on the future, school leaders must develop policies, practices, and programs that keep them in touch with the people whose support they need. It is not enough for school leaders to simply be responsive to the needs that are presented. They must understand the needs of those whose support the schools require, such as parents, students, nonparent taxpayers, and business leaders, even better than these people understand their needs themselves. School leaders must anticipate emerging needs and must bring to a conscious level needs that have yet to be articulated, shaping their own actions and the organizations they lead and manage in ways that are responsive to these needs. In simplest terms, this means that schools must develop marketing capacity. Whereas sales begins with a product, marketing begins with the customer in mind. The role of marketing is to identify customers, get to know their needs, find ways of gaining their trust and confidence, and create and shape products and services that respond to their needs.

For example, it is increasingly clear that if schools are to survive in most communities, they must respond to the needs of nonparent taxpayers in ways that have not been required in the past. Why is this so? Because nonparent taxpayers are becoming a growing majority in most communities, and the interests of nonparents in schools are inherently different from those of parents. Discovering what those nonparents' needs and interests are and determining how schools and school programs can be shaped to respond to those needs and interests are two of the major challenges confronting present-day educational leaders. Such discoveries are more likely to occur in schools that have a well-developed understanding of marketing processes and whose personnel and resources are committed to supporting marketing functions.

Any statement of beliefs nowadays that does not give specific attention to the principles that will guide the schools' relationship with senior citizens as well as with other nonparent taxpayers is inadequate. Further, any belief statement that attempts to define this relationship must first be submitted to those who are involved, in this case senior citizens and nonparent taxpayers, for review, comment, and reaction. This does not mean that every belief that guides the schools needs to be submitted to all stakeholders for review and approval, but when the beliefs or vision being articulated affect the lives of men and women or posit expectations for them and of them, they should be consulted about those beliefs, and their views should be accommodated, if it is possible to do so without violating the basic values that guide the system.

Keeping Everyone on Board

Good marketers understand that as important as developing new markets may be, maintaining existing markets is equally important, if not more so. Getting customers is only half the equation; the other half is keeping them. Thus, in addition to acquiring skill in gaining commitment (what marketers might call market development), if schools are to establish and maintain a focus on the future, they must give attention to the creation of programs and practices designed to ensure that shared understandings, once established, do not erode; that commitments, once made, are not forgotten; and that agreements, once arrived at, do not fall into disrepair.

At a minimum, leaders must continuously review the status of agreements and understandings, modify these agreements when it seems necessary to do so, and celebrate and highlight those that are retained. Serious induction programs for new employees and serious orientation programs for new citizens and patrons need to be developed. These programs should emphasize the beliefs that guide the system and what they mean for those who are entering the system, whether as an employee, a parent, or a nonparent taxpayer.

Maintaining Direction

In the effort to maintain direction, organizations confront a choice. Organizational leaders can either manage by programs or lead through values and commitments. If they attend to creating a strong system of beliefs and values, those beliefs and values can become the prime source of direction. When things go awry, the leader can call attention to the commitments and values as a source of direction and correction.

Management by Programs

Lacking a strong and compelling set of beliefs and values with which to maintain direction, the only alternative is for leaders to select programs or, if they are "democratic," to allow others to select programs and then ensure that they "do things right," because it cannot be assumed that program implementers have a compass to help them figure out for themselves what the right thing to do might be. Compliance with the programs' goals and objectives becomes the source of direction because there really are no system goals and objectives beyond those implicit in the programs that have been selected.

In such program-managed systems, it is much harder to maintain continuous direction precisely because it is so easy to change direction. All that is necessary is to change programs, and direction will be changed as well. Thus, when the new board member or new superintendent arrives and "sweeps out" existing programs, he or she is also sweeping out the only sense of direction there might be. In a program-managed system, followers are expected to find meaning and direction in the programs they manage or participate in, rather than in the values and commitments of the systems in which these programs are enacted. In such situations, programs become ends in themselves, whereas in systems managed by beliefs and commitments, they are a means to an end.

This is not to say that belief-driven systems do not give attention to programs and procedures, for they do. But this attention has to do with deciding which programs and procedures have the greatest potential for helping the organization realize its vision. In an organization that has no belief structure, programs and procedures take on a life of their own, and those associated with them find meaning in the *activities* they produce rather than the *results* produced.

As things now stand, most school districts manage by programs rather than by beliefs and values, and the pattern of leadership is more one of command and control than of leading and participating. If schools are to maintain direction, especially when change becomes real and resistance arises, school systems must create a culture that places value on managing by results, rather than on managing by programs. It is critical, as well, for the results pursued

to be consistent with beliefs and likely to assist in the realization of
visions.

Managing by Results

One of the desirable consequences of a belief-driven system is that
the programs that are adapted and the procedures that are employed tend, over the long run, to be supportive, coherent, and
more or less unified. In a system without beliefs, it is difficult to
govern the selection of programs or to guide the evaluation of programs once they have been selected, because programs tend to become fragmented and mutually destructive. The emphasis comes
to be on control rather than direction, on management rather
than leading. To create a culture where results are valued and beliefs provide direction, those who occupy official leadership positions in schools—including boards of education—must learn to
manage by results and to cause others to be results-oriented as well.
What does this mean? What do results-oriented leaders do?

1. They cause the groups they lead to arrive at consensus and clarity regarding what is to be achieved before they encourage or
   entertain discussions of how to do it.
2. They ensure that the decisions made by the group are consistent with a firmly held set of beliefs about the nature and purposes of the school or the school system.
3. They ensure that the groups they lead arrive at a consensus regarding what they will accept as indicators and evidence that the
   results produced are congruent with those that were intended.
4. They ensure that some individuals, groups, or agencies are assigned responsibility for collecting data and providing feedback on the present results and for linking the feedback to
   clear benchmarks of progress toward the intended results.
5. They ensure that the decisions made regarding what to do to
   achieve results are, in fact, the ones that are most likely to produce the results intended. Even in results-oriented environments, the special interests of decision makers can cause
   recommendations for action to show a preference for "solutions"
   that meet the needs of these interest groups as opposed to satisfying the conditions required to produce the intended results.

Transforming Action into Results

Results-oriented leaders see as one of their primary tasks the transformation of proposed programs of action into results. Take, for example, the classic problems associated with demands to reduce class size. Results-oriented leaders would ask and cause others to ask, What are we trying to achieve by reducing class size? They would understand that class size is not the problem. The problem is that teachers generally do not have enough time to plan, to reflect, and to provide useful feedback to students. From the students' perspective—and especially from the perspective of some parents—students in large classes do not get enough individual attention. Thus, properly understood, the results desired by those who advocate reducing class size are (1) to provide more time for teachers and (2) to ensure that students receive the personal attention they need if they are to perform at maximum potential.

On inspection, it becomes clear that unless a reduction is dramatic, reducing class size does very little to increase the time available to teachers. One or two, or even three or four, fewer sets of papers to mark do not yield much time. To provide real time—say, an hour or so per day—class size would need to be reduced by between five and ten students (assuming that a teacher spends between five and ten minutes per day per student marking papers and providing other forms of feedback). Similarly, if teachers and other adults are to interact with individual students more frequently than is now the case, and if reduction in class size is the way to make that happen, then the reduction will need to be equally dramatic. In a given day, a high school teacher confronting five classes with thirty students each would have available something less than two minutes per student, if she or he did nothing but confer with individual students. Reducing class size by one-third (from thirty to twenty students) would increase this meager average to about two and a half minutes.

It is little wonder that reductions in class size are not producing learning gains. Unless they are dramatic, they cannot produce the intended results (increased time for teachers and more attention to students). It would be better if leaders would frame the issue in terms of the intended results in the first place. A results-oriented leader should ask, How can we provide more time for teachers and more attention for students? rather than asking, How can we reduce class size and how can we afford to do so? The first question refers to the results to be achieved, the second to something to be done. Unfortunately, the culture of schools promotes discussions of what is to be done and discourages discussions of problems to be solved and results to be pursued. If schools are to have the capacity to maintain direction, school leaders must be as concerned about what is to be achieved as they are with the political viability of programs of action. Furthermore, they must develop a similar orientation in others as well.

Participatory Leadership

Given a results-oriented style of leadership, it is essential that teachers and school leaders learn the art and science of participatory leadership (leadership that assumes the commitment of followers) rather than a command-and-control style of leadership (leadership that assumes, implicitly at least, that followers are estranged from their task and will pursue a common direction only when they are coerced or bribed to do so). How do leaders encourage a participatory style of leadership?

- They constantly check to ensure that recommended actions are consistent with intended outcomes, they ask questions of others, and they cause others to engage in similar processes.
- They ensure that the groups they lead consult with others outside the group who have special information related to the decision or a special interest in the decision, in order to increase the quality of the decision as well as to guarantee maximum commitment to the decision once it has been made.
- They ensure that those who are likely to be called on to implement decisions are kept informed of what is occurring and that the reasoning behind such decisions is communicated.
- They ensure that when decisions call for action by others, the necessary training and support are provided for those people.
- They ensure that clear benchmarks are established that can be used to review progress and facilitate data-based decisions regarding whether or not to continue the present course, modify the program, or abandon the effort.

The Results-Oriented Leader

Results-oriented leaders are leaders who have learned to focus decisions on intended results, to link results to actions, and to enlist
the insights of others in ways that help to ensure success. Unfortunately, too often school leaders who gain attention for being results-oriented turn out to be top-down managers bent on holding
others accountable and being "tough-minded" (meaning willing
to dismiss nonperformers). Instead of using results to provide direction and as a source of encouragement, they use narrow measures of those results to instill fear. Instead of inviting inventions
to solve problems and improve effectiveness, they demand compliance and programmatic orthodoxy.

The consequence is that many teachers view demands for accountability and a clear focus on results as nothing more or less
than one more effort to scapegoat teachers and reinforce the
power of bureaucratic authorities at the district and state levels.
This is unfortunate, for only through a clear focus on results can
teachers and schools be empowered.

Site-Based Decision Making: A Good Idea Going Awry

In part because so few school leaders have learned to manage by
results and even fewer seem to have been able to connect a results-
oriented management system to a participatory leadership style,
and in part because of interest-group politics, a wide range of efforts has emerged over the past decade to enforce patterns of participatory leadership by requiring that decisions be "shared" and
that teachers and parents be empowered.

Much can be said in favor of positioning decision-making authority closer to the place where decisions are implemented and
finding new and better ways to involve parents and teachers in the
decision-making process. What is sometimes forgotten, however, is
that in the context of organizational life, the reason for broaden-
ing the base of decision making has little to do with a preference
for democracy or the rights of parents and teachers. Instead, the
reason for altering the way decisions are made is that it is assumed
that such changes will result in

- Better decisions
- Decisions more responsive to the needs and perceptions of parents
- Decisions more informed by the insights of teachers
- Decisions to which school faculties are more committed, because they have had a direct hand in making the decisions

In some instances, these results may be forthcoming; in others, probably not. But in fact, no one really knows or is likely to find out. Why? Because in implementing site-based decision making, the emphasis is too often on what to do rather than on what is to be accomplished. For example, it is commonplace for site-based decision making to be initiated through union contracts or state law. Usually the language of contracts and mandates related to site-based decision making is long on describing who will be on decision-making teams and what authority the teams will have. The language is usually brief or nonexistent regarding what results it is assumed the groups will produce and how to tell if these results are forthcoming.

In such a context, discussions of who has the right to make a given decision become more important than which decisions are the right ones to make. We need only review the literature on site-based decision making and training protocols for school-site decision-making teams to see that this is so. Much of this material is concerned with how such teams should be constituted (for example, how many parents and how many teachers) and what powers they should have (for example, the power to hire and fire principals and the power to make curricular decisions). Most of the training has to do with strategies for arriving at consensus on what to do and how to manage conflict as decisions are being made. Little, if any, attention is given to strategies for assessing the merit and worth of the results pursued, the way that teams can determine whether the decisions they make are producing the intended results, or what they might do if these results are not forthcoming.

Is there any reason to believe that site-based decision-making groups selected through political processes are more likely to produce the intended results than other politically elected bodies, like school boards? Probably not. Indeed, site-based decision making as it is currently being carried out in too many school districts may only aggravate further some of the problems that already exist in many of America's schools. For example, in extreme cases, parents and teachers at local school sites are under no obligation to take direction from the elected board of education with regard to such crucial issues as the curriculum, operating goals, purposes, and procedures. The only legitimate sources of direction for schools, outside of the council, are the state legislature and the state department of education.

In the long term, this is likely to result in an even more centralized system than is now in place, because isolated faculties and isolated groups of parents have less ability to confront state bureaucracies than do school boards, which have a broader community base. The only difference is that the point of centralization will be further removed from the local community than is now the case. Similarly, unless it is carefully designed, site-based decision making will further weaken the ability of systems to coordinate efforts among elementary schools, middle schools, and high schools. When each school site is governed by an autonomous group that may be under no real obligation to take into account the decisions made by other groups, the long-term interests of children are likely to give way to the momentary passions of particular groups of activist parents at a particular time.

Site-based decision making can either lead to or diminish support for schools. When the dominant decision makers at schools are parents and teachers and when school sites are the primary locus of decisions, those who pay the majority of the taxes—nonparents—may have even less ability to influence the direction of education in their communities and even fewer opportunities for meaningful involvement in matters that really count in the schools than they now have with unresponsive central office bureaucracies. The likely result will be that many nonparents will become even less supportive of public education than they are now. If the parents want to run the schools, some will say, let them pay for it.

The idea is suspect as well that when 10 to 20 percent of parents elect the school-site decision-making body (experience in Chicago and Kentucky indicates that this is about the proportion of parents who participate in such elections), schools can be responsive to all the parents of all the children. Elected parents may make schools more responsive to those who elect them and who share their views, but what of the majority of parents who have no interest in being involved in schoolhouse politics? It is doubtful that their needs and values will even be known, let alone taken into account in the decision-making process.

Responsiveness and Results

If the reader will review the role I have described for the results-oriented leader, as well as the general line of argument presented in the earlier chapters of this book, it should be clear that I am not unsympathetic to the idea of decentralization or to the idea that teachers need to have much more control over decisions about the allocation and use of resources, the design of the curriculum, and the management of the assemblage of students. My professional career has been committed at least in part to advancing the idea of decentralization and teacher empowerment, as my association with projects in Dade County, Florida; Hammond, Indiana; Louisville, Kentucky; and Rochester, New York, will attest. Where I differ from some of the extreme advocates of such things as charter schools and those who would grant "all power to parents and teachers" is in not believing that this is the best way to make sure that schools are more responsive to parents and students; nor do I believe that it increases the accountability of schools to the community.

Parents and teachers do have much to contribute to the decisions that are made in education, and they should be positioned to contribute and encouraged to do so. Many central office functionaries do behave too much like stereotypical petty bureaucrats, and too many school boards behave foolishly and in ways that are almost disgraceful. Therefore, some means must be found to attend more adequately to the needs and perceptions of parents and the wisdom of teachers in the decision-making process. Furthermore, if some means is not found to stop silly, destructive, self-serving, and interest group-dominated behavior on the part of school boards, the cause of public education will be lost. Bypassing school boards and destroying the district office will not, however, ensure greater responsiveness or accountability to parents. Indeed, it may do the opposite.

Decentralization Versus Divestiture

Those who would improve schools through such mechanisms as site-based decision making need to understand that decentralization and divestiture are different things. Decentralization does not cause fragmentation and destruction of the central core of the system. Indeed, it only works well when the central core is strong. This core nurtures the beliefs that guide the system and ensures that the direction of the system is established and maintained. Divestiture has to do with dispersal, breaking up, and fragmentation. Instead of a decentralized school system, those who advocate divestiture want, at best, a system of schools and, at worst, hundreds of thousands of little school districts with all the potential for mischief that is now built into the larger systems they find so abhorrent. Because this understanding is lacking, many site-based initiatives have created a climate of divestiture without really addressing the structures that make schools less than responsive to the needs of parents and students. What is more, some of the strategies employed to decentralize schools make the schools even less accountable to the local community than they were in the past and even more controlled by the bureaucratic interests of the agencies the state provides to regulate schools.

Instead of addressing the problem of developing a system that will result in local school boards' creating schools that are both responsive to parents and children and accountable to the taxpayers (most of whom are not parents or students), advocates of divestiture are creating thousands of little school boards, each of which will have the same problems that the central community boards now have. Some of these schools will be excellent and will function well. Some will be corrupt and will function poorly. Some will work out accommodations that will make the system do well in spite of itself. Programs will be implemented, but results will not be achieved, at least not on a consistent basis. And eventually critics will say, as some are now saying, "Site-based management does not work, so let's go back to the good old days," or, "Let's try some new panacea" (for example, charter schools or vouchers).

The only way to avoid such fickle and destructive behavior is to be clear about the intended results and vigorously pursue them. Programs are secondary; results are primary. Boards of education that fail to manage by results and that insist on managing by programs and serving special interests may inspire reformers to bypass them, but bypassing school boards and the problems they now represent will not provide the unity of purpose or constancy of direction that is needed if communities are to support the reinvention of America's schools.

Ensuring Continuity

Nothing is more destructive to the cause of school change than the tendency of schools to move by fits and starts, to reverse direction, to stop and take a new direction, and to generally behave in erratic and fickle ways. When a new principal is appointed, he or she often seems to feel obliged to deny the past and chart a new or different future. The same seems to be the case for newly appointed superintendents and new board members. Each new occupant of a position or an office seems bent upon leaving a mark, and that mark is too often made by first establishing a new or different direction from her or his predecessor. There is a similar tendency with programs. They are abandoned even before their effects are known, and the newest fad is put in their place, or so it seems. Indeed, faddishness, rather than innovation, more often than not characterizes the posture toward innovation that typifies many schools and school districts. As the Roman satirist Petronius Arbiter is said to have remarked, "No sooner do we come to understand what we are to do than the order comes down that we must reorganize."

Change produces uncertainty and feelings of incompetence: uncertainty because we are forced to deal with the unfamiliar, feelings of incompetence because we do not know how to do what we have never done before. In the face of fear and feelings of incompetence, people seek security, and the greatest security they know is found in the status quo. They therefore look for every reason they can find to justify their preference for the old and their resistance to the new. The belief that "this too shall pass" provides such a reason. It is essential, therefore, that those who would lead schools in a serious and systemic change effort do all they can to ensure that continuity is valued. For example, using personnel appointments as a means to "clean house and set a new direction" is a strategy that should be employed rarely and only after the impact on employees' confidence and willingness to take risks is assessed. New directions set by known leaders generally gain adherents more quickly than do those set by new leaders. There are times, of course, when this is not true and radical personnel changes are required, but in general, threats and fear do little to inspire the confidence and commitment needed to bring about real change.

Similarly, to abandon one relatively untested program only to start another is to establish a pattern of fickleness that will fail to inspire the kind of persistence in the face of adversity that is needed if real change is to occur. Of even greater concern is the tendency to go back to a program that was abandoned in the past because it was judged to be unsatisfactory. Once a direction has been set and communicated, leaders must persist and cause others to persist. They must remember what the research on change may teach if it is consulted, and they should help others to remember this literature and cause others to consult it. If they do so, they will certainly discover that in real change, a downturn in performance is likely to occur before the benefits of the change begin to become clear. Indeed, the fact that things often get worse before getting better is such a commonplace observation that change theorists have given it a name: the implementation dip (see, for example, Fullan, 1991).

Of course, it must also be understood that such dips can only be tolerated if students are not victimized in the process. For this reason, those who would lead a change effort—even more than those who manage existing systems—must be sensitive to the need for strong and powerful data, not only to bolster their claims but also to help them know when what they are doing threatens to be harmful to those they are trying to serve.

Acting Strategically

To act strategically is to act with a preferred future in mind. Preferred futures come in the form of visions that emanate from beliefs. Thus, again, the significance of beliefs is affirmed. Strategic action sometimes requires that we absorb temporary setbacks and short-term difficulties to obtain long-term benefits; it also requires that we abandon old ways and old habits as well as embracing new ways and new habits. Sloughing off the past is as much a part of the change process as is embracing the future (see Drucker, 1985).

If America's schools are to become more customer-focused and if concern about the quality of the work provided to students is to be of paramount concern in schools, then:

- The merit and worth of all programs, policies, and procedures must be evaluated in terms of their relevance to enhancing the capacity of the teachers and administrators to provide students with high-quality intellectual activities (knowledge work) that are responsive to students' needs and motivations and that produce learning results valued by parents, other members of the community—including the business community—and the society at large.
- Leaders and staff must develop skill in identifying problems and inventing solutions as well as in evaluating those solutions in terms of their capacity to produce the intended results.
- Collaborative action must be supported and encouraged, and institutional arrangements must be in place to support and sustain such collaboration. Furthermore, collaborative action must occur within the system (for example, between elementary schools and secondary schools or between the teachers' union and the board of education) as well as between the schools and groups and agencies in the larger community (for example, child- and youth-serving agencies, businesses, and civic groups).
- Contingency plans must be developed and constantly reviewed and updated to ensure continuity of effort in the face of personnel changes, funding changes, and other threats to persistent action.
- Those who are called on to change and to lead change efforts must be provided with the training and support they need to proceed with maximum confidence and efficiency. In addition to providing technical assistance and formal training opportunities, the district and its leaders must also offer moral, social, and political support for the change effort and must work to ensure that those who are involved in the change have no rational basis for fearing the consequences of the change.

How these things are done will vary from school to school, but the requirement that they be done is not optional. Not doing them will cause school reform to fail.

The Need for Flexibility

If teachers are to function as leaders and inventors, if students are to be the focus of all school activity, and if the business of schools is to invent knowledge work that engages students, then teachers must have considerable control over the methods that they can make available to students as they go about their work, and teachers must have control as well over the resources that give shape and meaning to these methods. At a minimum, this means that teachers must have considerable influence and control with regard to

- Decisions about time and the way it is used
- Decisions about physical space and the way it is allocated and used
- Decisions about the grouping of children and the assignment of adults
- Decisions about the way knowledge and information should be organized and presented to students
- Decisions about the kinds of technology needed by students

Unfortunately, in too many school systems, those in the best position to make decisions regarding these matters (teachers, building-level administrators, and parents) have little control over them. It is for this reason that many (including me) argue for decentralization. However, it is possible to decentralize decisions regarding the way a job is to be done without also decentralizing decisions about the intended results of the job or the values that are to be served in the pursuit of those results. Centralization and decentralization can go on simultaneously, and they should.

For example, in a properly led results-oriented system, the intended learning results and social results (for example, no child will be discriminated against, all children will be provided with the support they need, and the physical and emotional safety of children will be of supreme value) can be insisted on as a centralized or "corporate" expectation while the widest latitude is provided to teachers, building administrators, and parents in determining how these results might best be produced in a local school environment. As another example, consider the problem of expanding teacher access to new forms of technology. If schools defined technology as it should be defined (the means of doing a job, whatever the means and the job may be), it would be clear that textbooks, library books, television monitors, tape recorders, overhead projectors, and so on are forms of technology just as certainly as computers are. So a decision to purchase textbooks is also a decision that the presence of textbooks will *increase* the likelihood that intended results will be produced, more than the absence of alternative technologies, such as computers and interactive television, will *reduce* the likelihood that those intended results will be produced.

Certainly budget limitations will make it difficult, if not impossible, for schools and teachers to have access to all the various technologies that might be appropriate, but measures can be taken to increase the availability of specific technologies even if money is lacking. For example, noncategorical funding that allows teachers to choose whether to buy textbooks, library books, or computer software increases access, choice, and control. Giving teachers and building principals control over such budgets within the context of a results-oriented accountability system is another way to increase classroom and building-level control without giving up the ability to provide centralized direction.

Without decentralization, a customer-oriented quality-driven school is an impossible dream. The key to effective school operation, therefore, is to decentralize decisions that have to do with operations, such as how time is used and how technology is deployed, and centralize decisions regarding questions of value (for example, which students will be served, how the worth of programs will be determined, and what is to be learned and by whom). To bring about this kind of decentralization, however, the beliefs that guide the system must be clear. School systems that do not have a clear system of beliefs to guide behavior run the risk that decentralization will lead to anarchy.

The Need for Development

Change requires the adoption of new practices, procedures, policies, and programs. It also requires the abandonment of old practices, procedures, policies, and programs. During periods of economic expansion, when resources appear plentiful, it is commonplace to employ a *parallel systems* strategy in introducing change. The idea behind the parallel systems approach is that the new system or procedure can be introduced alongside the existing system, which can continue to operate until the new system has been "proved" and/or is accepted as preferable. Such an approach is given ideological support, in education at least, by the preference of educators to cloak their change efforts in the mantle of science and experimental design. In the conservative world of schools, the parallel systems approach has another advantage as well: the interests that are served by the status quo need not be threatened by the change, because such threats will not occur until late in the process, when the issue of program continuation arises.

As many of the experiences of the 1960s and 1970s illustrate, however, the parallel systems approach, at least in education, is much better at creating the illusion of change than at bringing about change. New programs, experimental programs, and innovations are viewed as add-ons rather than alternatives. Doctoral students and professors may get excited about "method A and method B" studies, but in the real world of public schools, method B (assuming that it is the traditional method) will, in the long run, win out over method A. When the new money that supports the experimental program disappears, the program is likely to disappear as well. The reason for this is that schools are not developmental problem-solving organizations. The presence of problems in schools is perceived to be synonymous with the presence of trouble, and problems are something from which people distance themselves, something to be avoided rather than solved. I would go so far as to say that the fundamental flaw in the design of public schools is that they are not positioned to take advantage of problems or equipped to invent solutions.

Most schools are, in fact, program-implementing, problem-avoiding organizations. Schools seldom are called on to invent solutions to problems. Instead, they are called on to implement solutions that others devise for them and to make these solutions work for problems that they may not have recognized or that they do not believe exist. This pattern is compounded by the fact that the maintenance needs of schools are so great and the resources to meet them are in such relatively short supply that when developmental resources are provided to schools, the odds are that they will be co-opted to respond to the maintenance needs of the system. Thus the foundation grant that was provided to encourage innovation will be diverted to underwriting the salaries of people whose positions were cut by the latest budget reductions. Money committed to supporting staff development will be used to support textbook adoption committees. And so it goes.

If schools are to change, school systems must create developmental capacity. Most importantly, school districts must find ways of ensuring that developmental resources are protected from being co-opted and are sufficiently flexible to support long-term efforts. Among actions that might be taken are the following:

- Teacher unions and boards might cooperate to provide protection for developmental resources by negotiating a development budget into a union contract. This has been done with limited success in New Orleans.
- The board of education could develop a policy that requires a minimum percentage of the salary budget to be committed to research and development.
- Overhead money from grants could be put into a special interest-bearing account to be used exclusively for developmental purposes.
- A quasi-independent developmental organization could be established and charged with a single mission: program and personnel development. Such an organization could have the legal status of a nonprofit corporation. This would make it possible to manage budgets on a long-term basis. (School leaders and program designers are almost forced to think short term with budgets, because in most governmental agencies, residual funds often cannot be carried over from one year to the next. "Spend it or lose it" encourages waste and sloppy thinking.) Such an organization also would make it possible to establish sustaining endowments from such sources as fee-for-service activity and special grants and gifts and to ensure that these funds would not be co-opted for maintenance purposes.

Numerous other examples might be provided. The important point is that if schools are to have developmental capacity, policies and structures must be in place that ensure the following circumstances:

- Developmental resources are available on a dependable basis.
- The size of the resource commitment is appropriate to the task. If healthy businesses are taken as a guide, a developmental budget, including staff development as well as other forms of development, of 6 percent of salary and wages is not out of line.
- Resources (including people, time, space, and technology) initially committed to supporting development cannot be easily co-opted or diverted to support the maintenance needs of schools and school districts.

Guaranteeing that things will not get worse is important, and that is the function of the maintenance system. Making things different and better—continuous improvement—is the function of the developmental system. Developmental resources must be protected from encroachment by maintenance needs if continuous improvement is to be ensured.

Collaboration

Collaboration is a commonly used term among educators, officials from philanthropic foundations, and government officials. The need for collaboration among agencies (for example, among schools, welfare agencies, and the juvenile justice system) and greater cooperative and collaborative efforts within school districts (for example, between unions and school boards or between elementary and secondary school faculties) is generally recognized. Furthermore, education is not without clear examples of the positive benefits of these efforts. However, anyone who attempts to further the cause of collaboration between schools and other agencies or to increase cooperative action between schools—especially schools in the same school district—will quickly learn that collaborative action and cooperative action take much more than goodwill and good intentions. There are many reasons for this, but chief among them is the fact that schools are threatened organizations living in what sociologists sometimes refer to as "hostile" environments. Schools react to the environment more than they act on it, and the results are frequently less than happy ones.

For example, intense competition frequently develops between schools within the same district. School faculties from one school look upon faculties from other schools as competitors from whom secrets should be kept and from whom little of benefit can be learned. (To confess that one can learn from the school next door is often seen as a confession of weakness or inadequacy.) Thus networking and collaboration between schools within a school district are often more difficult to establish than they are between schools from different districts, though this also has its difficulties.

Given these circumstances, if schools are to become capable of collaboration, two things must happen. First, school leaders must be able to maintain control over those areas of school life that any organization must control to provide direction and behave strategically. For this to happen, the system of governance and the policies that govern the operation of schools must undergo significant alteration. Those who are expected to lead must have control over the appointment, assignment, and evaluation of personnel; allocation of resources assigned to the schools (budgets, time, and space); and choices about technology—that is, the means of doing the job. Without control over these areas of school life, the school will remain too vulnerable to outside influence to operate with confidence in collaborative arrangements. Thus they will remain authoritarian and reactive rather than open and proactive. As Willard Waller ([1932] 1967) observed over fifty years ago, schools are authoritarian because they are threatened, and they are threatened because they are authoritarian.

Second, those who lead schools must conceptually distinguish between collaborative efforts intended to provide support for students and those intended to provide support for the operation of schools. In the latter instance, the school should be viewed as the senior partner—indeed the dominant partner—because the internal integrity of the system is involved. In providing support for students, school leaders and the school should be viewed as a community agency, just as child welfare agencies, the library, and the hospital and health services are.

The point here is perhaps a subtle one, but it is important. Children cannot succeed in school unless they have the support they need to do so. The family is usually assumed to be the primary provider of such support, but it is apparent that needed support may be lacking for some students, especially those from poor families and families in otherwise distressed situations. For this reason, a variety of agencies have been established to provide services and support. Unfortunately, children sometimes do not receive the services they need or they do not receive them in ways that are most helpful.

Other than parents, teachers and school officials are probably in the best position to ascertain the needs of individual children and to recognize when these needs are not being met. Recognizing this fact, educators often take on the task of providing support. The temptation is for schools to become full-service agencies, places where children and families can receive whatever services and support they need. The school is the one place where all children come and where their needs are most likely to become a matter of public concern.

Nothing is wrong with such thinking as long as it is understood that the school has two different functions vis-à-vis the child. First and foremost, the school is an educational agency. *The primary job of the school is to provide each child with rich and challenging experiences that will result in the child's being well educated.* Equally important, the school is or should be a community agency that is concerned primarily with the welfare of children and youth. As such, schools and those who lead them are obliged to ensure that each child has the support needed to be successful in school as well as in the life of the community. *But this does not mean that schools are obliged to provide this support. Rather, their obligation is to provide leadership and advocacy so that the community and the agencies it has created to provide support services can do what they are designed and funded to do with maximum effectiveness and efficiency.* Educational leaders must assert themselves as community leaders as well as leaders within the context of classrooms and schools. School leaders must ensure that needed collaboration happens, not simply between schools and other community agencies but between and among agencies external to the school as well. The community must provide the support children need; schools must provide the leadership needed to ensure that the community does what it must do.

The Community as Guarantor

Each child has the right to the support he or she needs to be successful in school and in life. The condition of a person's birth is not a matter of choice; a decent and moral society acknowledges this fact in its policies and its demeanor. No matter how reprehensible the parent, the child is innocent. When parents cannot or will not provide the kind of support the child needs to be successful, the community must serve as guarantor for that support. Nothing less will do. Well-meaning men and women disagree on how this community obligation should be met. Some argue that schools should become full-service agencies or one-stop shops where all the needs of children and families can be met. I have seen such places, and sometimes the results are impressive. I am not opposed to the notion, but I think there are better ways.

My concern about schools taking on the task of providing noneducational services such as medical and family welfare services to children and families is that such activities can divert attention from the primary mission of the schools, which is to provide children with high-quality schoolwork that results in their learning things that are important to them and to the continuation and progress of the society of which they are a part. However, it is clear that they cannot succeed in school if they do not have the support they need. It is equally clear that educators cannot stand on the sidelines and wait for the community to do what it should do but sometimes fails to do. What then is the solution?

It is here that thinking of schools as both educational agencies and community agencies is particularly attractive. As educational agencies, the mission of schools is quite clear—or at least I think it should be. As community agencies, schools bring two things to the discussion of the needs of children and youth that no other agency brings. By capitalizing on these things, educators can make a contribution to the overall health of the community as well as help to ensure that each child has the support needed to be successful in school and in the community.

First, the school system is the only community agency that comes into contact with all, or nearly all, of the children and youth in the community. Educators therefore are in a position to have a broader and more comprehensive view of the students' needs and the possibility of meeting those needs within the context of the community and the families that exist in it. Second, teachers are the only people in the community (with the exception of families, the rare cleric, and the occasional recreation director or Scout leader) who are in a position to get to know its children in enough depth to understand their longings and their needs, their hopes, their aspirations, their limitations, and their dreams.

Too few school systems and too few teachers take advantage of the position they occupy. Indeed, the very organization of schools often militates against these advantages being realized. The kind of data people in central offices have access to and seek are not those that will help them to make judgments about the needs of all students, both those who are doing well and those who are doing poorly. The relationship between teachers and students often is not shaped so that teachers have the time or the inclination to get to know their students well. Regardless of this reality, the possibility of knowing students well exists. And it is this possibility that I find of interest.

If schools were organized to take advantage of the possibilities described above, school leaders would be ideally situated to be the foremost advocates for children in the community. Educators today understand full well that they must be advocates for education, for schools, and for schooling. What too few recognize is that they must be advocates for children as well. It is up to the educators, I believe, to lead the community in bringing together coalitions to give all children the support they need to be successful in school and in the community. *It is also up to the educators to help members of such coalitions to understand that the primary mission of the coalitions is to guarantee support for each child, whatever the support may look like.* It is not the coalition's mission to rationalize the delivery of services to be more efficient, though that may be a side effect, or to resolve political and boundary disputes between child- and youth-serving agencies in the community, though that may happen as well. *The only mission of a community coalition worthy of being led, participated in, or otherwise encouraged by educational leaders is to fasten the attention of all community agencies on one thing: guaranteeing each child the support he or she needs to be successful in school and in the community.*

This may sound like much ado about very little, but I think not. Over the past decade, I have had occasion to spend considerable time in and around communities where great effort has been invested in building collaboratives aimed at supporting children. Most of these efforts could have been significantly improved if the parties to the collaborative had been clearer and more certain about its mission. Too often the mission seemed to be merely to collaborate, but to what end? Sometimes the mission seemed to be to coordinate the delivery of services in the name of efficiency. Sometimes the mission was determined to be child advocacy, with the biggest target of the advocacy the schools and school leaders. If all parties to such collaboratives could agree that their common mission is to ensure that each child has the support needed to be successful in school and in the life of the community, such groups would not be involved simply in school issues. They would be involved as well in ensuring that the streets children walk are safe; the parks they play in are available, clean, and safe; and the families from which they come have support and encouragement.

Collaborative efforts can be improved if educational leaders view themselves and are viewed by others as the leading advocates for children in the community. Unfortunately, educators, at least in the situations I observed, too often became the targets for other people who styled themselves child advocates, rather than sources of support for children. This sometimes forced educational leaders into the posture of defending the system they were charged with leading rather than leading the effort to change the system. Collaborative efforts can also be improved when it is recognized that, among all the agencies in the community, schools and school leaders are the most significant actors in the arena. Other than the family, no other group or agency can have as much impact on the lives of children and youth as the schools, and no other agency is as well positioned to lead the community in attending to the needs of its children, if school leaders can be encouraged and supported in their efforts.

In sum, I am suggesting that leaders of the educational system should stick to what they know or should know, which is how to continuously improve the quality of the intellectual activity provided to children. In their additional role as leaders of a community agency, however, they should be prepared to offer what the position of their agency in the community requires them to provide: advocacy for children and youth and leadership to ensure that the community and the agencies the community provides for the task are organized to give each child the support he or she needs to be successful in school and in the life of the community.

Conclusion

Schools are currently organized around the idea that the important work being done in them is the work of the teacher. Teacher performance, rather than student performance, commands the center ring. When principals come to visit classrooms with the state-approved teacher evaluation checklist in hand, the odds are that the focus of attention will be on what the teacher does and how she or he does it. Seldom are students the focus of such evaluative exercises. Similarly, when school principals develop schedules for students, they typically begin with such givens as the number of periods into which the day is broken, the amount of time assigned to each period, the size of the classrooms and state or contractual requirements about class size, the number of subjects to be taught, and so on. Students are assigned to classes and teachers according to these parameters and do whatever the teachers expect them to do within the structures given.

If schools were truly student-focused, educators would first decide what the students should be expected to do, and what circumstances would make them more willing and able to do what is expected, before making decisions about how time, people, space, information, and knowledge (that is, curriculum) should be organized and distributed. Indeed, decisions about how schools and classrooms should be structured would not be made until after decisions were made about what students should do to learn what they are expected to learn. Unfortunately, the culture of schools does not encourage a focus on the student. Rather the focus is on ensuring that students learn to fit into whatever structures the school provides and that they learn to learn within these structures.[1] It is largely for this reason that I have argued for some time now that education could be much improved if educators came to view the student as the primary or first-line customer of the schools.

Why think of students as customers rather than simply as students? The first reason is that the historical role of the teacher as

---

[1]Structure refers to the system of rules, roles, and relationships that shape and sometimes govern human behavior in groups and organizations. Thus the structure of some schools might be characterized as depending on rigidly enforced superordinate-subordinate relationships between teachers and students, a clear status hierarchy based on age and perceived performance, and so on. Similarly, the structure might assume that the time needed to learn most subjects and to master most content is relatively equal, resulting in a school day made up of five, six, seven, or eight periods equally divided with regard to time.

a transmitter of knowledge and the student as the recipient of that knowledge has loaded the term *student* with a sense of passivity. The teacher delivers; the student receives. Learning is an active process, and it involves voluntary action on the part of the student. But more importantly, the world of teachers and students has changed dramatically in the past fifty years, and the role structure of schools has yet to take these changes into account. Thinking of the student as a customer would move schools toward a role definition for teachers and students that would be more consistent with the social realities of our times.

In the schools of the future, students must be viewed as customers for knowledge work (purposeful intellectual activity that calls upon them to master and use ideas, propositions, facts, and systematic thought processes) invented by teachers (sometimes in cooperation with the students), and teachers must be viewed as leaders and inventors. In the next chapter, I will elaborate on the implications of this view for improving the performance of systems as well as for assessing system performance.

| Changing the System

Systemic thinking requires us to accept that the way social systems are put together has independent effects on the way people behave, what they learn, and how they learn what they learn. It also requires us to accept that the sources of these effects are frequently beyond the consciousness of those who are affected by them. Americans generally prefer explanations of human behavior that give emphasis to the attributes of individuals as contrasted with the properties of social systems (see, for example, Bellah and others, 1991).

The preference of Americans for individualistic explanations is further reinforced among educators by teacher education programs dominated by psychological modes of explanation (see Schlechty, 1976). It is not surprising, therefore, that coming to grips with the ideas upon which systemic reform is based is difficult for many in education. Even those who embrace the rhetoric of *systemic reform* sometimes tacitly assume that systems are simply the interference they must contend with as they try to figure out what difference individual differences make. The dominant modes of explanation in education continue to be psychological in origin. To think well about schools as systems, we must think as sociologists and anthropologists think.

Culture and Structure

Given the preference for individualistic explanations, it is important for those who advocate systemic reform to be very clear about the fact that systemic thinking requires us to look beyond the individual and individual actions for explanations. The structure of human relationships, rather than the structure of personalities and the structure of human intellect, becomes the focus of inquiry.

A systems perspective requires us to accept that in addition to the causal forces such as attitudes and intellectual abilities that reside within the human personality, causal mechanisms also reside in the structure of relationships and in the way these relationships come to be defined by the system of rules and roles that grows up to support them. More than that, we must understand that these systems of rules, roles, and relationships become so much a part of the habit patterns of people and organizations—indeed, entire societies—that they are taken for granted and no longer consciously considered. Rather, the resulting social system becomes a part of the tacit assumptions, beliefs, and cultural agreements upon which men and women operate on a daily basis.

Thus culture, as well as structure, is a part of the system and must be included in any useful discussion of systemic change and systemic reform. To change the system, we must alter the rules, roles, and relationships that define it. To make any *lasting* change in the structure, corresponding changes must occur in the shared beliefs, commitments, meanings, values, lore, and traditions in which structure is embedded and from which it gains its permanence and stability. It does little good, for example, to redefine the role of the teacher as that of leader and inventor unless the cultural assumptions that define the relationships between teachers and principals change as well. As long as we assume that the proper relationship between principals and teachers is that of bureaucratic superordinates and subordinates and as long as we assume that principals are—or should be—part of the command-and-control structure of the system rather than part of the leadership system (of which teachers are also a part), little real change will take place in the role of teachers.

Certainly principals can delegate additional authority to teachers if they choose or if they are compelled to do so by their own superordinates or the union contract. Some will call this teacher empowerment. It is not. It is simply a redistribution of official authority. Empowerment enables; it does not simply permit. Whereas delegation permits action but does not insist on it, empowerment insists on action. When teachers are empowered, they act as leaders and inventors because they believe they are leaders and inventors. No amount of delegation of authority will create such a belief, even though it may permit the behavior. Beliefs of this kind have to do with culture and the kind of developmental experiences a person has had in that culture. They have little to do with what appears on job descriptions and organizational charts.

Similarly, if schools are to operate on the assumption that the work of students, rather than the work of the teacher, should be the focus of school activity, it will take more than a change in structures to ensure that this is so. It is fine to speak of students as workers or as customers for the work the school provides for them and/or encourages them to undertake, but until this view of the world is embedded in the culture as well as in official rhetoric, little real change will occur, and even that little will erode quickly.

Structural change that is not supported by cultural change will eventually be overwhelmed by the culture, for it is in the culture that organizations find meaning and stability. For example, as I visit American high schools, I have observed on numerous occasions virtual shrines where the pictures of great former athletes are displayed and their records announced. From time to time, I also see pictures of former coaches and distinguished teachers. Obviously the culture of the schools supports the notion that what coaches, teachers, and athletes accomplish is important to the life of the schools. Seldom, however, do I see displays of great students: students whose academic performance was so impressive that myths and legends grew up around them and they are remembered and revered. Is there any reason to wonder why what students do in classrooms is less significant in the life of schools than what their teachers do and what athletes do on the playing field?

Perhaps the greatest difficulty systems thinking poses for those who would understand schools from a systems perspective is that it requires them to understand that social facts are real and that they are real in their consequences (see Durkheim, [1895] 1966). Men and women behave as they do not only because of who they are and the abilities they possess but also because of where they are and what those around them believe. More than that, much of who people are and what they believe is a product of the interaction between the self and social structure, history, and biography.[1] On the one hand, men and women create systems, and they can modify what they have created or even destroy what has been created. On the other hand, systems shape how men and women act and feel, even how they feel about the systems they have created.

"Them Bones," or It's All Connected

Because systems are made up of interconnecting parts, change in any part of the system is likely to require accommodating and supporting changes in other parts as well. Without such accommodating and supporting changes, little real change will occur, or if it does, it will not last. Similarly, change in any part of a system can affect other parts of the system, even though this may not be intended or desired.[2] These connections are not always obvious or well understood, even by those who are affected by them. In systems, things are not always rational. The functions and effects that one component of a system is intended to have may be totally lacking, but this apparently useless component may, in fact, have important effects on the system that may be unintended and largely unacknowledged.

Those who would change a system need, insofar as is possible, to devise a map of the possible connections between various components of the system. Such maps, properly drawn, can hint at the

---

[1]This phraseology closely parallels language used by C. Wright Mills in his book *The Sociological Imagination* (1959). It was in reading this book as an undergraduate that I first got a glimmer of what was meant by the concept of social structure and, consequently, what is meant by social systems. I have never recovered from what I found in the pages of this book. I commend it to the reader's attention.

[2]The idea that social facts are real and have real effects has a long tradition in the literature of sociology as does the idea of intended and unintended consequences. These ideas have recently gained some popular acceptance in the world of education through the writings of Peter Senge (1990), among others. Though my introduction to the concept of social structure and social systems and to the concepts of manifest and latent function came by way of the sociological tradition, I am aware that I am walking a path that parallels Senge's and that of a few other contemporary management consultants and writers.

collateral changes that may need to occur in the system to support the intended changes. They can also help us in understanding why these changes sometimes do not occur, and they may even suggest some new directions that might be taken to remedy the situation. Finally, these maps can illuminate connections between system components that might otherwise escape attention.

The remainder of this chapter is intended to present the broad outlines of such a map. Chapter Nine will illustrate how this map might be used to chart a course for inventing schools appropriate to the conditions of the twenty-first century.

Results for Whom?

Business leaders speak often of the bottom line, by which they usually mean what shows up on a profit-and-loss statement or a balance sheet. Educators, and educational critics, sometimes refer to the bottom line as well, by which they usually mean what shows up on measures of student learning such as standardized test scores. Student learning is to schools as profit is to business. It is also clear that there is a connection between system performance on such bottom-line measures as profit-and-loss statements or standardized test scores.

What is sometimes overlooked, however, is that such bottom-line measures, important as they are, are relatively unimportant to many who are affected by the organization and its outputs. For example, as a stockholder I am very concerned about the profitability of BellSouth Corporation. However, as a user of BellSouth's telephone system, I am not concerned with the profitability of the company, or if I am, I am worried that the company is making too *much* profit, which drives my rates up. As a direct customer of Bell-South, I want dependable service at the lowest possible price. As a stockholder (and thus a different kind of customer), I want a decent return on investment as reflected in dividends and stock prices. Thus, when we say that a system is or is not performing well, we must ask the additional question: For whom and under what terms? Failure to take this larger view can lead to distortions of action and eventually can result in an ineffective system. Indeed, one of the criticisms of some American businesses is that they pay so much attention to quarterly profit reports that they fail to attend to the kinds of investments that are needed to continue to grow the business.

Pushed far enough, attention to singular measures of results and measures of single results (for example, profitability or learning outcomes) can lead to very bizarre and counterproductive behavior. For example, many management experts contend that one of the reasons for a major decline in the overall health and productivity of Bausch & Lomb, Inc., has been that company's tendency to place heavy emphasis on quarterly sales in rewarding managers, which has led some managers to inflate sales falsely through a variety of means ("Numbers Game at Bausch & Lomb?" 1994). Similar cases of such shenanigans have been seen in education as well.

Measures of results are critical, but it is important to keep in mind that different customers and stakeholders want and need different kinds of results from the same organization. We must, therefore, be prepared to measure different things as well as to measure the same things in different ways. Most parents, for example, are concerned about whether their own children are doing well and are happy in school. On the one hand, if their children are doing well and are happy, a drop in the overall publicly reported test scores in a school is likely to be less distressing to them than it would be to business leaders or the local newspaper editor. On the other hand, if test scores generally go up and the performance of the parents' own children goes down, the parents are likely to be concerned with test scores.

Moreover, if the price of increased test scores for all children is that some children suffer great anxiety before tests are given, the parents of the latter will find the new strategies used to increase test scores less than satisfactory. Business leaders, conversely, may find the improvement in test scores a very positive indicator, not because they are callous but because they neither know about the negative effects on individual children nor think much about such matters, unless their own children are involved. Few school systems include measures of the rate of test-induced psychosomatic illness as a part of their measures of school performance, but many parents are quite aware that schools can produce these effects even though they are neither intended nor commonly recognized.

This does not mean that such bottom-line measures as test scores and profit-and-loss statements are irrelevant or should not be used in assessing system performance. Of course they should be used. A corporation that does not produce profits will not stay in business long, for it will not have stockholders. Schools that do not produce evidence that children are learning what the community wants them to will lose the confidence of their stakeholders. Without the confidence of stakeholders and stockholders, neither a corporation nor a school system can survive, particularly in turbulent times (see Drucker, 1980).

System performance cannot, however, be assessed with single measures or even with multiple measures of single things. What is needed are multiple measures of multiple things, because systems are complex and understanding system performance means understanding this complexity. If school systems are to be improved, educators must be able to control the components of the system that are critical to system performance. To do this, they first must understand them. As Deming taught so well, understanding precedes control, and control precedes improvement. The first understanding that a systemic perspective requires is that schools, like other complex systems, have multiple customers with multiple and very different needs they expect the schools to satisfy.

Different Customers, Different Needs

Commentators are often perplexed that year after year on the Gallup education poll sponsored by Phi Delta Kappa (see for example, Elam and Rose, 1995), parents are generally more pleased with the school their children attend than with the quality of education generally and tend to rate their own children's school much more positively than nonparents rate schools generally. One explanation for this condition is that parents have lower standards for schools than others do. Another explanation is that parents rationalize the quality of schools because no parent would intentionally put his or her own child in harm's way. A third explanation is that schools are better than is commonly believed and parents, who are more familiar with what is really going on in schools, make more accurate appraisals. At one time or another, I have heard each of these explanations advanced by people who were in a position to be taken seriously as commentators on the quality of America's schools.

I have not, however, heard an explanation advanced that I consider to be equally plausible and reasonable: it is that what parents want and need from schools is substantially different from what the community generally wants and needs and that many schools are doing a better job of meeting these needs than in meeting the needs of the larger community. Moreover, the measures and indicators parents use to make assessments of the schools their children attend are substantially different from those the community generally uses to assess schools or that the parents themselves use to assess schools with which they are not personally familiar.

From the perspective of business leaders, some political leaders, and some educators, especially those in higher education, the notion of the student as a customer of the school has little meaning. Students are products of the school, and these leaders and educators want these products to have particular qualities and attributes.[3] They seek measures that tell them something about the qualities these products bring to the transaction they are anticipating, for example, hiring the student or admitting the student to a college.

However, to parents, as well as to teachers and others inside the schools, students are not products, nor are they "members of the workforce" or "members of the entering freshman class at an elite university." For parents and teachers, students are sons and daughters, children and young adults, with immediate needs to satisfy and personal satisfactions, delights, and frustrations to be enhanced and dealt with. Thus the measures that parents use to

---

[3]Even though I have long insisted that those inside schools (teachers, principals, and so on) should view students as customers, I do not find the tendency of those outside the schools to view students as "products" particularly troublesome. The only time such a view causes trouble is when business leaders try to give advice to educators about how they should go about their business. When they do this and hang onto their perception of the student as a product, their advice is almost certain to be bad and useless, if not harmful. If, however, business leaders from truly customer-focused businesses can become Janus-faced and view students from the point of view of the school—that is, as customers as well as products—their advice can be powerful.

judge the worth of what the school provides may be very different from the measures that other members of the community use to assess system performance. These facts, though obvious, sometimes escape the attention of those who are endeavoring to establish standards for America's schools.

It is equally clear that what students want and need from school[4] often seems to have little to do with what parents and the larger community need and want. Few students come to school with a burning desire to think and reason and use their minds well, though many adults, including me, believe that schools fail when students do not learn to think, reason, and use their minds productively and well. I suspect that few students come to school because they need and desire to be culturally literate. Some probably do come with a desire to read or a desire to learn to read better, especially if their parents have read to them or they have observed older siblings reading. But even this need is not likely to be widespread among students.[5]

What Do Customers Want?

Table 8.1 posits four sets of customers who are relevant to school life. The first are the students themselves. Unless their needs can

---

[4]Here I am referring to immediate needs: conditions that must be satisfied now, conditions that motivate, drive, and orient action. I am not speaking of needs like "job skills" or the ability to communicate. These also are needs, but few first-graders come to school to gain job skills, nor do they care much about them. What they do care about is doing things that interest and engage them. The business of the school is to provide them with engaging work that results in their learning things that have to do with, for example, job skills or civic understandings and attitudes.

[5]The concept of the student as customer has already been discussed, as has the nature of students' needs (see Chapter Three). The discussion here simply points up that students' needs, although they are legitimate and important, are not the only ones the schools must satisfy, even if they are clearly focused on these needs. The art and science of leadership in schools is to find ways to meet the needs of the schools' primary customers and ways that also produce results that satisfy the needs of the others to whom the schools must respond if they are to continue to survive and thrive.

Table 8.1. Working on the Work.

Systemic Properties	Design Resources	Design Qualities	Results for "Customers"
Culture	Resource variables	Product focus	For students
Beliefs	Time	Clear and compelling product standards	Engaging work
Commitments	People		Compelling work
Meanings	Space		Satisfying work
Values	Information	Protection from adverse consequences for initial failures	For the school system
Lore	Technology		Students are engaged.
Traditions	Tools	Affirmation of performance	Students persist with the work.
Structure	Processes	Affiliation	Students learn what teachers want them to learn.
Rules	Skills	Novelty and variety	
Roles		Choice	For parents
Relationships		Authenticity	Students are happy.
		Organization of knowledge	Students are safe.
		Content and substance	Students learn what parents believe they should learn.
			For community and society at large
			What students learn is culturally significant and valued by the community and society at large.

be met, little else can be accomplished by the school, and in the long term the school will fail. Put directly, if schools cannot produce intellectual activity (1) that the students find engaging and so compelling that they will stick with it even when it is difficult and (2) that leads students to produce products, performances, and exhibitions of which they are proud, that they consider important, and from which they gain satisfaction and a sense of delight, the schools cannot possibly meet the needs of most parents or the larger community.

The second set of customers consists of teachers and others in the school, such as principals and superintendents, who have a direct interest in what students do in school. Teachers' judgments about the extent to which their expectations are being met are reflected in the grades and feedback they provide to the students. The fact that the students are expected to meet teachers' needs as they are expressed in performance expectations should suggest that the relationship between students and teachers is, in fact, a partnership. Although it is appropriate, in the larger context of schooling, to think of students as customers for work and teachers as inventors of that work, within the context of the classroom, Theodore Sizer's formulation (1984) of the student as worker and the teacher as coach (I would say leader) seems appropriate as well.

Though it is seldom commented on, teachers are generally much more attentive to what students do than to what they learn—as are parents, principals, and others who interact with students on a daily basis. Indeed, Lortie (1975) reports that teachers generally define a "good day" as a day when students do what the teachers want them to do, presumably with some enthusiasm and minimum resistance.

There is, in fact, considerable congruence between what students and teachers want and need. Students need engaging work; teachers want and need students to be engaged in the work teachers provide to them. Students want and need compelling work; teachers want and need students to persist in the face of difficulty, which means that teachers want the work to be compelling as well. Students need satisfying work that produces products and performances that bring feelings of accomplishment, pride, and delight; teachers are also gratified when these things happen. Teachers are perhaps a bit more concerned with what students learn than are most students, unless, of course, the students aspire to go to an elite college. When this is the case, it is likely that the students and their parents will be especially concerned that students are being taught what they need in order to compete for college entry.[6]

Of course, it is assumed that if students can be brought to do what teachers (and presumably parents) want them to do, students will learn what teachers intend that they learn. Perhaps, but this is not certain. It is at least possible that teachers could develop work that is highly engaging to students and so compelling that students will stick with it, even when the going is tough, but that students still might not "know" what their parents and the community expect them to. It is even possible for teachers to get students to do exactly what teachers want but fail to get them to know what the teachers believe they should know and have mastered.

There are those who will argue that what I have just written is wrongheaded, that it assumes a separation between doing and knowing that is not appropriate or assumes a dualism between thought and action that cannot be justified intellectually or empirically. Maybe so, but I am not trying to make a philosophical point or develop a new theory of learning. My point is that teachers can never assume that the work they assign students to do is the right work to get the learning they want. Discovering what work or activity will produce the desired learning for a particular student is as problematic as is the nature of learning itself. *That is why teachers must constantly work on the work they give students.* The right work for some students may not be the right work for other students or even for the same students in a different context or on a different day.

Teachers who design the right work for students to do and then find ways to get them to do it get more students to learn more of what teachers want them to than do teachers who design the wrong work or who fail to get students engaged in the work they design.

---

[6]One of the greatest barriers to school reform is the widespread perception that having students do unconventional and nontraditional things in school will result in a diminution in their learning of the conventional things they need to know to be successful on college entrance exams. If this is so, it is because those who are changing the work have not considered how they can increase the quality of the students' experiences and make these experiences more engaging for more students without decreasing the quality of the content.

This is not a profound insight; it is common sense, but common sense is often uncommon in discussions of schools and teaching.

The real problems for teachers arise when and if students for whom the work is intended do not find it engaging, compelling, or satisfying or when students find the work engaging but fail to learn what is intended. If students are viewed as customers, the first place to look for explanations of the problem is the nature of the work provided. The key questions would be, How might this work be modified or repackaged so that more students would be engaged or at least some students would be more engaged? and, How might the content in which the students are engaged be modified so that they are more likely to learn what is intended? Unfortunately, the more typical questions are, What is wrong with the student who does not engage the work? and, What is wrong with the student who did not learn what was intended?

The first set of questions, those dealing with the nature of the work, encourages teachers to consult with colleagues about ways of improving the work and may encourage them to think imaginatively and creatively about ways of redesigning it. The second set of questions, those concerning students, may result in students' being sent to see the guidance counselor or the school psychologist, but it is unlikely that the answers to these questions will really help the teacher to better understand what he or she might do to remedy the situation.

A third set of customers the schools must satisfy is the parents. Most parents, like most teachers, are concerned with what their children learn but, on a day-to-day basis, are much more concerned about what the children are doing in school than with what they are learning. Parents are concerned that their children are happy and safe as well as becoming more thoughtful and informed. Parents want schoolwork to both be understandable to them and have meaning for their children.

When test scores are made available, if a child's scores are lower than her or his parents think they should be, the parents may express concerns about test scores generally. But parents who are satisfied with the test scores of their own children seldom complain about test scores in the schools their children attend even when the local editorial writers are nearly frantic about the matter. Generally, low test scores may dissuade parents from sending their children to a school, assuming a choice is involved, but when youngsters are already enrolled in a school, low test scores will not drive the parents away as long as their own children are doing well, are happy, and are doing schoolwork that meets the moral standards the parents think appropriate.

The final set of customers that must be satisfied is the stakeholders other than parents whose support the school needs in order to continue, such as nonparent taxpayers and organizations that depend upon the schools to provide them with graduates who can meet the standards the organizations believe must be met if they are to continue to function as they would like.

As indicated by discussions of national standards, controversies over outcome-based education, and controversies over various statewide testing programs (for example, the debates in Kentucky and California), when we move beyond general principles, adult members of the community do not always agree about what constitutes a well-educated or even reasonably educated high school graduate. Agreement is substantially greater on the fact that graduates are not well educated unless they can read with facility, write passably, and compute with reasonable accuracy. But even this is controversial, for little agreement seems to exist on the operational meaning of words like *facility, passably,* or *reasonable accuracy.* People disagree, as well, about how old a student should be before he or she achieves a particular level or standard.

As was noted earlier, causing communities to engage in dialogue about these matters is an ongoing problem for local school leaders as well as for educational leaders at the state and national levels. It is unlikely, however, that consensus on these matters will occur anytime soon, so those who look for some magic statement of standards to be the bottom line in educational reform are, I fear, in for a disappointment. In the meantime, another bottom line must be considered. It seems clear to me that there is little possibility that students will learn whatever adults want them to unless the schools become much better than they are now at inventing engaging work for students. Attempting to make this happen seems quite enough to occupy the attention of most of us who are involved in the effort to reform America's schools.

Learning Is Not All There Is to School

This book, like most discussions of the quality of America's schools, focuses attention on the aspects of school life that most directly affect student learning. This is as it should be, because schools are designed to ensure that students learn what adults assume to be critical to the continuation of the culture, the progress of society, and the welfare of individual students. It is, however, important to observe that schools must and do meet many needs in communities in addition to those directly associated with student learning, just as businesses meet many needs in communities in addition to the most obvious ones. For teachers and administrators, schools provide employment and some degree of economic security. When schools' ability to meet these needs is threatened, employee groups are likely to become dissatisfied, and eventually this dissatisfaction will affect the ability of the schools to carry out their primary mission. Similarly, schools carry out custodial functions for families, and when decisions are made that adversely affect schools' ability to meet these custodial needs, parents may become disgruntled and dissatisfied, as any superintendent who has tried to make substantial changes in a school calendar understands very well.

Business leaders, especially those who are concerned with local economic development, are interested not only in the real performance of schools and schools' ability to provide businesses with a quality workforce, but also with the schools' reputation for quality education. Any reform effort that simply improves the schools and does not bring about a corresponding change in their reputation will not satisfy these interests. Therefore, it is in the interest of those who lead reform efforts to be attentive to these additional results. For example, nonparent taxpayers want to be assured that children are learning what these taxpayers want them to learn, but nonparent taxpayers also want to be assured that their tax money is being spent wisely and prudently. Any proper listing of results for customers would include such items.

In the discussion in this book, I have not included many results of schooling that should be a part of a comprehensive analysis, because I want to stay focused on the factors that most directly affect student learning. I believe that the most important factors affecting student learning over which schools and teachers have direct control are the qualities and attributes of the activities (work) the schools provide to students.

The Language of Classrooms and Schools

Educators, with the help of their colleagues in psychology, have developed a substantial language with which to talk about students. Labels for classifying students are abundant, ranging from "profoundly mentally retarded" to "gifted and talented." Learning styles have been described, and the brain has been segmented into two halves; "right brain" and "left brain" have special meaning in the discourse in teachers' lounges and college lecture halls.[7] A language of classroom behavior has been created as well. Phrases like "time on task" are commonplace in educational discourse. A language of sorts even exists to describe what teachers do—for example, "direct teaching," "Socratic dialogue," "modeling," "lecturing," and "processing." However, language to describe the work students are expected to do and teachers are expected to design is substantially more limited, although we do read about "the core curriculum," "the interdisciplinary curriculum," "the project-centered curriculum," and "the inquiry-based curriculum."

What is most clearly lacking is a language to talk about, describe, and analyze the nature of the work students are assigned. When teachers provide students with assignments that engage them, what makes those tasks engaging? Some will say that they are related to the interests of children. Good. Should the interests of children then be the guiding principle for schoolwork? *What if the children are not "interested" in things they need to know or that adults believe they need to know?* Teachers need to know how to get children interested in things they care not a whit about but need to learn to care about. *Discovering interest is important; creating interest is even more important.*

One of the greatest barriers to developing a language that permits us to describe the qualities of schoolwork is the penchant of educators for individualistic explanations. When students abandon

---

[7]I must admit that I am sometimes uncomfortable with these labels and meanings, but I will not voice my discomfort here other than to make note of its existence.

assignments, the usual explanation is that they have a short attention span, are undisciplined, lack persistence, or suffer from some other intellectual or moral shortcoming. It is true that some students have limited intellectual capacity and some have developed habits we call undisciplined and lazy. However, it is also true that some assignments are judged by students as simply not worth doing, especially in the face of all the other exciting options that are available to them. Teachers need first to work on the work they give students; only as a last resort should they work on the students. And to work on the work, they must be able to describe the qualities and characteristics of the work that are important to the students and that bear on the likelihood that students will find the work engaging, compelling, satisfying, and a source of delight.

Over years of reading about teaching and schools, teaching myself, watching others teach, and discussing with others what I have seen and think I have learned, I have come up with a set of categories that I have found useful when I have tried to answer such questions as, What makes one set of activities engaging to students and another less so? Why do students stick with some assignments even when they present them with difficulties and temporary setbacks, whereas other assignments are abandoned as quickly as possible? and, Why do activities that would seem to be boring and trivial, such as memorizing the multiplication tables or the names and locations of the states and continents, sometimes produce great satisfaction and delight among students and at other times produce precisely what we might expect—boredom and lack of attention?

The ability to get students actively engaged in and excited about matters that some might consider trivial is, in my view, one of the marks of a great teacher, not because I favor trivializing the curriculum or preparing students for cocktail party conversation and the appearance of being culturally literate but because this ability demonstrates that the teacher has somehow come to understand that much that we want students to do in school is not inherently interesting to them and that something must be done *to* the work if it is to be interesting enough to engage the students. Unfortunately, when this happens, the current tendency is to concentrate attention on what the teacher is doing rather than on describing and analyzing what the teacher is getting the students to do. This almost invariably leads to the conclusion that the teacher is extraordinary. I would suggest, however, that extraordinary teachers are those who get students to do extraordinary things. We have a much better chance of helping ordinary teachers to get students to do extraordinary things than we do of mass producing extraordinary teachers. First, however, we must be able to describe with some precision the attributes, qualities, and characteristics of the work teachers and schools provide to students.

The Qualities of Schoolwork

Work that is engaging to students is almost always focused on some product or performance (Sizer, 1984, calls it an exhibition) that is significant to them. The clearer the connection is between what they are being asked to do and the production of a product or performance that they perceive to be important to them, the more likely they will be to engage the task. Thus a clear product focus is a critical attribute of quality schoolwork.

Students also are more likely to engage and persist with work when the standards for the products and exhibitions are clear and compelling to them. Children and young adults—like most of us—prefer to operate in a world where they know what is expected and where what is expected is something they care about or can be brought to care about. Recent efforts to develop and communicate clear examples and models of such products to students and those who assess student performance (educators sometimes call these illustrations "rubrics") show that this need is coming to be better understood. What is less well understood is that until students learn to care about the products or performances suggested by a rubric, no amount of clarity and precision will suffice. *Standards only have relevance when those to whom they apply care about them.*

A third attribute of work that seems to affect the level of student engagement—especially that of students who are less quick and less precocious than some of the more gifted students—is the extent to which students have opportunities to engage in tasks at which they are not proficient without fear of embarrassment, punishment, or the implication of personal inadequacy. The unfortunate fact is that the way schools are organized makes this condition difficult to achieve. Consider, for example, grading practices. Each time a grade is given, rewards and punishments are distributed. Furthermore, any person who receives less than the highest grades is implicitly receiving a slight or heavy rebuke. (A's are excellent and B's are pretty good, but F's are failing.) Demanding that teachers have enough evidence in their grade books to justify the grades given makes it difficult for a teacher with 150 students in five sections of English composition to simply provide feedback to students without making the feedback count in the grade book. When this fact is combined with the rigid time frame within which schools typically function—even though we know that the rate of learning varies considerably among students—the linkage between failure and punishment is almost inescapable. Students, and sometimes their parents, do escape, however. The students simply begin to accept the fact that they are incapable of being more than C students, and their parents come to believe that their children's performance has to do with "ability" more than with effort.

A fourth attribute of work that is important to students is the extent to which the work is designed so that their performance is affirmed. We should not, however, confuse the word *affirm* with the word *praise*. To affirm is not to approve or disapprove; it is to declare that what happened matters and is important. Affirmation suggests significance and thus attaches importance to the event or action.

Performance that counts matters to people who count in the lives of the students. If the performance expected in school is of little concern to these people (sociologists call them "significant others"), then the likelihood is that it will not count to the students. Who are the people who count? First and foremost are the significant adults in the nonschool life of the students; second, their peers; and finally, the teachers and others who are officially employed to instruct them. It is unfortunate that the myth has grown up that teachers are always significant influences in the lives of students. Sometimes they are, but often they are not. Few high school dropouts report that they had great teachers who influenced them, though most teacher education majors report that they were influenced greatly by one or more great teachers in high school. No surprise here that I can see.

Individual teachers are more likely to be in a position to affirm student performance in ways that are important to the students in the early grades than later in the students' lives in school. Why? Because as children grow older their social networks expand, and those who become significant referents for them change. On average, parents and teachers are much more powerful sources of affirmation for little children than for older youngsters. This is perhaps why the expectations of first-grade teachers have such powerful effects on student performance, whereas those of sixth-grade teachers are less salient (Rosenthal and Jacobson, 1968).

Few adults other than teachers are in a position to affirm the performance of students in school because, in most cases, that performance is concealed from everyone except the teachers and perhaps a few peers. This is one of the reasons that portfolio assessment has such great appeal. It makes the performance of the student available for scrutiny by a variety of potential sources of affirmation, whereas conventional systems of grading and reporting make only the *teacher's evaluation* of a student's performance available to others.

The critical point here is that teachers who are able to get students engaged in work that seems inherently boring and uninteresting do so partly because they find ways to get the performance affirmed as important by people who count in the students' lives, whether they are peers, parents, or others outside the school. They do this by finding ways of making the performances and products produced by students visible to others and by causing others to show that they take them into account. (The spelling bees and ciphering matches that were public events in many rural schools in years gone by probably had such affirming effects.)

A fifth attribute of work that is important to students is the extent to which the work is designed to permit, encourage, and support opportunities for students to affiliate with others. It is generally understood that most students enjoy and are motivated by being members of vital and well-organized groups. (Many students even enjoy poorly organized groups, and some students participate in actions that look a great deal like mob activity.) Groups and the affiliation they provide are powerful forces for good or ill in the motivational structures of schools and classrooms. Teachers and schools that produce the highest levels of engagement seem to understand the power of groups and how to use them, as well as how to offset the negative effects that groups may have from time to time.

Skillful teachers design work so that affiliation is one of the rewards students get from doing it. Sometimes this reward comes in the *process* of doing the work (in so-called *group work*) and sometimes it comes as a *result* of doing the work (for example, lonely practice at home may get a student into the school band). Skillful teachers also understand that group work is not simply work that students do together; very small children engage in parallel play long before they have learned the skills of cooperative action. Group work requires interdependence as well as independence.

Those who advocate cooperative learning as a pedagogical strategy (for example, Slavin, 1991) understand this very well. Unfortunately, sometimes teachers and administrators do not understand this strategy and end up with five or more students working independently together on a common task and calling it group work. The result is that group work in schools sometimes develops a bad reputation, especially with the parents of students who are quick, aggressive, and intellectually gifted. On the one hand, parents see such work as holding their child back; on the other hand, they see their child doing all the work and others getting credit for it.

This ill-deserved reputation is largely the result of poorly designed group work. The affiliation and affirmation provided by properly constructed groups is a critical element in good design of quality work for students. The skeptical reader should recall that many of the most highly engaging activities in schools, such as band, choral music, team sports, and drama, are multiage and multitalent and are organized around groups and cooperative ideals. Yet individual attainment is not stifled, and stars are born and recognized. Maybe it is the classroom based on James Garfield's vision of Mark Hopkins on one end of a log and a student on the other that needs to be reexamined.

Building novelty and variety into schoolwork and classroom tasks is a sixth area that should be of concern to teachers. Furthermore, it is well to keep in mind that *novelty* and *frivolity* are not synonyms. Novelty adds freshness and new life to the tired and the repetitious. It improves performance because it insists that one continue to learn to master the new situation. Frivolity is activity without substance. Novelty can be, and should be, substantial. Giving students novel things to do and novel ways of doing them is simply one more way of increasing the likelihood that they will engage the work. For example, the introduction of computers into writing classes sometimes motivates students to write who otherwise would not do so. What is sometimes forgotten, however, is that novelty has a way of wearing off. What is new today is taken for granted tomorrow. The motivational power of computers, and other forms of electronic technology, will only be realized when they are used to provide students with new forms of work to do and new products to produce as well as new ways to do old work and produce old products.

Choice is yet another attribute of work that should be considered in designing activities for students. Choice implies some degree of control over events. Individuals who have choice are empowered, and empowerment increases the likelihood of commitment. Unfortunately, like the term group work, the word choice has become tainted in schools. During the 1960s, it became relatively commonplace for radical reformers to assert that students needed choice in what they learned. Some even went so far as to argue that the students' interests should dictate the curriculum. This argument is still being advanced by some people. I am not one of them, and I think those who do argue this way are wrong.

Schools exist because the present generation of adults believes that the young need to learn certain things in order to ensure cultural and social continuity. The young are given little choice about these matters. They need to learn to read whether or not they come to school wanting to read and whether or not their parents insist on this endeavor and support them in it. Children are not simply family members; they are citizens as well, and as such they have duties and obligations that cannot be adequately fulfilled unless they can read. Other learnings are basic as well. For example, though I would not go as far as some of the list makers in the cultural literacy movement seem willing to go, I do believe that all adults need to be generally conversant with the history of America and the world.

I also think that it is not a bad idea for everyone to have a general grasp of basic geographic facts, skill in the use of maps, and so on. But for now at least, I am willing to leave to others debates about what learnings are essential. I will simply stipulate that I am not as interested in providing "learning choices" as I am in providing "doing choices." I am also interested in bringing to a level of consciousness the obvious fact that students have choices about what they will and will not do whether adults like it or not. Anyone who does not believe this has not been in schools, churches, synagogues, or other places where adults try to get the young to do things they do not see some sense in doing. Certainly, through coercion, rebellion can be stopped and minimal compliance assured. But commitment, which is needed if learning is to occur, must be earned. Certainly the young can be compelled to attend school through coercion, but their attention at school must be earned.

It is critical, therefore, in building the schools of the future that we understand that students, like other customers, are volunteers and have choices. By recognizing this fact and by providing choices that are attractive to students and that cause them to work with knowledge and information they need in order to be culturally literate, personally competent, and (I hope) the possessors of civic virtues, the schools may indeed be able to satisfy the critics who believe that the schools are not doing their job. To provide such choices, we must first acknowledge that what students do determines what they learn and that they can find many ways to learn the same things. Variety in "doing" is the only way I know to ensure constancy in learning.

The authentic nature of the work students are expected to do is another feature of significance to student engagement, persistence, and satisfaction. The word *authenticity* is bandied about quite freely among educators, so freely that the power of the concept is sometimes lost in rhetoric. (I once threatened to write an article entitled "Let's Get Real About Authenticity.") Though I find it difficult to understand how it is possible for people to have "inauthentic" experiences, I do understand how they might experience things that are in themselves inauthentic. And when they authentically experience these inauthentic things—the artificial, the contrived, the meaningless, and the inconsequential—the likelihood that the experience will be compelling enough to produce a high level of engagement is low. Conversely, if experiences seem to be real—for example, if they carry real consequences such as winning or losing a football game—it is more likely that engagement will be increased.[8]

Authenticity is obviously enhanced by attention to building affirmation into students' work. Few teachers have failed to note how much more attentive most students are when they are preparing for a performance their parents are likely to attend. The parents' presence not only affirms the performance; it gives it authenticity as well. Authenticity is also enhanced by associating the work with real-life products from which the student gains feelings of pride and satisfaction. For example, a documentary videotape on the Civil War produced by a group of students is much more likely to possess a modicum of authenticity than a series of lectures on the same topic whose only benefit is in helping the students to pass a test indicating that they were listening to what the teacher said and were smart enough to figure out what was important—that is, what was likely to be on the test.

A seventh attribute or quality of work that is critical to engagement, persistence, and satisfaction is the way the content to be worked on—the information, the concepts, and the ideas as

---

[8]Adam Urbanski, the president of the Rochester, New York, Teachers' Union, argues that the most critical difference between private and public schools is that private schools have the ability to uphold standards (by excluding students), whereas public schools lack this ability. His solution would be to enable schools to exclude students who cannot meet or refuse to meet standards and to provide these nonperforming students with alternative schools to attend (Urbanski, 1996). This would certainly increase authenticity, as would high-stakes testing, at least for students who place value on attending a particular school. I have considerable sympathy for Urbanski's argument, and I am not totally opposed to the idea of high-stakes testing. However, until I have some degree of assurance that the quality of the experiences provided students is the highest possible, I find punishing students for the failure of the schools a dubious enterprise, something like imposing tariffs to ensure that Americans will buy American cars even when the quality of foreign cars is judged by the customer to be superior. Conceptually, at least, a tariff punishes the customers for not choosing the product provided, just as high-stakes testing punishes the customer for not doing the work the school provides. Before imposing tariffs or high-stakes testing, I think we should ensure that both the quality of American goods and the quality of the work schools give students are truly superior.

well as the materials in which they are contained—is organized and made available. Sometimes content is presented in ways that are fragmented and disjointed; sometimes it is unified and focused. Sometimes the information is easily accessible; sometimes it is difficult to access, difficult for the student to organize, or difficult to manage. Such things make a difference in the likelihood that the work will be engaged, and any content that is not engaged will not be learned.

Finally, the issue arises of the richness and profundity of the knowledge upon which students are being asked to work. Rich and profound knowledge requires students to expend considerable energy and gain control over complex and difficult processes if they are to employ the knowledge with positive effect. Learning to write complete sentences and to decode words is not the same thing as learning to write persuasively and to read critically, thoughtfully, and well. If, however, students are to function in the world of educated men and women, they must write persuasively. If they are to gain access to the ideas contained in great literature, they must be able and willing to read well, not just passably.

Unfortunately, because so many students and adults fail to acquire the skills needed to write and read well, it is assumed that the acquisition of these skills and abilities has to do with the characteristics of particular students. Some people say that not all students have the ability to read well, and they leave the matter there. It is my view that this is no place to leave the matter, especially in a democracy where the ability to access, control, and use information is becoming the currency of the realm. Those who cannot read well, think well, and present their views persuasively or who are incapable of mathematical reasoning and the ability to compute will find themselves increasingly excluded from the opportunity structure in America's economy and will become dangerous to the survival of democracy, for they can be manipulated by those who do possess such skills and who lack a moral rudder.

If it is indeed the case that mastery of profound knowledge and rich content is necessarily limited to the children of the rich and well-born and to those among the less economically and socially fortunate who were born, in present school terms, relatively gifted, then the dream of democracy cannot be realized. If, however, nearly every person is capable of benefiting from an "elite" education through hard work, it is time educators committed themselves to inventing work that is engaging to all students, not just those who were born with a predisposition to the kinds of work schools now require them to do.

The Disgraceful Compromise

The statement "all students can learn" is meaningless unless one is prepared to assert what they should learn and at what level. Unfortunately, as writer Henry Levin (1987) makes clear, the answer too many educators give to the question How much can all children learn? is that many, especially the poor, those who have nonsupportive parents, and those with ordinary intellectual equipment cannot learn very much. And as Levin makes painfully clear, schools have responded to this perception by providing those who are perceived as being unable to learn much with experiences that are not worth much. In fact, in many schools, most students are not expected to learn anything of significance. Consider, for example, the meaning of the grade C as it is communicated in most schools in America. C is said to be an average grade and, therefore, an acceptable grade for most students.

That the grade of C does not represent the attainment of high academic standards is attested to by the fact that colleges and universities that pride themselves on requiring evidence of the ability to perform at high levels in academic pursuits do not find the grade of C a positive predictor of performance. Students who go through their academic careers with a C average do not meet high academic standards—or even reasonable academic standards. Most likely the only standards they consistently meet are compliance standards, such as turning in homework on time, filling in all the blanks on tests, and constantly doing extra-credit work.

If the grade of C does represent the expected attainment of the average student, then the critics are right: the standards of America's schools are indeed quite low. Unfortunately, many teachers, especially those who grade on the curve (a terrible practice, by the way), really do not expect more than 15 to 20 percent of their students to meet high academic standards, which, theoretically at least, are represented by A's and perhaps B's.[9] The practice of defining C's as average grades that are appropriate to most students is, I believe, an organizational compromise that is disgraceful in its impact if not its intent. The grade of C—and more so the grade of D—legitimizes and makes acceptable marginal and submarginal academic performance. Indeed, in many schools, the C grade should probably stand for *contrite* and *compliant,* for what is required to get the grade is skill in doing extra-credit work that may not be good but is at least abundant.

I can see only one way out of this compromise. First, educators must complete the sentence "All students can learn . . ." differently than is commonly done. Adding the phrase "and learn at high levels" helps a bit, but it is still not adequate. The statement "all students can learn, and learn at high levels" still does not answer the question posed by Deborah Meier: "Learn what?" In response to this query, I suggest the following assertion: *All students can learn, at high levels, the forms of knowledge, skills, attitudes, and habits of mind that are judged by relevant adults to be both important to the happiness and welfare of the students and socially and culturally significant. Furthermore, it is the obligation of schools, and those who work therein, to provide students with engaging work that ensures that students learn what they are expected to learn.*

To be sure, schools are incapable today of achieving such a lofty goal, and it is also doubtful that this goal will be achieved in the short run. The intent of school reform should be to learn how to meet this goal. The belief that all students can learn substantially more than they do now and that what they can learn is itself substantial should guide any effort to reform schools. School reform must work to create conditions where this belief can be realized. Anything less is a disgraceful compromise.

---

[9]It is not my intention here to get into the issue of grade inflation or to comment on the relative merits of the ABC grading system. Whatever one thinks about this matter, I believe that what these grades have come to mean in the vocabulary of educators is evidence of the problem I am raising here: too few students are expected to meet high academic standards.

Design Resources

Thus far I have discussed two basic components of Table 8.1. The first component had to do with results, the second with design qualities. Here I want to discuss what is referred to in the table as design resources, of which technology is a central feature.

The most critical resource in education, as in most enterprises, is the technology that is available. It is important to understand, however, that textbooks and slate boards are forms of technology just as computers are forms of technology. Technology is the means of doing the job, whatever the means and whatever the job (see Chapter Three).

Technology comprises three components:

1. Tools, including such things as computers, computer software, books, magazines, chalkboards, chalk, and laboratory equipment
2. Skills, including the understandings and insights required to use the tools available
3. Processes, including the processes by which skills are developed and tools are accessed and made available

Skill in reading is really a part of the technology of schools and schooling. Students who cannot read cannot use books, as students who cannot type cannot effectively access computers. Further, students who cannot read are limited in the extent to which they can work with or on profound (as opposed to trivial) knowledge because much of this knowledge is to be found in books. Students who cannot use computers will also be severely limited, at least by contemporary standards, in the range of information they can access, because more and more information is being stored and transmitted through electronic means.

A clear linkage can be seen between the kinds of tools available to students, the skills students possess, and the possibility of controlling and enhancing the design qualities discussed above. Students who have considerable facility in reading and writing, which

I define as skills, are able to participate in the creation of a much wider range of academic products than are those who have more limited skills. Skill development is really technological development, and it is also a means of enhancing the ability of schools to produce engaging work for students. The key, of course, is to design work that calls upon students to develop these skills while they are mastering the information and gaining the profound understandings to which these skills provide access.

A linkage also exists between the technology available to students, the tools and skills available to them, and the other resource variables of concern in schools: time, people, space, and information (see Table 8.1). This linkage is not as obvious, however, since time, people, space, and information find their connection to technology through the processes employed in developing skills and using or gaining access to tools.

Consider, for example, the development of skill in reading. There is considerable evidence that developmental differences between children account for much of the variability in success in learning to read in the early years of schooling; cultural differences and differences in the level of parental support are critical as well. Evidence also supports the assertion that children who fail to learn to read early are more likely to fail to learn to read well later than are early readers. All of these conditions aside, the way schools are organized, and especially the way time is assigned and distributed, makes it difficult and often impossible to take these variations into account. A first-grade reading level is assumed with first graders who are more or less six years old. Six-year-olds who do not read at the first-grade level are already behind.

The fact is that it is generally known which six-year-olds will be behind before the first grade even begins. Children who are considered to be at risk are the most likely to be behind, but children from more affluent homes who are not as developmentally precocious as some of their peers are likely to be behind as well, as are children who are substantially younger than their classmates. In most schools, time waits for no one, and the schools are indeed "prisoners of time" (see National Education Commission on Time and Learning, 1994). Thus many of these children who are behind in the beginning will also be behind in the end—not because it is foreordained but because the way time can be used in schools is generally so inflexible.[10]

Similar illustrations could be provided regarding the difficulty of using people, space, and information in a flexible way and the adverse consequences this has for the kinds of technology students and teachers have available to them. Enough has been said, however, to illustrate the primary points I wish to make:

- The technology available largely determines the degree to which teachers and administrators can vary the qualities and characteristics of the work provided to students or that students are encouraged to undertake.
- If the quality of the work provided to students cannot be varied, it cannot be improved, and if the quality of work cannot be improved, it is not reasonable to expect much improvement in the performance of schools.
- The availability of technology can be enhanced by increasing the ability of teachers to use time, people, space, and information in a flexible manner and by ensuring that it is understood that choices regarding technology are choices about the means of doing the job rather than simply about computer hardware and software.

Stating the matter differently, budgets and financial figures are nothing more or less than proxy statements for resources. The

---

[10]Many schools and communities are endeavoring to use time more flexibly. Preschool programs such as Project Head Start are efforts to provide at-risk students with more time in enriched learning environments, with the intent of compensating for the developmental disadvantages produced by poverty. Anyone who has worked to establish and maintain such programs, however, knows that the idea that school begins after Labor Day and that children start to school when they are five or six is deeply embedded in the thought ways of America. The inflexibility and scarcity of time is one of the greatest barriers to improving the quality of the work provided to students. Many students do not have the time to develop the skills they need to use the tools academic work requires them to use, and teachers do not have the time to think about and invent new work that will engage more students.

relevant resources in schools are the forms of technology employed and the time, people, space, and information that provide the context for the use of these technologies. In the enthusiasm generated around the purchase of new computers, distance learning opportunities, interactive computer programs, and fiber-optic connections, it is sometimes forgotten that the way time is organized in schools may preclude the effective use of these new tools. Skilled and well-educated teachers still must make decisions about which technologies are most appropriate to produce a given type of work and which students need special skills to use these means of doing the job. If teachers are not skilled and well educated, they will be less likely to make good decisions.

Some forms of technology simply cannot be used in the physical spaces now typical of some schools. Therefore, unless physical space can be rearranged, some sound decisions about what students should do are precluded from consideration.

If students do not have the skills and insights needed to turn information into knowledge as well as the conceptual tools needed to figure out how information might best be organized and used, then all the hardware and software in the world will not help them. In this age of fact, students and the citizenry do not need more facts. Indeed, we are all overwhelmed with facts and supposed forms of knowledge. What we need are ideas with which facts can be disciplined and tools to help students discern which parts of the information they are getting are truthful, useful, and relevant to them and the tasks they are undertaking.[11] This is the challenge that confronts teachers and other educators who take up the task of working on the work as opposed to working on the students. The quantity and quality of information available to students cannot be improved by simply turning on a computer and dialing up the Internet.

Systemic Properties

Systemic reform of schools involves changing the systemic properties of schools. These properties are of two types: structural and

---

[11]Much of the sentiment and some of the phraseology used here is attributable to C. Wright Mills (see Mills, 1959, p. 5).

cultural. Broadly speaking, as stated earlier, structural properties have to do with systems of rules, roles, and relationships. Cultural properties have to do with systems of beliefs, commitments, meanings, values, lore, and traditions (see Table 8.1).

More narrowly speaking, structural properties have to do with the way systems are given direction and coordinated, organizational boundaries are established and maintained,[12] evaluations are conducted and enforced, status and rank are accorded, and so on. Cultural attributes have to do not only with the way things are and what people really do—that is, practices—but also with what John Cuber, a sociology professor I once knew, called "the preachments of the system," by which he meant the "ought norms," or the way things are supposed to be, even if they are not so (Cuber with Harroff, 1965). Contained within the same culture are the accepted explanations for the discrepancies that exist between preachments and practices (Cuber called these "pretenses"; Robin Williams, 1960, refers to them as "cultural fictions").

To bring about systemic change, therefore, leaders must deal not only with objective reality but with subjective realities as well. Many times structural changes do not occur because the myths and fictions in the culture conceal the effects of the present structure. In schools where children are doing poorly, lore supporting the

---

[12]Organizational boundaries are much more than district lines and attendance zones. They include areas of the lives of participants over which the organization endeavors to exercise some control or influence. For example, schools try not only to control the behavior of students in schools but also to exercise some influence over what students do at home, as when teachers assign homework. Organizational boundaries go well beyond the schoolhouse door and geographic lines in districts.

On another topic, much of what I am suggesting here was first introduced to me by Ronald G. Corwin (1965) in a paper he wrote many years ago where he endeavored to describe the organizational properties of schools (what would nowadays be called systemic properties). Unfortunately, his framework has been overlooked by most of those who write about systemic reform in schools. Grounded as he is in sociology, Corwin has the ability to distinguish between social systems and their effects. Too many of those who write about systems—both in education and in business—are apparently so unfamiliar with the literature of sociology that they fail to see much that would be visible if they stood on the shoulders of some of these intellectual giants.

notion that variance in student performance is largely attributable to factors beyond the control of the schools is likely to prevail. In schools where students are doing very well, the power of schools and teachers to make a difference is likely to be celebrated. In both cases, a great deal of mythmaking occurs, and these myths serve a common function—the maintenance of the status quo.

Culture is inherently conservative. It embodies the past and the assumptions of the past and thus places limits on what the future can be. Anyone who would change the future by changing the structure of schools must be prepared to change the culture of the schools as well, for the culture provides the foundation upon which structures depend. If cultures do not change, structures will not change in the long run either.

The Restructuring Error

In the decade following the Russian launching of *Sputnik I*, from approximately 1958 to 1968, educational reformers placed their faith in curriculum reform as the means of improving schools. Large national curriculum projects like the Biological Sciences Curriculum Study and the High School Geography Project were the order of the day, and Jerome Bruner's notion (1966) of "the structure of the disciplines" was the organizing principle for much of this order.

By the mid-1970s, it was clear that faith that curriculum reform would bring about a rebirth of America's schools had been misplaced. Critics were just as concerned about geographic illiteracy in 1975 as in 1957 and as they are today. Scientific illiteracy, at least as the critics viewed the matter, had not been abolished in spite of the active intervention of scholars from the disciplines in the curriculum development process and in spite of efforts by academic departments to update and upgrade teachers perceived to be woefully unprepared. Today, concern that America's youngsters are scientifically illiterate continues unabated. In 1976, when many critics were asserting that school reform had failed, with some going so far as to claim that schools could not be reformed until and unless society itself was reformed, I wrote the following (Schlechty, 1976, pp. 266–267):

Unfortunately, many Americans are coming to believe that school reform has failed because the schools cannot be reformed. Some defenders of schools attempt to counter such charges by attacking the research used to demonstrate the failure of school reform. From the point of view presented in this book, one can accept the idea that school reform has failed—perhaps even as badly as some of the radical critics suggest—and yet retain faith in the viability of schools and the promise of school reform. From the point of view presented here, it is possible to suggest that the reason school reform has failed lies not in the fact that schools are not reformable but in the fact that reformers too often start from faulty premises, premises that insist that personalistic variables are more important in schools than are structural ones. Perhaps it would be better to assume that the affairs of men are as much shaped by the institutions men build as by other men[13] and that reform of institutions involves structural as well as personal changes. To try to change the behavior of individual school participants can lead to little more than personal frustration and the failure of reform. It is reasonable to believe that schools can be reformed, if we but understand the level at which reform is needed. Knowledge of the structural sources of classroom behavior will provide a clearer view of where needed reform might be instituted.

Subsequent to the publication of the now famous *A Nation at Risk* (National Commission on Excellence in Education, 1983), in which the "rising tide of mediocrity" sweeping over America's schools was noted with alarm, and the spate of other reports and reform-oriented books that appeared at about the same time, restructuring schools became the watchword of school reform. Curriculum reform was passé; structural reform was in.

Now, lest the reader believe that I am making a claim for somehow causing the restructuring movement of the mid-1980s, I want to be clear that no such claim is being made. Very few read my 1976

---

[13] Today I would say "women" as well, but in 1976, my consciousness of gender bias was not as keen as it is today. Two daughters, a strong woman for a wife, and many female graduate students and colleagues have done much to make me better understand what men of my generation did not. The only defense I have is that I did not know better, and I meant no harm.

book, and most who did were professors and graduate students aspiring to be professors. Professors did not inspire the restructuring movement in education. Union leaders, business leaders, governors, and state legislators started the movement, supported by a cadre of consultants and professional change advocates. Organizations like the Education Commission of the States, the National Governors Association, the American Federation of Teachers, the National Business Roundtable, and the Southern Regional Education Board had much more to do with inspiring this movement than did any group of professors or the American Educational Research Association (AERA).

I say this not to disparage either professors or the AERA, nor to lay blame for one more failed effort at school reform at the feet of the business community, teachers' unions, or politicians. I only make the observation that both a largely university-based and academically based reform effort (the curriculum reforms of the sixties) and the more experience-based and activist-oriented reforms that typify the restructuring movement have met the same fate. Both have come to be seen as failures, and once again critics are saying that schools cannot be reformed (see, for example, Chubb and Moe, 1990) or that school reform cannot succeed outside the context of reforms in the larger society (see, for example, Berliner and Biddle, 1995).

My position on the matter is much as it was in 1976, though I am now clearer on what I am thinking because I have had numerous clarifying experiences in the intervening twenty years. The reason curriculum reform did not work is because the structure of schools could not, and cannot, support new technologies and new work for students. Radically different curriculum designs are not accommodated by the existing structure of schools. I made this case in my 1976 book, and I stand by what I said then.

The reason structural change has not worked is that efforts to change the structures of schools proceeded without real attention to the reasons such changes were needed. The consequence has been that in spite of many structural changes, for example, teaming in middle schools, the emergence of site-based councils, and decentralization, little has happened that necessarily affects the quality of the work provided to students. *Until restructuring is coupled with improving the quality of work provided to students and curricu-*

lum reform is coupled with providing students with access to profound knowledge through work that is engaging, compelling, and satisfying, there is little chance that either restructuring or "recurriculuming" the schools will produce the results for students, teachers, parents, or communities that they promise to deliver.

Conclusion

If the period from 1958 to 1968 was the decade of curriculum reform and the period from 1983 to 1993 was the decade of restructuring, then the period from 1997 to 2007 must be the decade in which we take the lessons learned from our recent past and reinvent schools so that each child, each day, is provided with engaging, compelling, and satisfying work. Work that, when it is done, will result in the student's developing the skills, understandings, and habits of mind that will serve both the student and society and will help to preserve the best of American culture as well.

Chapter Nine

| **Working on the Work**

Student engagement, persistence, and satisfaction are key indicators of the potential effectiveness of schools. However, the fact that students are engaged, do persist, and are satisfied does not necessarily mean that a school is effective. It is possible to engage students in trivial work: work that fails to bring them into contact with the substantive content they need to master to be well educated. Engagement is not the only result one must have to ensure a quality school. The presence or absence of desired learning is—in the long run—the determining factor in assessing the quality of a school. Absent engagement, however, there is little possibility that students will learn anything the school intends for them to learn.

In the short run, therefore, teachers and administrators must concentrate their attention on factors and conditions that increase engagement, ensure persistence, and foster satisfaction. Thus it is important to understand the attributes of the work and tasks students are assigned or encouraged to undertake. In Chapter Eight, I described some of these properties or qualities. When they are present in the work schools and teachers provide, students are more likely to engage the work, persist with it, and find satisfaction in it. The properties mentioned were these:

- The work or activity is product-focused.
- The standards for assessing the product or products associated with the activity are clear to the students and the students find them compelling.
- Students are provided with opportunities to fall short of standards on initial tries without suffering adverse consequences.

- The work is designed so that student performances are affirmed.
- The work is designed so that affiliation with others is encouraged and supported.
- Novelty and variety are present in the task structure.
- The work is designed so that students have choice in what they do, although this does not mean choice in what they learn.
- The tasks have a sense of realness and authenticity about them.
- Knowledge and information are arranged in such a way that they can be focused on products and problems; that is, they are integrated as opposed to segmented.
- The content presented is rich and significant as opposed to pallid and trivial.

Analyzing the Work

If the work presented to students is to be improved systematically, teachers and administrators must be in a position to analyze its qualities. This analysis should be aimed at determining whether the desired qualities and attributes are present in the work and the extent to which they are present. The goal should be to design or redesign the tasks and activities assigned in order to increase the presence of attributes found to be missing or found to be present in insufficient quantities to appeal to students.

Following is a list of questions the reader may find useful in guiding such an analysis and the discussions it may produce. Teachers who have used these questions to guide their work have reported that they are useful in assisting teachers both in thinking through plans and in analyzing actions when things go wrong and students for whom work is intended do not become engaged with the work or fail to persist with it when they experience difficulties.

Product Focus

Is the work assigned clearly linked to some product, performance, or exhibition?

Are students aware of the product toward which the work or activity is directed? Do they understand the connection between what they are doing and what they are expected to produce?

Do students place value on the product or performance they are being asked to create or provide? Do they care about, want to produce, or see meaning in this performance or product?

Clear and Compelling Product Standards

Are the standards by which the product or performance is to be assessed clearly articulated? More specifically, are students provided with concrete examples, prototypes, or rubrics that illustrate what the finished product or performance should look like?

Are the attributes and qualities desired in the performance or product identified and distinguished sufficiently for students to assess the progress of segments of the performance or product as well as progress toward the whole?

Are students persuaded that it is important for them to produce products and performances that meet the desired standards? Do they perceive that they have a realistic prospect of doing so?

Protection from Adverse Consequences

Are students provided with feedback and judgments about the quality of their products and performances other than on occasions when they are being graded and evaluated for the record?

Are people other than the teacher invited to inspect the students' products and performances and to provide feedback in settings where that feedback will not affect the students' status among their peers or within the evaluative structure of the school?

When the students' performance or product fails to meet the standards that have been set, are the students provided with additional opportunities to produce a product or a performance that meets these standards without having the failed effort count against them in some subsequent evaluation?

After a reasonable number of tries, do all students produce products and performances that meet standards in nearly all cases?

Affirmation of Performances

Are the students' products and performances made sufficiently public (observable by others) so that people other than the teacher—such as parents and peers—who are significant in the lives of the students have the opportunity to inspect them, comment on them, and affirm their importance and significance?

Do people other than the teacher inspect students' performances and products and affirm their worth, importance, and significance?

Affiliation

Are tasks designed in ways that encourage cooperative action among students as well as between students and adults?

Are many of the products and performances that students are encouraged to produce complex enough that their successful completion requires and encourages cooperative action?

When tasks assigned to students require independent work and work in isolation, is the result of the work linked to products and performances that require cooperative action for completion?

Novelty and Variety

Do the tasks assigned call upon students to employ new or varied means of completing the tasks, and are the products and performances students are expected to produce varied in kind, complexity, and length of time anticipated for completion?

Are students' tasks designed so that students are called on to use new skills as well as new and different media, approaches, styles of presentation, and modes of analysis?

Are the information and knowledge students are called upon to process, consider, think about, and command presented in a variety of formats and through a variety of means?

Choice

When students are given limited choice with regard to the product they are to produce and the performance they are to provide, are they given a wide choice in the means they will employ as well as in the amount of time, sequence, and order used for the completion of the tasks?

When students are given minimum choice in the time to complete tasks and the sequence and order with which tasks are to be completed, are they given optimum choices with regard to the product to be produced and the nature of the performance to be provided?

Authenticity

Are the products to which the tasks are related perceived by students to be "real"? For example, do they perceive that the quality of their products will have consequences for them, and do these consequences have meaning and significance for them?

Are the conditions under which the work is done similar to those under which similar work is done in the "real world"? For example, is the interaction between a teacher and a student author of an essay like that of an editor and an author or is it more like that of an inspector and a supplier?

Organization of Knowledge

Are information and knowledge organized in ways that make them accessible and inviting to students?

Is the knowledge students are expected to master and use organized in a way that makes it accessible and focused? For example, if they are presented with problems that require the use of information from a variety of subjects, is the knowledge presented in a way that encourages them to see the connections between disciplines?

Are students provided with opportunities to develop the skills they need to access the knowledge and information they are expected to process and master? More specifically, are they provided with explicit instruction in the use of tools relevant to scholarly crafts, such as seeking context clues when reading, examining the logical structure of arguments, and distinguishing fact from opinion?

Content and Substance

Is the content with which students work—facts, opinions, cultural artifacts, books, and materials—rich and culturally relevant?

When content from the various disciplines is presented, are the ideas, propositions, facts, and insights presented consistent with those generally agreed upon by scholars in these disciplines?

Is the content with which students are expected to work appropriate to their maturity level, experience, and background, and is it packaged and presented in a way that optimizes its attractiveness?

Beginning the Dialogue

Using questions like those listed above, groups of teachers are in a much better position to assist each other in improving what goes on in classrooms than they are if the focus of conversation is on the behavior of the teacher, a situation that is advocated by proponents of clinical supervision. The focus of the conversation will be where it should be, on the following questions: What are students doing and what is the teacher expecting the students to do? and, What has the teacher built into the work or activity that appeals to the needs of the students, and what more might be built in if attention were given to the matter?

Conversations among teachers regarding such questions cannot help but lead to improved experiences for students. Furthermore, these questions may help teachers to learn from others what they cannot learn from them now. For example, a charismatic, dynamic, and entertaining teacher has a difficult time teaching a more reserved teacher what he or she knows. Short of a personality transplant, the reserved teacher will never be able to perform in the same way as the more dynamic teacher. It is possible, however, for both teachers to learn more if they begin to examine what the dynamic teacher has students do and how he or she gets them to do it. Is the work product-focused? Could it be more so? Do students have opportunities to try and fail without being punished?

Unfortunately, what will often be found is that many apparently dynamic teachers really are not much better at engaging students than their more reserved colleagues, though they are better entertainers. And as entertainers and performers, they do meet a vital need of students in many schools: the need for relief from boredom.

Accessing Resources

Proposing actions to improve the quality of the work with which students are provided opens up possibilities, but it also reveals limitations. For example, it is clear that the use of a variety of electronic information-processing technologies, from audiotape recordings to video recordings to compact discs, opens up possibilities for a wide range of intellectual products for students that were not possible forty years ago. Unfortunately, teachers may find that they do not have access to such technologies or, if they do, they do not have the skills they feel they need to assist students in using them. Lack of skill on the individual teacher's part can sometimes be offset by teaming arrangements. Unless schools can use personnel in flexible ways, however, this solution becomes problematic as well.

Similarly, students are sometimes discouraged from considering the possibility of producing high-quality products such as essays or exhibitions because they do not work fast enough or do not work as fast as others do. To pursue high standards, in this case, is to pursue failure, so the students settle for lower standards and come to define themselves as marginal students capable of only marginal academic performance. If teachers had control of time and could use it as a flexible resource, rather than being "prisoners of time," such problems might be more easily addressed.

Listed below are questions related to technology and resources that I have found useful when I have taken seriously the question, What might schools do to make teachers better able to systematically improve the quality of the work they provide students?

Technological Resources

Tools and Equipment

Do students use a variety of means for collecting, organizing, and presenting data? For example, in addition to conventional written work and reading assignments, do students regularly use computers, create multimedia presentations, access the Internet, and interact with adult community members, including senior citizens, in the course of their work?

Are the materials and equipment, including computer hardware and software, textbooks, and library materials, adequate to support the tasks and assignments provided to students?

Are the materials and equipment easily accessible to students?

Has provision been made to ensure that tools and equipment are always up-to-date and in good working condition?

Processes

Are systems in place to ensure that tools and equipment are accessible and usable?

Is ongoing training provided to ensure that teachers and students are aware of the kinds of tools that are available to them as well as to ensure that they have the skills needed to use them? (This refers to library research skills as well as to the skills needed to use more sophisticated electronic information-processing technology.)

Do the school board policy, budget, and planning documents reflect the understanding that the quality of the tools and equipment that are available to students and teachers is of concern?

Skills

Do students and teachers possess the skills needed to use the materials, equipment, and tools that are provided effectively and efficiently? If not, are these skills being developed?

Are skills in a variety of means of doing tasks, as well as skill in selecting the most effective means, taken into account in assessing student and teacher performance and the performance of other school personnel? Are students, teachers, and others provided with feedback regarding the skills they possess and/or need to develop?

Have the skills needed to support effective use of the available tools and equipment been clearly identified?

Have training programs been designed to support the development
of these skills, and are these programs supported by appropriate staffing, budgetary allocations, and time commitments?

Other Resources

Time

Do those with instructional responsibilities have sufficient control
of the way time is used to be able to vary the way it is allocated
to tasks?

Is time assigned to tasks in a way that ensures that each student will
be able to perform at his or her optimum levels, or is the time
allocated, rather than the quality of performance, the highest-
priority concern?

Have district-level policies and procedures on the use of time been
examined? If policies and procedures constitute constraints
and barriers to quality performance, have they been changed?
If they have not been changed, why not, and what plans are in
place to address the problem?

When schedules are being developed, calendars established, and
time lines created, is the focus of decisions on the quality of
the performance and products, or is it elsewhere (for example,
on ensuring that all conceivable topics are covered)?

People

Are systems in place for identifying human resource needs and for
recruiting or developing staff to meet these needs?

Are patterns of grouping and staff assignment sufficiently flexible
so that people can be assigned to tasks according to their needs
as well as the requirements of the tasks?

Do barriers exist to the flexible assignment of staff—for example,
rigid certification requirements, seniority rules in contracts, or
board policies—and have they been identified? Similarly, do
barriers exist to the assignment of students, and have they been
identified?

Where barriers to the assignment of staff exist, has the rationale for the barriers been considered by the parties who are charged with upholding them?

Where the rationale for barriers to flexible assignment of students cannot be defended in terms of the publicly articulated beliefs and vision that guide the system, have strategies been developed to remove the barriers?

Do the budgets of the school district and individual schools as well as the commitment of time and staff indicate that human resource development and the support of quality performance by both staff and students are top priorities of the system?

Do the policies, programs, procedures, and practices of the schools and school district support easy access to external sources of human resource support—for example, sharing staff with businesses, using parental involvement programs, or networking with senior citizen groups—and are external personnel routinely employed in supporting students and the work they do?

Space

Is the physical environment in which school activities are carried out appropriate to the tasks that are being undertaken? Is the environment attractive and aesthetically pleasing to students and staff?

Does the space provided have the necessary infrastructure (for example, proper wiring and acceptable work spaces) to support the use of a variety of technologies and approaches?

Are the physical structures such as school buildings and classrooms in which students and teachers meet and conduct their work designed in ways that provide flexible use and, therefore, the capacity to incorporate new and emerging technologies? If not, are top-level leaders aware of the need to ensure flexibility, and do they take this need into account when making renovation plans or plans for new buildings?

Do school leaders, including teachers, envision nonschool sites such as museums, zoos, business settings, and other community meeting places as potential educational spaces, and do school personnel work with and support those in charge of such spaces to ensure that they are designed in ways that optimize their use and potential?

Information

Do teachers and other school personnel have a clear understanding of what parents, civic leaders, business leaders, and other community members expect students to learn?

Is the information needed by students to produce products, performances, and exhibitions that are meaningful to them readily available, and is it organized in a way that makes sense to students and attracts their attention?

Structure and Culture

Rules, roles, and relationships (structure) and the beliefs, commitments, meanings, values, lore, and traditions in which they are embedded determine, to a large extent, how time, people, space, information, and technology will be organized, deployed, and used. People who believe that the primary function of schools is to select and sort students on the basis of their presently demonstrated abilities to do particular types of work will find a graded school structure quite congruent with their beliefs. Those who believe that schools should develop such abilities as well as identify them may, at some point, find this structure too limiting.

Much of the conversation on school reform has centered on some of the more obvious of these structural and cultural features. Site-based management, for example, is, regardless of form, a purported answer to the question: What should be the *relationship* between the central office and the school? It may also be proposed as an answer to the question: What should be the *role* of parents in the decision-making process? Efforts to deregulate schools are efforts to change the *rules*. Similar efforts to bring about change in some of the more obvious features of school culture have also been undertaken as a part of the current school reform movement. For example, many school reformers hold that bringing school faculties to *believe*—in the sense of being willing to act as though—all students can learn at high levels is the first step in school reform.

Considerable energy and a great deal of rhetoric have been expended in pounding this belief home.

If the recommendations I have been making were taken seriously in schools, the questions teachers and school administrators would bring to the failure of students to do what teachers ask would be different. Rather than asking, What is wrong with the students who do not do the work provided? they would be more likely to ask, What might we do to the work we provide students to make it more engaging and compelling? Bringing about such changes is difficult. Indeed, they are not likely to occur without strong and persistent leaders who have a vision based on a well-articulated set of beliefs. Unfortunately, as difficult as these more or less obvious structural and cultural changes are to bring about, it is even more difficult to bring about changes when the condition that needs to be changed is less obvious.

Tacit Understandings and Presumed Causes

Tacit understandings are understandings that are so deeply rooted in the thought ways of individuals and in the culture of the systems in which people live out their lives that the assumptions upon which they are based are seldom, if ever, submitted to critical examination. They are taken for granted, and as such they are the most change-resistant of all the understandings, assumptions, and supposed forms of knowledge that undergird organizations, including schools. Even the language used to describe events is based on these taken-for-granted assumptions, and this language often, if not always, directs action and controls experience.

In schools, and in the research on schooling and teaching, the performance of teachers is the presumed cause and the learning of students is the presumed effect. The assumption that teaching causes learning is taken for granted, and it is so widespread that many argue that unless learning has occurred, teaching has not occurred. Because of this assumption, many proponents of "pay for performance" schemes in education see absolutely nothing wrong with using test scores as a basis for distributing rewards and imposing sanctions on individual teachers.

Still, most reasonable men and women understand that the basis of the assumption that teaching causes learning is more shaky than some of the more rabid advocates of pay for performance and "method A versus method B" researchers would like to acknowledge. Usually, when pay schemes based on the idea of teacher behavior as cause are advanced, their proponents acknowledge that some sort of adjustment will need to be made to take into account differences in the backgrounds of students, the resources available, and so on. Thus they acknowledge that causal forces are at work other than what the teacher does, though most often these other forces are assumed to reside within the students or to be attributable to conditions they experience outside the school and over which the school and the teachers can exercise little control. Similarly, researchers interested in comparing teaching method A to teaching method B almost always control for extraneous variables, thereby acknowledging that school learning has many causes other than the behavior of the teacher or the decisions she or he makes.

Teachers and administrators are usually quick to see the difficulties of a too-tight linkage between teacher performance and school performance when this linkage affects paychecks and careers. They are, however, less likely to see the difficulties the linkage causes when they go about their work inside the school. Teachers, for example, are constantly seeking new ways to "motivate" students, which implies that motivation is something one person can do to another—a dubious notion at best. Many teacher evaluation systems focus primarily on what the teachers do and how they perform. This is reasonable, of course, if we assume that teacher performance causes student performance in some direct and understandable way and that these causal connections are well understood and codified. The research on teaching notwithstanding, I do not believe that this is so. Indeed, I would argue that the effects of teachers' behavior are situationally determined and that we cannot develop a context-oblivious system for evaluating those effects.

The critical point here is that if systemic change is to occur in schools, educators must learn to think and act systemically. The history and traditions of schooling, from the way teachers are educated and trained to the way schools are organized, teachers are evaluated, and educators go about their craft, are clinical, individualistic, and particularistic.

But teaching is not learning. Teaching consists of inventing activities for students to undertake that will result in the desired learning, and encouraging students to invent such activities for themselves. Teaching is an interaction between leaders and assumed or intended followers, between the self and others. The proper focus of sociological and anthropological studies is what goes on between the self and others, as well as the way the structures men and women create and the cultures they cling to and participate in shape and mold what goes on between the self and others. This is why sociological and anthropological insights are so useful to those who see systemic reform as a means of improving education in America.

Teachers as Leaders: One More Time

The language of the teachers' lounge and the curriculum of the teachers' college would encourage the view that the primary task of teachers and schools is to diagnose students and to work on them in terms of what the diagnosis reveals. Diagnosing students' learning styles and learning to adjust one's teaching style to the learning style of each child are as much a part of the curriculum of teachers' colleges as discussing what is wrong with students today is a part of the conversation in the teachers' lounge when students fail to do what teachers want them to. This view, informed as it is by reliance on medical models, squares well with the overly scientific aspirations of a large part of the educational research community. It also squares well with the aspirations of teachers for a truly professional status, given that the primary professional models educators use for comparison are law and medicine.

Clinical professions like surgery, radiology, and pharmacy operate on the basis of some hard-won understandings that have been codified and elevated to the status of state-of-the-art practices. People who have mastered these state-of-the-art practices are licensed and certified to work "on others" or on behalf of others. All service delivery professions, of which law and medicine are examples, assume that members of the profession provide some service to others that they cannot or should not provide for themselves. Being a member of a service delivery profession, especially one that is based on science and empirical research, clearly elevates one's status and turns what might otherwise be a mundane baby-sitting job into a calling and a profession. Many interests are served by the assumption that teaching causes learning, even if these interests are generally not acknowledged.

As one who has long argued that teaching should be a high-status profession and a calling, I wrote the preceding paragraph with a great deal of trepidation. As one who early on in his professional life made something of a career of comparing teaching to law and medicine and arguing that the route to professionalization in teaching was by way of disciplined research, I wrote it in fear and trembling. *I want to make it clear, therefore, that I have not renounced my commitment to the professionalization of teaching or to the relevance of research to that profession. I have, however, changed my mind about the kind of profession teaching is and should be.* This change of mind has also caused me to change my view regarding the kind of research that is relevant to teachers and regarding what they need to know and be able to do if they are to teach well and boldly in the twenty-first century.

I foreshadowed my change of mind in 1990 when I wrote *Schools for the 21st Century.* In that book, I advanced the argument that teachers were and should be thought of as leaders. Indeed, even in 1976 I was taken by the idea of teachers as leaders, as Chapter Three of *Teaching and Social Behavior* will indicate. I had not, however, given the implications of this view the kind of thought that I have given to them since 1990. And the more I have thought about it, the more I am convinced that teaching is not a service delivery profession; it is a leadership profession. Teaching is more like being an executive in a corporation than a physician in a clinic or a lawyer in a law office or courtroom.[1]

---

[1]The idea that teachers should be thought of as executives was first suggested to me by Royce Angell, a manager with the BellSouth Corporation, and I began developing this notion at that time. Some time later, I ran across a very useful article by David Berliner on the same subject (Berliner, 1983). Although our basic ideas are similar, our formulations diverge at some points. Therefore, those interested in the analogy between teachers and executives should read Berliner's article as well as the present discussion.

Teachers, like other leaders, should be evaluated and assessed on the basis of what they get others to do, not on what they do themselves.[2] Like other leaders, they must assess their own success through others rather than directly through their own performance. Teachers are not surgeons, and they should not be viewed as actors. They are leaders, and what they do should be understood in terms of theories of leadership, as opposed to most existing theories of teaching and learning.

Conclusion

Those who would change school systems must think systemically. They must first believe that social facts are real and that they are real in their consequences. They must believe that the way systems are put together shapes and molds how men and women behave in them. This is not a deterministic view, nor does it deny the importance of the individual in human systems. Men and women create systems, and they can destroy or modify them. Furthermore, as Peter Drucker has observed, real change in an organization is almost always started by some individual, and the greater the change, the more likely that person is to be a monomaniac with a mission. Now monomania is not far from megalomania, so people must be careful when attaching themselves to a great leader. But great leaders are needed if real change is to occur. My hope is that this book will find such leaders and that they will find this book useful.

---

[2]At the present time, I and members of the staff at the Center for Leadership in School Reform are working with the Cincinnati Public School System and the Newport News Public School System in an effort to design a personnel evaluation system that reflects these understandings and that is consistent with the view that "working on the work" is the business of schools.

Chapter Ten

Measuring What Matters Most

If we accept the proposition that America needs and deserves a system of education where nearly every student graduates from high school and where all who graduate meet high academic standards (as opposed to minimal standards of compliance), then America's system of education stands in need of great improvement. To bring about such improvement, we must first understand that the intended results, which I will summarize as improved student learning, cannot be improved directly. What can be improved are the processes that affect or produce learning results and over which schools and teachers can exercise control. Improvement requires control, just as control requires understanding.

Measuring results is important precisely because it is only through measurement that we can know when processes are out of control or when the system is not performing as well as it should. But these measurements provide little assistance in figuring out what to do when this happens. To understand why systems do not perform well, we must look to factors other than results and measure things other than the attributes and qualities of end products. Measures of the quality of end products are powerful tools for evaluating the health of organizations, but they are almost useless as tools for improving them. Even if we accept that students should be thought of as products of the school, which I do not, measures of student performance are not very useful in measuring school improvement, though they may certainly be useful in helping us understand how desperate the need for improvement is.

The Standards Issue

Too many of those who are advocating the creation of "standards for schools," especially state and national standards, seem to fail to understand that school performance and student performance are not synonymous. Consequently, rather than establishing standards for school performance, they establish standards for student performance. The assumption is, of course, that if schools are performing as they should, students will be performing up to standard.

I have no more quarrel with the idea that student learning is the bottom line in the business of schooling than I have with the notion that profit is the bottom line in business. Further, I will not argue with the fact that the presence or absence of desired learning results or desired levels of profitability is an indicator of how well schools and businesses are performing. Schools that do not produce desired learning outcomes need to be fixed or abandoned just as businesses that do not produce desired levels of profitability need to be fixed or abandoned. Where I do have a quarrel is with the idea that measures of student learning are useful tools for directing efforts to reform schools, or worse, that measures of student learning in school are also measures of school quality. Neither proposition holds up under scrutiny.

Measures of student learning may indicate that something needs to change in schools. Such measures can even give some indication as to the general areas where change needs to occur; for example, measures of learning in science may be unsatisfactory, whereas measures in history meet desired standards, thereby indicating a need to work to improve science instruction.

Profit-and-loss statements can serve similar functions for business. As I write this chapter, Federal Express is reporting that fourth-quarter profits are below expectations because of losses in the overseas market. You can bet that the top-level executives will focus attention on the operating areas where their analysis indicates that they may have problems. But top executives at Federal Express can review all the profit-and-loss statements their accounting department can develop and not get a clue as to what to do. For those clues, leaders at Federal Express must study and measure the internal operations in the domestic and overseas markets, then factor in the effects of New England weather as well.Changes may be needed at Federal Express, but the accounting department is not the place to go to figure out what those changes should be, any more than the test-and-measurement department is a useful source of direction for school reform.

Five Kinds of Measures

Generally speaking, five types of measures are of concern to those who would improve the performance of schools or for that matter any enterprise:

1. *Measures of results.* Standardized test scores are illustrative of such measures, but they are not the only ones. Teachers' grades are summary statements of other measures, as are absentee rates.

2. *Quality-control measures.* These are measures of the presence or absence of some quality or attribute in a product or service. For example, gas mileage is a quality of concern when purchasing an automobile. I suggest that if measures of student engagement were developed, they could serve similar functions in education.

3. *Process measures.* These measures indicate the extent to which needed processes are in place and working as they are intended to. For example, if the framework suggested in Chapter Eight were to be taken seriously, it would be necessary to develop and use measures of such things as product focus, novelty, and authenticity. The presence or absence of these qualities or attributes in the work provided students and the degree to which they are present or absent could go far toward helping to explain why students are or are not engaged in particular tasks. Such measures might also provide clues as to which processes need to be worked on and controlled to ensure that the desired results, such as improved test scores, are produced or produced more dependably.

4. *System performance measures.* These are measures of the way the system itself works, for example, measures of the kinds of technology employed, the presence or absence of skills needed to use particular tools and procedures, the availability of qualified personnel, or the adequacy of spatial arrangements.

5. *Measures to describe and analyze the properties of the system itself.* Such measures, when they are focused on cultural and structural

properties such as rules, roles, and relationships, permit us to describe and analyze how coordination occurs in the system, how direction is maintained (and lost), how status is gained (and lost), and so on. System measures and descriptions are critical to anyone who is serious about school reform, for bringing these system properties under control is the only way to bring the processes that produce student engagement under control. Without controlling the processes that enhance or militate against student engagement, there is little likelihood that continuous improvement in the performance of students or schools will be forthcoming.[1]

What Standards Cannot Do

Many policy analysts and business leaders view the creation of national standards as a primary driver in the effort to improve public schools. Some advocates of national or statewide standards for student performance argue that assessing student performance on a common yardstick will give parents and other taxpayers a better basis for determining whether students are being educated as they should be and thus will provide a better basis for action; this is a position that is hard to dispute. It is clearly the obligation of adult members of the community, through whatever processes they deem appropriate, to decide what they want the young to know and be able to do. Schools are established to ensure that the young learn what their elders deem it important for them to learn. To fail to establish clearly what these things are and then to fail to check to see if students do, in fact, know what they need to know and can do what they need to be able to do is irresponsible. Furthermore, without such sources of direction, school reform is a meaningless activity.

My disagreement with many of the advocates of high standards and high-stakes testing is that they really have very little to say about what educators should do when their school or their system fails

[1]It might be better to think of six types of measures and add measures of capacity as described in Chapter Five as the sixth type. At present I have not separated them. Capacity measures are, I think, just a special case of the measurement of system properties.

to meet standards, and what they do have to say is often punitive and potentially harmful. For example, among the more "tough-minded" and "realistic" of these advocates of high standards, the most highly touted improvement strategies to be used "on" non-performing schools are negative sanctions and threats to survival, such as instituting school choice, firing the superintendents and reducing central office bureaucracy, removing the school board, and denying tenure to teachers.

Deming's notion that one of the first obligations of change leaders is to drive out fear (Walton, 1986, p. 35) has somehow escaped the attention of this segment of the reform community. The assumption seems to be that in schools where student performance is down, teachers and administrators really know how to do better—they just are not doing so.

I agree with Samuel Johnson's adage that "when a man knows he is to be hanged . . . , it concentrates his mind wonderfully." The performance of many schools would clearly be improved with a bit more focus. I also know that an enterprise that employs more than two million people must include some teachers and administrators who are lazy, slovenly, incompetent, foolish, or downright stupid. Such people should be removed from schools, as they must be removed from hospitals, law offices, and corporate boardrooms. However, I am not persuaded that all the focus school leaders can stand and all the accountabilities communities can muster can overcome the fact that as things are now, neither schools, nor the districts of which they are a part, nor the communities in which they are embedded have the infrastructures in place to ensure the success of a substantial effort to improve America's schools. Furthermore, I am persuaded that until such infrastructures are created, standards and accountability will do little more than provide fodder for speeches by politicians and papers from think tanks. Punishing people for system failures is not smart; fixing the system is more important than fixing the blame.

A second line of argument that defends the quest for standards as a primary tool for school improvement proceeds from the assumption that part of the reason schools are performing poorly is that students have no incentive to perform well. Given incentives, most students will perform better. Among the incentives commonly recommended are (1) *high-stakes testing*, where youngsters who fail to meet standards are denied access to jobs, colleges, and universities, or at least to their driver's licenses, and (2) *two-way choice,* where schools can refuse to accept students just as students can choose the schools they will attend or even whether they will attend. Indeed, any educator who believes that the present dissatisfaction with schools will not result in major change—with or without the consent of educators—should reflect on the fact that serious consideration of the abandonment of compulsory attendance would not have occurred thirty years ago. Yet Colorado seriously considered such a move and similar discussions are occurring throughout the nation (see Miller, 1995).

Again, I have no problem with the basic assumption that part of what is wrong in America's schools is that children and young people no longer feel compelled to do what adults would have them do just because the adults say they should or because it is good for them. I also believe that children and young people must do many things to learn what must be learned, and some of them are neither pleasant nor particularly entertaining. The ability to tolerate boredom and inaction is certainly as much a sign of an educated person as is the need for stimulation and excitement.

Unfortunately, schools have always been better at teaching tolerance for boredom and passivity than at providing students with engaging work. This may be why students place such great value on teachers who are charismatic and great performers. At a minimum, watching others work should be entertaining and somewhat enjoyable, and if the primary work going on in the classroom is the performance of the teacher, about all students have to do is watch.

In the past, when the traditional authority of adults was upheld in the family as well as in the community, teachers could expect students to engage in what would otherwise appear to be meaningless and trivial work simply because many students believed that they were expected and required to satisfy the demands of the adults in their lives. Some students still have such a view and some families are able to enforce it. But in the face of *Beavis and Butt-Head, The Simpsons,* and the many movies that depict adults as incompetent in the face of children and in the face of the messages contained in some popular music and literature, it is increasingly difficult to sustain this view.

One of the reasons students are not learning what the community wants them to and what is most likely to be measured on standardized tests is that they are learning many things their teachers and parents would prefer they not learn from very engaging electronic media. More than that, compared to the power of these media to command their attention, the work and activities that schools provide pale in comparison. Like the American automobile industry of the 1960s, the public schools have new and stronger competition. And like the leaders of the automobile industry, educational leaders often do not recognize this fact, or if they do, only respond by imposing the educational equivalent of tariffs (for example, getting parents to turn off the television set). School leaders need to learn what some business leaders have learned: improving product quality is a better long-term solution.

Those who would use standards as leverage to cause students to engage the work schools provide misunderstand the problem. For students to accept the standards suggested by adults as binding on them, they must agree with the adults regarding those standards; in a word, they must have internalized them. When traditional authority is available to teachers, the relevant standards are those that insist that the most important standard is compliance with the directives and wishes of adults. However, when this authority is no longer available, other means of gaining commitment to standards are needed. Coercion in some form is the most obvious strategy, though it is not the most productive. Coercion, which includes denial of access and limitation of mobility as well as the infliction of pain assumes alienation and causes alienation as well (see Etzioni, 1961). What teachers want and need is not further alienation and estrangement but students who are morally involved and committed to the standards, norms, and values that guide the system.

If standards are to have meaning, much more than compliance is needed. Students must be brought to internalize these standards and make them sources of guidance and direction throughout their lives. The strategies employed should aim for and encourage moral involvement with the standards, rather than assuming alienation as a permanent condition. As Etzioni (1961) points out, prisons are the archetype of institutions that assume alienation as a permanent condition. *Bird Man of Alcatraz* notwithstanding, few prisoners find work in prison that engages them. My fear is that the use of standards as tools for exclusion and as coercive instruments will produce too many punitive principals and not enough inspiring teachers.

As I have observed elsewhere (Schlechty, 1976), schools vary considerably in their ability to engage students in the moral order of the schools. Those schools that are most successful renounce the use of coercion in favor of the exercise of normative strategies that assume consensus on core values and core standards. In creating this consensus, schools must sometimes employ strategies that assume most participants are calculatedly rather than morally involved in the system. For example, schools must first provide students with work the students consider to be worth doing before expecting the students to value what the adults in their lives believe they should learn.

The so-called accountability movement in education has made teachers and administrators especially sensitive to discussions of standards, and sometimes they behave defensively when confronted with the charge that schools are not up to standard and educators are not accountable. This defensiveness is understandable, and sometimes it is justified. There is no doubt that there are those who would like to bypass public schools altogether, and some of these people see the drive for national standards as a means of hurrying along a process they believe has started. "After all," they argue, "it is already proved that private school students do better on standardized measures of learning like Scholastic Aptitude Test scores than public school students. Once high and rigorous standards are established and enforced, the superiority of private schools over public schools will be demonstrated once and for all."

Of course, many in the private school business do not feel this way and do all they can to avoid having the performance of their graduates compared to that of public school students and other private school students. Many private schools, for example, work hard to be excluded from statewide testing programs and will almost certainly work to avoid the imposition of national standards on their students.

What Standards Can Do

Standards, as I see the term being used in education, means judgments by the adult community regarding what students should know and be able to do as a result of going to school. Measures of standards include tests and other forms of observation that provide data for judging how well schools are doing in helping students meet those standards. Given this definition, it should be clear that standards and measurements are important to school reform. I do not believe, however, that the creation of standards is the most important single task confronting school reformers. Building community consensus regarding what schools are about and what beliefs should guide them is more important. The quest for standards can help to create the dialogue that will lead to this consensus, but it is the consensus that is important rather than the standards that may result from it.

It is only necessary to attend a few school board meetings or read letters to the editor in the local newspaper for a few days to understand that little consensus exists in communities regarding what the purpose of schools should be, which people schools should serve, or how schools should go about serving these people. This lack of consensus is most likely to be amplified and made clear in the debate over standards. The quest for standards can, therefore, help to clarify issues. The opponents of outcome-based education, for example, are not opposed to education having outcomes. They prefer it that way. They simply do not like the outcomes that some of the more secular-minded and nontraditional proponents of outcome-based education would provide.

Indeed, the opponents of outcome-based education might easily become proponents if they could be assured that the outcomes being pursued are consistent with the values they hold and if the methods of producing those outcomes were consistent with their views of how schools should be organized and managed. It is lack of consensus on the ends and means of schooling that leads to battles royal in boardrooms and editorial papers, not disagreement about the fact that schools should produce results. The question is, what results and for whom?

Unfortunately, the battles over results that occur at the local level are often conducted by people who have little experience in the art and science of consensus building. Further, they occur in a context where the effects of factionalism and the demands of special interests are amplified rather than redirected in support of the common good. It is also important to understand that these battles are likely to be much more real and visceral at the local level than at the state or national levels. At the local level, the abstract student presented in the state curriculum guide as "the student Will" becomes a concrete reality whose name is not only Will but also Susie, George, Juan, Carletta, Tyrone, Lakisha, or even Dick or Jane. The student Will is an abstraction in the state capital, but in local communities, he goes to school with many other students whose parents care what they learn and what the school is promising and threatening to teach them.

Because of the passion in local politics and the failure to control the effects of factionalism at the local level, it sometimes appears easier to arrive at consensus at the state and national levels than at the local level; this may encourage leaders to believe that the real discussions about standards must occur at those levels. Among the reasons that discussions of state and national standards proceed more smoothly at the state and national levels are these:

- Discussions at the state and national levels are further removed from local passions and local interest-group politics.
- National and state groups are likely to represent the interests and concerns of the officially organized segments of the educational policy establishment, that is, the educational and business interests that are housed in and around the state capital or Washington, D.C., or whose lobbying organizations are housed there. These interests are supplemented by infusion of the interests of elite universities, with some ritual attention to the interests of parents and perhaps a governor or state legislator or two.
- People who represent organized interests are usually competent and experienced negotiators who understand the art of the deal. Their hearts are less likely to be involved than their heads, since they are not dealing with matters that affect them as personally as does the life of one's own children or of children one knows. To be sure, careers become involved in national debates over standards, and career interests shape the debate over standards, as do academic concerns and serious theoretical and empirical concerns.

None of this is to deny that interest-group politics affects discussions of national standards, but those who engage in these discussions are likely to be professional discussants. Most of the participants in the discourse over standards at the national level understand how rules of evidence and rules of procedure work (to say nothing of politeness and common courtesy), and generally they adhere to these rules. Those who do not often find themselves unheard, no matter how loudly they shout.

When states go about setting standards, they usually turn for advice and counsel to those who have led, or are leading, national standards efforts; this advice is used to inform how state standards might be developed and who should be involved in their development. The consequence is that at both the state and national levels, those who are called on to establish standards are likely to have considerable expertise in the business of arriving at consensus and developing documents that communicate intentions. They will also have access to people who have considerable facility with language and a knack for stating things in sufficiently general terms (called *principles*) so that most people feel comfortable with their pronouncements. Who would be opposed to all children being ready for school? Who last voted against all children being literate in science, mathematics, history, and foreign language?

However, when groups, even national groups, move from the general and the abstract to the specific and the concrete, which they must do if tests and observations are to be devised, the lack of real consensus, even at the national level, becomes apparent. *All we need do is follow the controversy surrounding the results of the proposed standards for history instruction to see how far from agreement Americans really are about what students should know and be able to do.* This does not mean that the quest for consensus is meaningless or pointless, but if the quest for standards is to be productive, the idea that they should be fixed, permanent points must be abandoned. *Standards, especially student performance standards, are moving targets, representing the best agreements that can be reached at the time among those who have a stake in what students learn in school. It is likely that standards will be much more attentive to the needs of parents and individual children at the local level and much more attentive to the needs of business and academic elites at the national level.* It is in reconciling such competing needs that society's interests and individuals' interests are worked out.

What must be understood is that for schools to survive and thrive in American democracy, they must serve the interests of all children, not simply the children of the poor or the children of the economic, academic, or political elite. *Schools are concerned with the common good and the common culture, and the quest for standards should be an effort to define that good and to identify that culture.*

Measuring Results

Different constituencies want and need different things from schools. What parents want and need is not the same thing that business leaders or nonparent taxpayers do. Furthermore, these differing wants and needs are not necessarily contradictory or mutually exclusive. They just differ. The kinds of measures different groups want and need vary as well. When people are considering buying stock in a company, they look for various financial measures and consult *Barron's,* the *Wall Street Journal,* and perhaps an expert on stocks. When they are considering the purchase of a product produced by a company in which they own stock, they do not call their broker; they study *Consumer Reports* or some similar source where measures of the quality of products are presented. Unfortunately, the tendency in education is to seek a one-size-fits-all measure or, at best, to develop multiple measures for the same thing. It must be kept in mind that what is measured and how it should be measured depend upon whom the results are intended to satisfy. All results are not relevant to all customers and constituencies.

For example, there is currently much conversation around the topics of authentic assessment and portfolio assessment. Much of the controversy regarding the relative merits of standardized tests, especially standardized multiple-choice tests, and other forms of testing and assessment, such as observations, interviews, and the development of portfolios containing exhibits of student work, could be more enlightened if the discussants would first acknowledge that each form of testing has its place and that each meets different needs for different customers at different times. On the one hand, portfolio assessment provides much richer and more detailed data upon which to make judgments about the performance of individual students, and those who are concerned about individual student performance have every reason to find it a useful tool. Teachers, parents, university admissions officers, and potential employers (if they are serious about personnel screening) can find much in a well-developed portfolio that would be totally lacking in a student file containing nothing but grades, attendance records, and scores on standardized tests. Those who make decisions regarding the needs and performance of individual students need such data.

On the other hand, such data are much too cumbersome to be used as a basis for assessing the ability of schools to meet the expectations of the community regarding what students should learn. For this task, other measures are needed. Well-designed standardized paper-and-pencil tests are very useful as broad measures of the extent to which the system is producing the kind of learning that the community or subsets of the community want it to produce. They are much less useful in attempts to assess the performance or the performance potential of individual students.[2]

Those who would improve schools and who believe, as I do, that measurement is an essential element in the improvement process need to keep in mind that some measures are much better as measures of system performance than as measures of individual performance. Profit-and-loss statements, for example, tell us much more about the performance of total enterprises than they do about the performance of any individual salesperson or middle-level manager in a corporation. Standardized test scores are probably much more useful in determining whether the schools are producing the kind of learning results desired by powerful community stakeholders than they are in determining the extent to which the schools are meeting the needs of students and their parents. And, I hasten to add, all of these needs and all of these customers must be satisfied if schools are to survive and thrive.

---

[2]Tests such as the Scholastic Aptitude Test and the Graduate Record Examination are purported to be useful predictors of performance, and they probably are. However, such tests are only proxies; direct observations of performances are much more reliable as predictors if they are done by many people over a sustained period of time. A too-heavy reliance on tests can lead to some bizarre behavior. I recall once working in a university setting where it was common to permit graduate students to enroll in graduate classes without first being admitted to graduate school, sometimes for as long as two semesters. Many of these students did very well and received honors grades in their coursework. From time to time, however, a student with a record of honors grades would be denied entry into the graduate school on the basis that his or her GRE scores were too low. When this happens, something is wrong.

Assessing Results

Measurement begins with questions to which measures attempt to provide answers. Customer-focused schools begin with the customers to be served and the schools' endeavor to produce results that will satisfy these customers. Assuming that the reader will accept, at least for present purposes, the line of argument I presented in Chapter Seven regarding the kinds of results wanted and needed by different segments of the "market" for school results, the following questions might be used to guide a useful assessment process.

Results for the Community

High school completion. Do all, or nearly all, students who enter the school district before age nine graduate from high school?[3]

Test performance. Do all students who have been enrolled in the school system for at least eight years perform on tests and assessments valued by the community at or above the performance levels recognized by the community as indicating possession of the skills and understandings needed to function effectively as citizens, employees, and lifelong learners?

Subsequent academic success. Do all students who choose to pursue education beyond high school qualify for entry into the institution of their choice? Are those who pursue education beyond high school successful?

School-to-work transitions. Are students who move directly from high school to the world of work judged by their employers as

---

[3]I have inserted the caveats "before age nine" in this statement and "at least eight years" in the following one. There is nothing particularly magical about these numbers. I am simply trying to signal that when we attempt to assess the effects of school, we should be sensitive to the fact that a possible reason schools seem not to have the desired effects on students is that the students were not present long enough for the effects to occur or were not present when the schools could be most effective. For example, many students drop out of school because they fail to develop basic skills in the early grades. If children transfer into a school system after they have been miseducated elsewhere, we should not expect the same level of success that we would in a generally healthy system. Remediation programs can help and should not be abandoned, but remediation is not a substitute for adequate schooling in the first place.

possessing the skills, attitudes, and work habits needed for entry-level employees?

Results for Parents

Satisfactory progress. Are most parents satisfied with the rate of progress and the level of performance of their children?

Appropriate content. Are most parents satisfied that what their children are learning in school is "the right stuff"? Moreover, do nearly all parents believe that what their children are learning is congruent with what they want them to learn and supportive of the values the parents hold for their children and for their families?

Safety. Do most parents believe that their children are safe in school, and are the schools safe in objective terms?

Inviting environment. Do parents voluntarily interact with teachers and school officials, and are these interactions routine or do they only occur in times of crisis and difficulty?

Results for Teachers

High performance. Does the teacher expect and intend that all students will perform at a level deserving of being labeled, by the teacher, as good or excellent, and are most students judged to be deserving of this label—that is, do they receive A and B grades?[4]

---

[4]Some will see this as an argument for lowering standards or inflating grades. It should not be so. If an A means that a student's performance is excellent, then it should also mean that his or her performance exceeds expectations by a degree so notable that few would argue otherwise. A grade of B, which most schools suggest is good or very good, means that students have met or exceeded the performance standard. In practice, the grade of C, which in the normal curve of many grading systems means average, also has come to mean mediocre. Unless we want mediocrity to be the standard for the schools, the grade of B should signify the standard. Of course, schools could abolish the letter-grade system altogether, but I doubt that that will happen in the foreseeable future. We should at least abolish D's and F's and substitute in their stead the grade of incomplete or "NY," for "not yet." (I borrowed this idea from someone, but I do not know who.)

Desired actions. Do all, or nearly all, students do what the teacher wants them to do, and do they do so voluntarily and without coercion?

Excellent products. Do all, or nearly all, students regularly produce products and other kinds of academic performances that, in the judgment of the teacher, deserve to be labeled "good" or "excellent"?

Getting and Keeping Customers

Peter Drucker has frequently made the point that too many business leaders fail to understand that the business of business is to get and keep customers. Without customers there can be no profit and without profit there will be no business. But the business of business is not profit; it is customers. Business leaders who think that their business is to make a profit can drive their business into bankruptcy. Those who understand that their business is to produce products and services that attract and retain customers and increase customer loyalty stand a good chance of producing a decent return on investment.

It is my view that a parallel argument can be made about schools. Satisfying the community, even satisfying parents, is critical to the survival of schools. It is unlikely, however, that student performance will ever meet the expectations of communities or parents unless schools can invent and design products (intellectual activity, or knowledge work) that the students find engaging, compelling, and satisfying. Just as getting, keeping, and satisfying customers is the true key to the bottom line in business, engaging students, getting them to persist with difficult work, and ensuring that the work produces products that are satisfying to the students is the business of schools.

It is important, therefore, that schools develop measures of student engagement, persistence, and satisfaction as well as measures of student learning. Some of the questions around which such measures could be developed are listed below.

Student Engagement

Do students understand why they are doing what they are being asked to do, and do they believe that what they are being asked to do is important for them or relevant to something they consider important?

Do students continue to work on assigned tasks even when they are not under the direct supervision of the teacher, or are they easily distracted from the task?

Do students give priority to completing the tasks assigned?

Student Persistence

When students experience difficulty mastering skills associated with a task or when the products and performances they produce fail to meet standards, do they continue to practice to attain mastery of the skills, reworking or starting anew on the product, or do they abandon the effort or return to the task only after considerable urging by the teacher or other adults?

Student Satisfaction

Do students evidence pride in the products they produce? For example, do they seek opportunities to show the products to others? Do they express feelings of satisfaction to the teacher and their peers?

Conclusion

The reader who observes that I have provided very little technical advice on issues of measurement is correct. I have not. There are two reasons for this. First, I am not an expert on measurement, and the construction and evaluation of *some* measures (especially psychometric measures) require a great deal of expertise. For example, the creation of really useful standardized tests or even teacher-made short-answer tests designed to "sample learning and test for mastery" requires considerable expertise and would entail more discussion than I am prepared to offer here.

The second reason for my reluctance is that, *for the most part,* measurement is a commonsense act: an act we engage in every day and one that is very dependent on local environments and local circumstances. Expert advice about these matters of measurement is likely to appear silly and misguided. For example, it is possible to imagine ways of creating measures of student engagement that would be quite elaborate, highly reliable, and very dependable and that would require large amounts of resources. When precise measures are needed, such an expenditure of effort may be worthwhile.

However, such precise measures may not always be needed. Sometimes we can measure student engagement by identifying the students we expect to be engaged, asking them simple questions: Did you find this task or project interesting? Would you recommend that I [the teacher] do this with next year's students? Why? Such questions do not require experts in measurement or assessment. All they require is the will to ask them and the ability to hear the answer.

Chapter Eleven

Leading the Change Process

Superintendents, top-level union leaders, and board of education members—if they have the will and the inclination—are the people in the school district who are positioned to relate to the larger community and to sources of political and economic power in ways that make it possible to sustain serious change efforts over a long period of time. The key to systemic reform, therefore, is the development of the capacity of school districts to support and sustain reform efforts at the building level and to ensure that those who occupy top-level positions in the system have the inclinations and skills to use this capacity to the fullest. To do this, educational leaders must think and act in strategic ways, for it is through strategy that the future is invented.

Three Types of Change

At least three types of change exist: procedural change, technological change, and structural and cultural (systemic) change:

1. *Procedural change* consists of altering the way the job is done. Such changes usually have to do with the sequence in which events occur, the speed with which they occur, or the forms that give shape and direction to action. For instance, in determining the process by which a patient is admitted to a hospital, it makes little

Parts of this chapter appeared in Phillip C. Schlechty, "On the Frontier of School Reform with Trailblazers, Pioneers, and Settlers," *Journal of Staff Development*, Fall 1993, *14*(4), 46–51. The author would like to thank the *Journal of Staff Development*.

difference whether blood pressure is taken prior to, concurrent with, or after taking her or his temperature. What does make a difference is ensuring that all the necessary steps are taken. However, some sequences are more efficient than others, and often the quest for efficiency leads to procedural changes. For example, taking patients' temperature concurrently with assessing their blood pressure saves time.

2. *Technological change* consists of changing the means by which the job is done, for example, switching from typewriters to word processors to prepare manuscripts or switching from a mercury to an electronic thermometer to take patients' temperatures. In both examples, the job being done remains the same; the means by which it is done is all that has changed.

3. *Structural and cultural (systemic) change* consists of changing the nature of the work itself, reorienting its purpose, and refocusing its intent. For example, many American businesses are now attempting to focus their activity on customers and their needs, whereas in the past their focus may have been on the technical properties of products. Such changes require alterations in rules, roles, and relationships as well as in beliefs, values, and orientations. It is this kind of change that is suggested by the term *systemic change,* for it requires alterations in both the structure of the organization (the system of rules, roles, and relationships) and the culture (the system of beliefs, values, and orientations) in which the structure is embedded.

In the life of healthy organizations, procedural change and incremental technological change are relatively commonplace occurrences; consequently, leaders have considerable experience in managing these types of changes. Equally important, researchers and consultants who write about these changes have numerous cases to use for study and discussion. Until recently, in fact, most empirical studies of change have focused on technological and procedural change rather than on systemic change. For example, studies in agriculture and medicine regarding the processes by which innovations are adopted and adapted were typically interested in determining the characteristics of early and later adapters. To the extent that they were concerned with systemic and cultural issues, they usually dealt with the attributes of people rather than of systems. Thus procedural and technological change are much better understood than is systemic change.

It should not be surprising that structural and cultural change in organizations is relatively uncommon, for it challenges the roots of an organization and the assumptions upon which it is based. It focuses on an organization's purpose (its reason for being); the rules, roles, and relationships that determine how that purpose will be pursued; and the beliefs, values, and commitments that give meaning to the rules, roles, and relationships that give rise to the sense of purpose that gives direction to the life of the organization. Such changes are not undertaken lightly or often, for they are cataclysmic events in the life of the organization. Thus they are not as accessible to study and analysis as are technological and procedural changes.

Implications for Leaders

Procedural change is largely a matter of communication, monitoring, evaluation, and enforcement. The new procedure must be described and communicated to those who are to use it. Sometimes this is done in writing, sometimes in workshops, sometimes in one-on-one conversations. Persuasion may be involved if old habits have come to be valued, and even in the simplest forms of procedural change, those who must act on the change need to have some ownership of it, but the complexity of this leadership task is relatively low.

After the change has been communicated, some means must be established to ensure that the new procedure is implemented and old patterns are not reestablished. Sometimes this involves nothing more than a cursory inspection, but it may require intensive feedback and support sessions. Much depends on how deeply ingrained the old procedure was, how much value the workers placed on it, and how convinced they are that the new procedure will, in the long run, make their lives somehow better.

Finally, some effort should be expended, though it often is not, in determining whether the change in procedure produces the intended results and does not produce any unintended and undesirable results. For example, Northwest Airlines, which historically had a poor on-time record, has become known as the "on-time airline" through two procedural changes: adding time to each flight, which gave the airline some leeway in the schedule, and rigidly enforcing on-time departures. As a result, Northwest Airlines regularly appears as the leader in percentage of on-time departures and arrivals.

But the story does not end there. It is also the case that, on average, Northwest flights take longer for passengers, and Northwest personnel feel much less able to respond to some situations: for example, delaying a departure by two minutes might allow a customer coming in on another flight to make a connection, but that delay isn't allowed under rigid enforcement of on-time rules. As a result, although on-time departures have increased, flexibility and response to the needs of individual customers may have suffered.

The Northwest Airlines illustration indicates one of the greatest dangers confronting leaders who are bent on procedural change: they need to be clear on the goals to be served by the change. Northwest's leaders must ask if the goal was to improve customer service or to improve on-time performance. If it was the former, then a too-rigid adherence to on-time rules may have led to negative consequences; if the latter, then rigid adherence to the rules may be appropriate, in spite of the impact on individual customers. Procedural changes that are not evaluated in terms of the values of the system can distort those values in the long term.

Technological change, like procedural change, requires communication, monitoring, and evaluation. However, technological changes require considerably more attention to training and support than procedural changes. The development of new skills is likely to be necessary if technological changes are to be implemented effectively. People cannot do what they do not know how to do. It is therefore the obligation of leaders to ensure that those they lead know how to do what is expected of them.

Much of the best thinking about staff development in education is associated with the implementation of technological changes, that is, changes in the means of doing the job, whatever the means and whatever the job. Bruce Joyce and Beverly Showers (1987) have much to say about these matters, and I will not try to add or detract from what they have said. Suffice it to say that supporting technological change requires much more than instituting awareness workshops; it requires as well the creation of opportunities to practice and observe and opportunities to be coached and to coach others. When the effort to install technological changes fails, it is likely that leaders have simply not appreciated and provided for the quality of training and support that is required. Or the effort may fail because of the fact that in schools, as in other organizations, technological changes often require structural changes too.

Systemic change, which usually involves procedural and technological changes as well, calls upon leaders to do all the things they must do to lead procedural and technological change—and more. It also calls on them to think, to conceptualize, to see relationships between and among events that might escape others, to help others see these relationships and overcome fear, and to assure, cajole, coach, and inspire hope. Most of all, systemic change calls upon leaders to be wise and sometimes demanding but always to be supportive of and reassuring to teachers.

Four Key Questions

As a leader who teaches, a leader who would promote systemic change must be prepared to answer four key questions:

1. Why is change needed?
2. What kind of change is needed and what will it mean for us when the change comes about?
3. Is what we are being asked to do really possible? Has it been done before? By whom? Can we see it in practice?
4. How do we do it? What skills do we need and how will they be developed?

These questions, properly framed, suggest four different types of lessons that leaders must teach and that need to be learned if the change process is to be properly directed. The first question—Why change?—calls for the analysis of values, beliefs, and commitments and context; studies of the past; and anticipation of the future. The type of lesson required is a *value clarification* lesson. The second question—What is it?—is asking that a vision, direction, or intention be clearly stated and articulated in a way that allows the person asking the question to understand the answer and make it his or her own. The type of lesson required is a *concept development* lesson.

The third question—Can it be done?—is a request for real-life hands-on experience or testimony from those who have had such an experience. The type of lesson required is a *demonstration* lesson. The final question—How do we do it?—is a request for assistance in developing the skills and habits required to do the job. The type of lesson required is a *skill development* lesson.

Value clarification lessons rely heavily on dialogue, discussion, and logical analysis. Such lessons require detailed attention to the values participants bring to the discussion, the values the proposed change promises to enhance or serve, and the values the change is likely to threaten. Among the values most likely to be threatened by any radical change is that of security. Consequently, those who would promote systemic change must be carefully attuned to the significance various actors give to this value, for some of the greatest resistance to change can occur in protecting this value.

Those who are best at concept development often seem to rely heavily on the Socratic dialogue, focused discussion, and pointed questions, combined with the use of figurative language (indicating what the concept is like) and counterexamples intended to distinguish the concept from other notions with which it might be confused. For example, I began this discussion with a distinction between three types of change. Now I am using the fact that I made this distinction as an example of another concept, the concept of a concept development lesson.

Demonstration lessons require the existence of models and exemplars—real or contrived, empirically demonstrable, or theoretically described. Those who ask the question, Can it be done? are seeking assurance that what they are being called on to do is possible and that if they commit effort to the task, it is likely that they can do what the concept or vision calls on them to do. The techniques associated with demonstration lessons are those commonly referred to as modeling and illustrating and—where real-life situations do not yet exist—simulating actions based on theoretically derived models.

Skill development lessons, like demonstration lessons, usually rely heavily on modeling and simulation, but they are more likely to be active and involve coaching, experimental tries, corrective feedback, and opportunities to practice than is the case with demonstration lessons. Demonstration lessons are intended to be persuasive, to show that things can be done. Skill development lessons are intended to develop the understandings, skills, attitudes, and habits of mind that permit people to do with confidence and ease what at first is exceedingly difficult, awkward, and perhaps even threatening and frightening.

Five Types of Actors

As I view the matter, at least five types of actors participate in any change process. Each of these types requires a different kind of support from those who are charged with responsibility for leading the change effort. Furthermore, those who play different roles in the change process have different needs for some of the lessons described. It is therefore critical that leaders understand whom they are addressing at different stages in the process, for the needs of different actors will be different from time to time.

Trailblazers

Paradigm-breaking journeys are not for the timid, and we should not expect everyone, or even almost everyone, to willingly be among the first to undertake such a trip. Those who take the first steps in systemic change are *trailblazers:* they are willing to go, in terms understood by *Star Trek* fans, where no person has gone before, without maps and without the benefit of empirically based models and with little to guide them except belief in themselves, a desire for novelty, the freedom to try, and the vision that motivates and guides them.

The most important requirement for trailblazers is a clear, guiding vision. Trailblazers want to know that they can go someplace that is different; they are motivated by novelty or excited by risks. Once they have found a vision in which they believe, all they want and need is encouragement to pursue it and support for that pursuit. Most of all, trailblazers want to be recognized for their unique brand of courage and to be celebrated, recognized, praised, and honored.

Trailblazers are not egomaniacs, but they are often mono-maniacs with a mission. They know where they want to go, even if they are not quite sure how they are going to get there or what obstacles they will confront on the way. When they do confront obstacles, they are likely to view them in highly personal terms, for their vision is a personal vision, and anything that stands in the way of the pursuit of that vision is a personal threat. As a result, trailblazers have a need for a great deal of personal and personalized support.

Leaders should be sensitive to the fact that trailblazers need to be reinforced constantly in the view that the vision they are pursuing is worth the quest and that others, especially powerful others, see what they do as important enough to give them unusual latitude and provide them with unconventional forms of support, such as noncategorical funding, flexible schedules, or special access to the human and physical resources of the system. Equally important, trailblazers need to be reminded constantly that they are on a community quest, not a private venture. The vision the trailblazer is pursuing is a private one; it is up to other leaders in the system to link this to a larger vision. (Daniel Boone may simply have wanted "elbow room," but national leaders saw that he, and especially those who followed him, could have an effect on America's claim to be a nation that spread from shore to shore, which was later articulated as America's "manifest destiny.")

Because trailblazers are leading the way into a new world, whether that world is a physical frontier or the creation of a new system or new way of doing business, they seldom have access to a body of research and experience to guide them. What, then, do they use as guides? First, they use experiences they and others have gained in circumstances that are analogous to those they are about to confront. It is not coincidental, I think, that the language of space travel is laced with terminology that refers to early explorers who took voyages on the ocean, just as spaceships now take voyages to the moon. Even the names of spacecraft often refer to other explorers in other times. Trailblazers need, therefore, the opportunity to visit with and read about trailblazers from other fields (for example, from business, the military, or medical services), and they need time to discuss and assimilate what they learn from these encounters. From these experiences, relevant analogies are discovered and come to be understood. (I have found that leaders whose language is rich with figures of speech and who argue by analogy are particularly good at inspiring and directing trailblazers.)

A second source of guidance for trailblazers is the experiences of other trailblazers who are moving in roughly the same direction and over the same terrain. The rendezvous was one of the ways early trailblazers on America's frontier got information from other trailblazers. Today we refer to this as networking, a process in which people who are endeavoring to move in a common direction develop mechanisms to ensure regular interactions. Providing opportunities for networking is one of the primary contributions change leaders can make to the continuing growth and development of trailblazers.

It is important to understand that networking and rendezvous do much more than provide opportunities for sharing information. Networking provides opportunities for self-affirmation and more than a bit of bragging and storytelling. Trailblazers need opportunities to meet with other trailblazers, and networking turns lonely ordeals into shared ones. Lonely ordeals debilitate; shared ordeals inspire and motivate. Leaders who listen in on these stories can learn much that will later be of value to pioneers. Furthermore, if leaders watch carefully, they can get some insight as to which of the trailblazers have the temperament and the style to be guides as well as trailblazers, for those who come later will need guides as well.

In addition, it is up to leaders and trailblazers to create conditions in which what the trailblazers learn is not lost. Trailblazers tell stories, but they seldom turn these stories into lessons for others. It is up to leaders, therefore, to ensure that the stories are turned into lessons that can serve as sources of guidance for those who would follow, much as mapmakers translated the tales and reports of the early explorers into crude maps that later "researchers" refined and rendered increasingly accurate. Change leaders should never forget that trailblazers need public acknowledgment for their efforts; they need the opportunity to tell others about where they have been and what they have done. Such storytelling serves not only as a source of information for others but also as a continuing source of motivation for the trailblazers.

Staff development budgets that do not make provision for sending trailblazers to conferences where they can brag a bit are, therefore, inadequate. And leaders are not doing their job if they do not seek every opportunity to put local trailblazers out in front, including helping them write proposals to get support for their work and proposals that will permit them to share their work at conferences.

Pioneers

Closely following the trailblazers are the *pioneers*. Like the trailblazers, pioneers are an adventurous and hardy lot who are willing to take considerable risks. Pioneers have many of the same needs as trailblazers. Concept development lessons (the development of a vision that links a personal quest to a larger agenda) are the most important lessons leaders can offer pioneers, but pioneers also have a considerable need for assurance that the trip upon which they will embark is worthwhile. More than trailblazers, pioneers need demonstrations that help to assure them that the journey they are about to take can, in fact, be made. However, they understand that very few people can teach them how to do it, because no one other than the trailblazers has gone to the frontiers the pioneers are set to explore. Thus pioneers need concept development, value clarification, and demonstration lessons. They do not need skill development lessons, and staff developers would be ill advised to try to provide them.

So what does all of this mean in practical terms? First, it means that when change leaders approach pioneers or are attempting to recruit them, their best allies are those who find the trailblazers of sufficient interest to write about them (see, for example, Fiske, 1991; Sizer, 1992). Rather than providing research data, these authors provide anecdotal accounts, reports, and stories. Such stories can inspire prospective pioneers to take the journey, and contained in them are some possible lessons to be learned regarding what pioneers need to know and be able to do to survive the rigors of the journey.

Even more useful to leaders committed to systemic change in schools are the trailblazers themselves, especially if they are colorful and good storytellers. Davy Crockett, for example, did much more to inspire pioneers than he did as a true trailblazer. Indeed, one could argue that he was a staff developer rather than a trailblazer, because what he often did was take the stories of others, embellish them a bit, and then use them to inspire others to act.

I have found that trailblazer teachers and administrators are invaluable as sources of inspiration and direction for pioneers and even for settlers (see below). But here a caution is in order. Too often, in their quest for authenticity, change leaders, especially staff development specialists, remove trailblazers from their natural habitat on the frontier and move them into the central office or, worse, to the university campus, in the hope that the stories they will tell will reach a wider audience. Sometimes this works, but more frequently it is a bad experience both for the trailblazers and for those with whom they are to work. The teamwork that it takes to build community, which is what pioneers must do, requires a different style than does the early exploration of new frontiers.

Monomaniacs with a mission can quickly come to appear to others to be egomaniacs whose only mission is to advance themselves. Trailblazers are needed, but they are not easy to live with in the sedate environments of committee meetings and seminar rooms.

Settlers

After the trailblazers and the pioneers come the *settlers*. Settlers need to know what they are expected to do and where they are going to go. They need much more detail and more carefully drawn maps than do those who have gone before them. Settlers are bold, but they are not adventurers. They need to be persuaded that the venture upon which they are being asked to embark is worthwhile. Consequently, leaders must give careful attention to developing good value clarification lessons that help the settlers understand why the change is needed. Settlers also want assurance that they are not set on a fool's mission and that what is being suggested can be done; thus, they have considerable need for demonstration lessons such as site visits where pioneering work is already under way, conversations with pioneers and trailblazers, testimonials from those who have tried, and books and articles that provide rich descriptions of what can be expected.

Much more than either pioneers or trailblazers, settlers want skill development lessons. They want to be sure that they know how to do what they are required to do. Indeed, many potential settlers will not move until they are assured that the requisite knowledge and support are available to them. Change leaders and staff developers who support them must therefore give attention to providing systematic training supported by coaching, opportunities for feedback and critique, and above all, protection from negative consequences for faulty tries and failed efforts. (It is here that the ideas of writers like Joyce and Showers, 1987, regarding the design and delivery of staff development become especially useful.)

Perhaps the most critical thing to remember about settlers is that they need strong, constant, and reassuring leadership that inspires them to keep going when they are tempted to turn back. Those who would work with settlers must understand that systemic change does not make things better or easier in the short run; instead, it is likely to create uncertainty, doubt, and confusion. The new practices called for are likely to be frightening and demanding, and the results may be no better—at least in the short run—than doing things the old way. Fullan's notion (1991) of the "implementation dip" comes to mind here; it assumes that a natural part of the change process is short-term deterioration in performance capacity, because the old way of doing things, although perhaps not as good as the new way, has one advantage: it is familiar and people know how to do it. The new way is unfamiliar and requires learning and practice.

Without persistent leadership by people who have been there and without encouragement from others who are going there (this country's settlers traveled in wagon trains, not alone), it is unlikely that settlers will stay the course. Accordingly, it is critical that leaders understand the terrain well enough to point out progress, especially when those who are unfamiliar with the terrain become discouraged. Benchmarks of progress are, therefore, essential, and feedback regarding progress toward these benchmarks is critical. Assessment and constant monitoring, coupled with public appraisals of progress toward restructuring goals, are important. For example, improved student performance is certainly a goal of restructuring and systemic change, but an intermediate goal might be to have teachers and building administrators become more systematic in using data regarding student performance to evaluate the merit and worth of decisions they make.

Helping settlers learn how to use such data and evidence of progress in the use of the data are necessary antecedents to answering the question, Does restructuring and systemic change improve student performance? Until such changes have occurred, this question cannot be answered. The first-order assessment questions for those who are engaged in the change are, therefore, What evidence do we have that we are, in fact, doing our business differently today than we did yesterday? and, Why do we think the new way of doing business will improve our results? Settlers need the answers to such questions, both to keep them going and to provide assurance that where they are going is worth the effort.

Stay-at-Homes

Two situations motivate change:

1. Present conditions are so intolerable or dangerous to people's interests and values that the only alternative is to do something. The Puritans who left England to settle in America were driven by such motives.
2. A new and compelling vision inspires so much hope of a new day, a better life, or a full realization of existing values that risks seem tolerable when measured against the rewards. The utopian settlements on the American frontier are examples of such vision-driven change.

However, as the Declaration of Independence states so eloquently, basic changes are not lightly undertaken, and people will tolerate a great deal rather than give up what is known. Furthermore, intolerable or threatening conditions, although they can serve as an initial impetus for change, cannot sustain change. In fact, negative forces are seldom adequate to motivate fundamental change and almost never adequate to sustain it. The *Mayflower* Puritans, who had among them some trailblazers, some pioneers, and a substantial number of reluctant and frightened settlers, may have left England because of oppression, but it did not take their leaders long to recognize that a new and compelling vision would be required to sustain them. This new vision, expressed first in the

Mayflower Compact and reinforced by visions based in religious symbols, was as important to the settlement of the New World as were the oppressive conditions that motivated at least some of the *Mayflower* passengers.

Yet it is sometimes forgotten that many Puritans stayed behind; not all boarded the *Mayflower*. Some came to America later, and some never came. Many wanted to come to the New World but could not get up the nerve to try. Others gave up the faith rather than go, and a few even joined the oppressors. Indeed, most of the *Mayflower* Puritans had earlier gone to Holland to escape oppression. Furthermore, not all who came on the *Mayflower* were Puritans; some were adventurers bent on personal gain. And not everyone signed, or ascribed to, the shared vision as expressed in the Mayflower Compact.

Stay-at-homes are not bad people, but in the long term of history, they are not likely to be viewed as remarkable or memorable. How many Tory supporters of King George are American students today expected to recall? At the time a change is being contemplated, however, stay-at-homes receive a great deal of attention—I think too much. The reason they receive so much attention is that leaders of systemic change tend to be gregarious people who need approval from those they want to lead. People who do not respond enthusiastically, or at least compliantly, to the desires of change leaders are often viewed as problems and, unfortunately for the change process, such problems get attention.

Effective change leaders understand that early in the change process it is probably not wise to spend too much energy trying to convince the stay-at-homes that they, too, need to move to the frontier. These leaders accept the fact that some stay-at-homes will never come along, that those who do change will only do so after the pioneers and settlers have done their work very well, and that some will only come to the new land for a visit.

One of the greatest dangers when dealing with stay-at-homes in the restructuring process is that the strategies used to entice them to change may backfire and convert these relatively benign actors into supporters of the saboteurs (discussed later in this chapter). And saboteurs, whose favorite strategy is to sow distrust through rumors and misinformation, will destroy even the best-organized wagon train if they can gain enough followers. The most likely sources of recruits for the change resisters and saboteurs are the stay-at-homes and the more timid settlers who feel pressured to move before they have the assurances they need and before they have identified leaders whom they trust.

I have found that the best strategy to use with stay-at-homes, at least in the early stages of structural and cultural change, is benign neglect, coupled with as much generosity of spirit as is possible. We must remember that those who do not particularly want to change are not necessarily opposed if others choose to change. Many stay-at-homes stay at home because they truly love the place. Of course, some people simply are too timid to go to unfamiliar places. Such people are not likely to be encouraged to move by direct assaults on what they currently value or threats to what little security they now enjoy. Instead, they will join with those who for other reasons do not want to change: the saboteurs.

Saboteurs

It is important to understand that *saboteurs,* unlike garden-variety change resisters—that is, the stay-at-homes—are actively committed to stopping change. Not only do they refuse to take the trip; they do not want others to go either. Why is this the case? Obviously, this question calls for more profound psychological insight than I can provide. But I do know that most who take on the role of saboteur do so because they get something out of this role that they do not see themselves able to get out of supporting change. I have also observed that some of the most effective saboteurs have many qualities and needs that are strikingly similar to those of the trailblazers: they are often "lone rangers" and they are not afraid of taking risks.

The difference is that whereas trailblazers will go where others fear to go, saboteurs are likely to stay when others are beginning to be afraid to stay. Loneliness does not have the same meaning to them as it has to the settlers, and isolation often inspires them to even greater effort. To be persecuted, it seems, is to be appreciated and, in a perverse way, to be isolated or excluded is to be honored.

It is certain that saboteurs can cause trouble no matter where they are, but I have found that the best place to have them is on the inside where they can be watched rather than on the outside where they can cause trouble without its being detected until the effects have been felt. Certainly, saboteurs can be disruptive, and some will not cooperate even enough to communicate their concerns. However, if change leaders continue to reach out to saboteurs and critics and try hard to hear what the saboteurs are saying, they sometimes will learn a great deal. Among the things to be learned is that some saboteurs were once trailblazers and pioneers, but the leaders whom they had the misfortune to follow did not give them the support they needed and abandoned them at the first sign of trouble.

Resistance and Commitment

Creating commitment to change is not the same thing as overcoming resistance to change. To create commitment, leaders must understand motives. Trailblazers are motivated by novelty, by excitement, and sometimes by the possibility of fame and glory. Pioneers often begin their journey because of intolerable conditions, but they will stay the course only if they become convinced that the new world is really better. Settlers need to know, almost certainly, that the world they are being asked to move to is better than the one they are leaving and that the way to get there is known. And, most of all, they need to know that they are not taking the trip alone.

Stay-at-homes will only move when nearly all of their friends and neighbors have deserted them or when they muster the courage to "come for a visit" and find that they like it better where their old acquaintances are than where they themselves have stayed. Some saboteurs will never come along, and even if they do, they may make the trip as difficult as possible. But as mentioned earlier, saboteurs—quite frequently in my experience—are simply people who behaved as trailblazers and pioneers in some prior movement to another frontier and were betrayed by their leaders. As a result, these people became cynical about the prospects of change or the likelihood that those who espouse the newest clarion call for change really mean it and will stay the course.

Whether the present demand that our schools be restructured will be positively responded to remains to be seen. But I am confident of one thing: without leaders who will stay the course and without staff developers who understand what leads men and women to the frontier in the first place and what these men and women need to keep on going, all our efforts to reform our schools will fail.

Conclusion

Sociologists and anthropologists have long been aware of the effects of structure and culture, but it is only relatively recently that those who are concerned with more pragmatic matters related to leadership and the management of change have begun to consider the systemic properties of life in organizations. The result is that most of what is known about leadership in the area of structural and cultural change is derived from studies of political leadership in revolutionary periods and religious leadership in times of reform and upheaval. James McGregor Burns's book *Leadership* (1978), which has contributed so much to our thinking about leadership and change (Burns originated the concepts of transactional and transformational leadership), is a clear illustration of this type of work.

Until recently, however, structural and cultural change has been viewed by many as largely beyond the direct control of leaders and planners. Therefore, rather than asking, How can organizations be reoriented so that they do new things and serve new ends? leaders and planners have asked, How can organizations be made to serve the ends they now serve more efficiently? and, How can organizations do the jobs they now do better? Given these latter questions, culture and structure are likely to be viewed as impediments to change, rather than as the content that must be changed.

In any event, this condition is now being changed. Over the past fifteen years, largely through the work of authors like Deal and Kennedy (1982), Peters and Waterman (1982), Ouchi (1981), Pascale and Athos (1981), and others operating out of the tradition of the McKinsey & Company consulting firm, business leaders and educators have been made more aware of the impact of culture on performance and the significance of leaders in shaping symbols and traditions. Writers such as Rosabeth Moss Kanter have done, and are doing, much to help us gain insight into the role of leaders in bringing about change in organizations and the culture of organizations, as are scholars like Warren Bennis. Certainly the work of scholars and consultants such as W. Edwards Deming, Peter Drucker, and Philip B. Crosby has given great impetus to this movement.

But the fact remains that, at an empirical level, much more is known about the management of procedural and technological change than about the management of structural and cultural change. This is particularly true in the field of education. Perhaps what I have written in the preceding pages will encourage the kind of discussion needed if educators are to take advantage of what American business leaders are just now beginning to learn: that much of the variance in performance of all organizations and of the people in those organizations has to do with the properties of the systems themselves rather than with the attributes and motives of individual men and women.

Chapter Twelve

Inventing the Future
The Task Before Us

The capacity to establish and maintain a focus on students and the quality of the experiences they are provided, the capacity to maintain direction, and the capacity to act strategically are the most critical components to be attended to if we are serious about developing an action plan to improve the quality of America's schools. In the preceding chapters, ideas, questions, tactics, and tools have been provided that should be useful to the reader who is intent on developing such a plan.

Such plans are not likely to be implemented effectively, however, until and unless the issue of school governance is effectively addressed. Focus, direction, and strategic action result from strong and clear messages from the top of the system as well as imaginative and creative action in schools and in classrooms. The present system of governance does not promote the creation of the conditions necessary to revitalize and reinvent the schools of America. Just as schools must be reinvented if they are to serve the nation well, so too must the system by which they are governed.

Defining the Problems

The primary source of the problems that beset boards of education is the dominance of interest-group politics in the election or appointment of school boards and in the daily operation of board

Parts of this chapter appeared in Phillip C. Schlechty and Robert W. Cole, "Why Not Charter School Boards?" *The American School Board Journal*, November 1993. The author would like to thank *The American School Board Journal*.

members after they have been elected or appointed. Parents of students with handicaps demand that the schools provide appropriate services to their children, regardless of cost; at the same time, the taxpayers' coalition insists that the costs of education be contained, if not decreased. The Religious Right demands that abstinence be the only form of birth control discussed in school, while liberals maintain that condoms should be distributed by the school nurse. In every such case, special-interest groups see acquiring control of seats on the school board as the key to gaining the influence needed to safeguard their particular interests.

Some would argue that all of this is "democracy in action" and a sign that grass-roots democracy is alive and well on the school board. I am not one of them; I do not see the factionalism that typifies the operation of many boards of education as a sign of a healthy grass-roots democracy. This factionalism is harmful to democracy and democratic control of public education; it supports and encourages the view that public schools cannot be reformed as long as school boards and the factional interests they represent control school policy and programs. Those who would destroy local boards of education, and their numbers are growing, appreciate such encouragement.

The Federalist Papers

Speaker of the House Newt Gingrich is quite fond of advising any who will listen to attend carefully to the content of *The Federalist Papers*. Those who would save local school boards might do well to heed the Speaker's advice, at least on this score, and they could do worse than to give special attention to the words of James Madison as he recorded them in Federalist Paper No. 10 ([1787–1788] 1961) In expressing his concern about the potential of factionalism and interest-group politics to destroy democratic institutions, Madison wrote:

> A zeal for different opinions concerning religion, concerning government, and many other points, as well of speculation as of practice; an attachment to different leaders ambitiously contending for pre-eminence and power; or to persons of other descriptions whose fortunes have been interesting to the human passions, have, in turn, divided mankind into parties, inflamed them with mutual

animosity, and rendered them much more disposed to vex and oppress each other than to co-operate for their common good. . . .

. . . .

It is in vain to say that enlightened statesmen will be able to adjust these clashing interests and render them all subservient to the public good. Enlightened statesmen will not always be at the helm. Nor, in many cases, can such an adjustment be made at all without taking into view indirect and remote considerations, which will rarely prevail over the immediate interest which one party may find in disregarding the rights of another or *the good of the whole* [emphasis added].

The inference to which we are brought is that the *causes* of faction cannot be removed and that relief is only to be sought in the means of controlling its *effects* (pp.79–80).

Madison also sees remedies for factionalism.

There are two methods of curing the mischiefs of faction. The one, by removing its causes; the other, by controlling its effects.

There are again two methods of removing the causes of faction: the one, by destroying the liberty which is essential to its existence; the other, by giving to every citizen the same opinions, the same passions, and the same interests (p. 78).

He observes, however, that the first method destroys liberty and the second is impossible. He goes on to argue for controlling the effects of factionalism. Then he writes:

Democracies [that do not have control over the effects of factionalism] have ever been spectacles of turbulence and contention; have ever been found incompatible with personal security or the rights of property; and have in general been as short in their lives as they have been violent in their deaths (p. 81).

Intended Results

Any effort to redesign the way schools are governed needs to promise to produce at least the following results:

- *Increased responsiveness.* Our existing system of governance in no way ensures that all those who work in and around the schools are responsive to the needs of students and parents. The current method of electing school board members encourages them to see themselves as representing primarily the interests of the constituencies that elected them and only secondarily the interests of young people. This problem was not so pressing a generation or two ago, when the majority of taxpayers either had children in school or anticipated having children in school. Nowadays, nonparent taxpayers are becoming the majority of the voting public, and this trend is likely to continue. We have no assurance that the interests of nonparent taxpayers and the interests of children and youths will always be congruent.

- *Continuity of leadership.* As W. Edwards Deming, Peter Drucker, and many others have observed, strong and persistent leadership is a key to continuous improvement. This leadership requires continuity; however, the situation today encourages discontinuity. The rapid turnover rate of superintendents is well documented, and the tenure of individual board members is also becoming shorter. As the lives of board members become overtly political, many members appear to be deciding that one term in office is all that they can endure.

In the past, community leaders often served on the school board as a civic duty. Today, more and more board members seek election to the board in order to *become* community leaders. There is often a vast difference between the operating styles of board members who bring status to the board and those whose position on the board defines their status in the community.

- *Accountability.* It is often assumed that school boards are made accountable through the election of individual school board members or through an appointive process that is somehow responsive to the existing political system. It is easy to overlook the crucial fact that individual school board members—in theory, at least—have no power to cause anything to happen in the school system. Only the board acting in concert can act and cause others to act; only the board *as a collective body,* not any individual board member, has the power to move the system.

Presently the board of education as a collective body is accountable to no one. Indeed, in the case of elected boards, board members, as individuals, can do precisely what their constituencies want them to do and can still cause the schools to produce nothing at all. Gridlock is not unique to Washington, D.C.

* *Equity*. One of the major gains for minorities in the past thirty years has been their increase in access to positions of power and authority in the governance of schools. School boards are, in fact, probably more representative of the racial and ethnic makeup of local communities than any other elected public body.[1] These gains should not be lightly regarded. Whatever changes are advocated must be designed to ensure that issues of equity are addressed, including those related to vital representation from racial and ethnic minority groups.

The Limits of Board Training

Many of those who agree that factionalism is harmful to the cause of democratic control of public schools see the solution to the problem to be simply a matter of electing or selecting better board members and providing better training for board members once they have been chosen. Certainly, high-quality board members and solid training may help to alleviate some problems, but such efforts will not solve the problems, for the problems with school boards are structural; they are not individual and idiosyncratic.

Largely because of the factionalism and political nature of school boards, those who already hold clear leadership positions in the community are increasingly less likely to run for the board of education. Why? Because to run for such a position makes them beholden to the special interests to which they must appeal to be elected. Those who bring status to a board because they are already recognized as leaders in the community become members in order to serve the common interest. Most of those who are willing to

---

[1]Although it is true that the absolute number of minority school board members, as a proportion of all school board members, is disproportionately low, this disproportion is due, at least in large part, to the fact that the vast majority of school boards serve communities with very few minority voters. Minorities are not equally distributed among school districts; this is one of the structural problems that America's courts have been trying to address ever since the *Brown* v. *Topeka Board of Education* decision.

incur political debts in order to be elected have further political ambitions or see themselves as serving the narrow constituency that elected them.

Put directly, because of the way school boards are elected and selected, those who are motivated to run for seats on factionalized boards often are those who want to get on the board in order to gain status, to get public visibility, and to advance narrow causes and narrowly defined interests. Advocacy rather than pursuit of the common good is more likely to be their goal, and all too seldom are the interests for which they are advocates the interests of *all* children. The prospect of improvement in the quality of candidates for election to school boards is not, I fear, very good. It is more likely that, unless the system changes, we now have the best boards of education we will ever have. Training and development opportunities for board members can be improved, and quality training may lead to some improvement in board performance. However, the incentive systems for board members work directly contrary to the direction in which sensible board training would try to move a board.

For example, the National School Boards Association and many state school board associations provide training programs in which board members are warned of the dangers of board interference in administrative matters and told of the importance of boards' playing the role of policy makers, goal setters, ensurers of direction and continuity, and so on. Most board members I know can describe quite well what an effective board would look like and how it should operate, yet school boards continue to behave in dysfunctional ways. Men and women who seem reasonable when they are approached individually somehow become unreasonable in the collective body of the board.

The Charter School District: A Proposed Solution

Most states are now considering some form of legislation that would make it possible for school boards to grant charters to faculties and parents to organize and run schools for the school district under conditions specified in the charter. As the reader is by now aware, however, I am not overly impressed with efforts to reform America's system of education one schoolhouse at a time.

Such an approach may be emotionally appealing and politically popular, but it is simply too slow. Furthermore, the creation of any meaningful number of charter schools assumes an inexhaustible supply of men and women of heroic quality. But heroes and heroines are in short supply (that is why they are so much admired).

That said, however, the notion of having schools operate under a charter or constitution is an appealing one. Such a constitution or charter would cause those who work in the schools and those who govern them to operate on the basis of an explicit consensus regarding who they are and what they intend to do. This leads to the question: Why not *charter school districts,* as opposed to charter schools? Rather than the school board granting charters to others to run individual schools, the *board itself* would be chartered, *by the voters in the community.* (Therefore, under the system I will propose, a board still could grant charters to others if the board itself were chartered to do so.)

The Primacy of Community

Educational systems include entire communities, not simply the children and families who are most directly affected by a particular school at a particular time. Education is about the future as well as the present, the universal as well as the particular. Arguing for charter school districts rather than charter schools acknowledges this and at the same time recognizes the merit of operating schools under the direction of a clear charter to which those who are responsible for the schools are clearly and publicly committed.

Emphasizing the community need not denigrate the family and the values it brings to the educational enterprise. Indeed, properly drawn, a charter system could give the needs and values of families and children a much more central place in the decision-making processes of our schools than is now customary. There is no reason, for example, that a community could not insist that a charter include provisions for ensuring that the needs of children, youths, and families be central to the operation of the schools. Today when boards of education try to use child and family benefit as a measure of worth, they often run head-on into interest-group politics that militate against this goal.

Where to Begin

How might such a charter system be initiated? In fact, any number of approaches might be taken. The first need, of course, is for enabling legislation that would specify how groups could go about forming a slate and creating a charter. (More on this soon.) Once this legislation is in place, any group of citizens that is willing and able to create a qualified slate would be permitted to do so. Of course, the slate would need to be constituted in a manner prescribed by law, and its composition would need to conform with whatever legal requirements state legislature might impose.

When a slate has been formed and other qualifying actions have been taken—for example, gathering a required number of signatures on a petition—the slate would be given a grant to support activity leading to the creation of a charter. Once this has been done, the charter would be submitted to a designated state agency, either an existing state department of education or a special commission created specifically for the purpose of overseeing the operation of charter school districts. The only function the state agency would fulfill at this point would be to certify that the charter submitted was complete; the state could neither approve nor disapprove the content of the charter. Approval or disapproval would be vested in the local community.

When the charter has been certified as complete, the slate of candidates would be in a position to campaign for election, using the charter as the basis for its campaign. Because there would likely be more than two slates, runoff elections could ensure that a majority of the voters would support the dominant slate. This method of election would not excuse *individual* board members from accountability measures. The means of ensuring accountability would be through action by the board as a collective group rather than through direct action by the voters.

The total board would bear the responsibility for monitoring the behavior of its individual members. If individual board members misbehave and are not satisfactorily dealt with by the rest of the board, voters would retain the authority to dismiss the entire board and install a new slate. And if the community was dissatisfied with the functioning of the board as a body, it could dismiss all of them and elect a new slate.

Enabling Legislation

As indicated above, the first step in implementing this idea would be to persuade a state legislature to enact enabling legislation. The content of the legislation would depend on local circumstances and values. However, two essential elements should be included:

1. Issues of equity and of geographic representation are key considerations in the composition of any slate. A slate seeking certification, for instance, might be required to be representative of the racial and ethnic composition of the community, to contain proportionately at least as many parents and guardians as there are parents and guardians in the community, and to be drawn geographically from around the community.

2. For a slate to qualify to stand for election, its members would need to prepare a detailed charter or constitution that they would submit to the community as their official platform. This charter should be quite specific and provide a clear indication of where the slate stands on such issues as these:

- *The purpose of schools, whom the schools should serve, and the intended results of the experiences to be provided to children.* As discussed earlier, intended results should not be limited simply to *learning* results but should be expanded to include results for the family, the community, and the various constituencies that make up the community. (If a slate believes that the only results worthy of pursuit are narrowly defined learning results, it should say so and submit its view to the judgment of the entire community.)
- *The ability of students to learn.* Of particular importance here are questions of how the slate views differences in rate and style of learning and what its members propose to do about their beliefs. For example, will they offer gifted and talented programs and maintain tracking or will they seek to abolish them? What will they do about special education programs?
- *The factors that account for the quality of learning in schools and the degree of responsibility the board will accept and assume for controlling these factors.* Will the board use "lack of parental support" as a rationale for shortcomings in student performance or will it

be the schools' responsibility to ensure that each child has the support she or he needs, whether or not the family provides support?

- *The relationship among schools, families, and other agencies that serve children and youth, as well as the relationship between the schools and the groups and agencies that have a special interest in what children are taught, such as the business community, ethnic- and minority-interest groups, and religiously oriented interests.* Here the issues concern collaboration, responsiveness, and responsibility. What, for example, will the board do to ensure that the needs and concerns of parents are heeded quickly and appropriately? How will the board communicate with and gain input from the various constituencies in the schools? What kind of support will the board expect from these constituencies?

- *The rules, roles, and relationships that will govern behavior within schools, between schools and the district-level office, and between schools and the community.* Will the board's style of operation be centralized or decentralized? If it is decentralized, how will accountability and direction be maintained? If it is centralized, how will responsiveness be ensured? How will relationships with employees be managed? What about issues of employee involvement and empowerment?

- *The obligation of the system to employees and the role of the system in encouraging and supporting innovation.* How will teachers be selected? What qualifications will be required of administrators? What kinds of training will the system provide its employees? What incentives will be provided to encourage innovation? How will the effects of innovations be evaluated?

- *The accountability measures the board will use to judge its own progress.* What measures will the board present to the community as a basis for community assessment?

3. To create a charter that could provide satisfactory responses to questions such as those raised above would require a great deal of work (and probably staff support). Therefore, a legislature would be wise to provide some funding to a qualified slate, in the form of a grant, to create the charter. It is reasonable to expect substantial start-up costs for the first round of charters, because of competition between groups vying to become the dominant slate.

These costs could be controlled by requiring that a slate, to be eligible for a grant, present a petition containing the signatures of some percentage of the electorate.

Possible Consequences

One attendant peril of election by slate is that a special-interest group could put forward a slate and win. Such an outcome would be unfortunate, of course, but with proper recall provisions, the long-term consequences could be minimized.

For the first round of elections, at least, a great deal of lead time would be required for implementation, possibly two or even three years. The entire community would need to be educated about the new process, and slates would need to be formed and provided with considerable training and support. In terms of time and dollars, the start-up costs could be substantial. Over time, however, these costs would lessen and eventually disappear as election by slate became understood and accepted as a part of the fabric of community life. The short-term costs of this method would be outweighed by the potential benefits, including the following:

• The creation of a slate of representatives from diverse constituencies would force the forging of a consensus around some of the more difficult issues that now tear school boards asunder. For example, if the guidelines for creating a slate required racial and geographic distribution, the white community leader from the suburban fringe of an urban school district would need to find common ground with the African American activist from the inner city. Troublesome issues, rather than tearing a board apart at each meeting, would have to be resolved as a condition of forming a slate and during the process of creating a charter.

• The community would be provided with clear choices and a clear direction for its schools. Indeed, if it is properly conducted, the election of a slate could be a major community-building activity. The school system might become a part of the glue that binds the community together rather than the irritant that helps to divide the community, as is so often the case.

• Gone would be the hit-or-miss, start-and-abandon-policy framework that dominates so many boards today and that is caused primarily by the shifting coalitions generated by staggered elections combined with the extreme vulnerability of individual members to the pressures of interest-group politics.

• Election by slate would heighten board concern about and commitment to the success of the superintendent and the school district, because the success or failure of the superintendent would directly reflect the success or failure of the board. (Rhetoric suggests that this is now true; in reality, however, factionalized boards—especially in urban areas—frequently distance themselves from the administration and develop a them-and-us mentality.)

Responsiveness and Accountability

The goal of school reform is to ensure that schools are increasingly responsive to the needs of children and parents *and* clearly accountable to the community. Properly framed, the approach suggested here can serve to increase the responsiveness of schools to the needs of parents and children. When they are handled with care, schools and those who are responsible for their direction can also be made accountable to the community. The method of accountability is one that is honored in democratic societies: the ballot box. The easy way to approach the issue of accountability for boards elected as slates would be to have the boards seated for a certain period (for example, four years) and then to have a new election in which new slates could organize and run. Or election could be for a longer term (perhaps eight to ten years), with provision for direct recall through a petition by a set number of voters.

Relatively short terms for slates have several disadvantages. First, a short term threatens to weaken what should be one of the strengths of election by slate: the capacity of a slate to provide continuity of leadership. Second, the complexity of running elections by charter will necessarily make school board elections, when they occur, more time-consuming and expensive than would be the case if individual candidates were to develop their own platforms and run independently. Thus short-term reviews could be very expensive, probably prohibitively so.

Longer terms of election, with provision for recall elections based on a petition by a proportion of the voters, have some appeal. At virtually any time and in virtually any district in America, however, it seems likely that enough anti-current-board votes could be mustered to cause a recall to occur. All that would be necessary would be a dedicated group committed to a single issue, like the Religious Right. This would not solve the problems that election by slate is intended to solve.

One attractive alternative is to assign a state board of education the responsibility for certifying slates as eligible to stand for election and monitoring their performance. Every two years, the state board would conduct a performance audit and report its findings to the community. In the off year—the year between performance audits—an item would be placed on the ballot asking whether or not a new election should be held and raising the possibility of installing a new slate. If 50 percent plus one person desired a new election, it would be held the following year. This would give new slates time to constitute themselves and would provide the present slate with an opportunity to take corrective action. Such a procedure would make the school board accountable to the voters without submitting it to the kinds of pressures that can now be generated by vocal but nonrepresentative interest groups.

Encouraging Continuity

The procedure outlined here would, if properly implemented, help to ensure board continuity. It is possible to imagine a case in which a board would be installed for a relatively long period—perhaps eight to ten years—subject only to the recall provisions suggested above. If a board member were removed, resigned, or became disqualified, the seated board members would appoint a replacement. This would make the process of board selection somewhat similar to the process by which corporate boards are selected, with the exception that the total school board would be subject to recall and required to stand for reelection on a periodic basis. (It is important to remember that the *board* would be elected, not individual board members.)

Similarly, the superintendent would function much like a chief executive officer in a corporation. It is possible to imagine a scenario in which the charter under which a board operated would permit, or perhaps even require, the superintendent to serve as a voting member of the board. The board and the superintendent together could then be held accountable for the operation of the district. Such a condition would do much to foster mutual support between the board and the superintendent, because the success of each party would clearly be tied to the success of the other.

Election by slate could provide the incentives needed to produce the kind of civic conversation that communities must have if they are to arrive at consensus regarding two of the most important questions any community can address:

1. Who should run our schools?
2. In whose interests should the schools be run?

Equally important, such a change has the potential to ensure the survival of community control of schools and the continuing functioning of one of the most vital of America's democratic institutions: the community-controlled board of education.

The World Is Changing Rapidly but the Schools Are Not

The basic premise underlying this book is that the demands of modern society are such that America's public schools must now provide what they have never provided before: a first-rate academic education for nearly all students. In the past, this was not necessary and the schools did not do it. Indeed, as academic institutions, America's schools have always been suspect. Going back to the good old days will not do the job. The good old days were not so good after all. Going back to the basics will not work either, for the schools of America have never taught the basics to most students, if by *basics* we mean the ability to read critically and with comprehension, to use arithmetic to solve problems as well as to solve arithmetic problems, to speak well, and to reason logically.

What is needed are schools that make it possible for the vast majority of students to do what a generation ago it was assumed that perhaps only 15 to 30 percent of the students could do: think creatively; master intellectually demanding concepts; analyze propositions in their cultural, historical, and economic contexts; reason well; and argue persuasively—in sum, evidence the traits of well-educated citizens who are prepared to participate fully in the life of a modern democratic state and in an economy where the ability to think, reason, and use one's mind well is the key to access and to success. And these things must be done in an environment where most of the assumptions upon which the traditional structure of schools is based are no longer valid.

For example, schools proceed from the assumption that parents understand and accept their responsibility to be partners in the educative process and are positioned in such a way that they can carry out these responsibilities. When this is so, traditional approaches to schooling do work better, and children in these traditional schools do better than other children. Unfortunately, more and more children, from affluent homes as well as from poor families, do not come from environments that reflect Dick and Jane, Mother and Father, Spot and Puff. The structure of the family has changed, but the structure of the school has not changed as well to accommodate these new realities—at least the change has not been as dramatic and widespread as it needs to be.

Schools also proceed from the assumption that children receive the information they come to school with from their parents and from other "moral" institutions, such as religious institutions, that have the interests of the child at heart and will therefore not provide the child with age-inappropriate learnings. Unfortunately, CNN and MTV are not age-graded, and students come to school knowing many things that their parents and teachers do not even suspect they know and certainly do not believe they should know.

Teachers and parents can work hard to persuade youngsters that adult authorities (parents, teachers, and elders) deserve respect and that the youngsters "owe" these sources of authority attention when it is demanded, but the message of *Beavis and Butt-Head* is not always consistent with the message of parents and teachers.

The task that confronts those of us who are serious about reinventing America's schools is daunting. But the alternative to revitalized schools in America is too awful to contemplate. I sincerely hope that some of what I have written here proves useful to the men and women who are leading and will lead the school reform effort in America.

Action Plans for School Restructuring

Memphis City Schools, Memphis, Tennessee

N. Gerry House

The Vision

The Memphis City Schools' district-wide theme for this year is "Building Tomorrow Today." The ideas and imagery conveyed in this slogan capture the urgency and the importance of preparing today's youth to be our city's and our nation's citizens, parents, and leaders for the twenty-first century. We cannot guide our children into tomorrow without first envisioning what we want them to be today. Vision is simply the act or power of seeing things, not as they are, but as they can be. This is the vision toward which we are working in Memphis City Schools (MCS). We want every school to be like our imaginary Promise Street School.

Promise Street is a large urban school very similar to many of our own. Eighty percent of its students are young people of color. The average family income is only slightly above the poverty level. The dropout rate is less than 1 percent. Parent involvement is among the best in the district. Colleges from throughout the nation actively recruit its students and provide scholarships and financial aid. Ninety-two percent of its graduates continue their postsecondary education. Ninety-eight percent of the students are

N. Gerry House is superintendent of the Memphis City Schools. This report was written in 1994. I would like to thank Dr. House for permission to publish this document.

present on any given day. The building is old, but the campus is safe, clean, and well cared for.

The curriculum is comprehensive and balanced—the arts, additional languages, and global education are included alongside mathematics, English, social studies, and science. Increasingly, the boundaries that have traditionally separated these subject areas are giving way to a more integrated approach to student learning. Each teacher in this school has a strong background in at least one subject area specialty and has frequent opportunities to renew and extend knowledge across the curriculum. Together, the faculty forged a cohesive learning community, one where classroom teaching is not isolated. The school provides access to a unified system of social services to ensure that students' physical, social, emotional, and health needs are met. Scheduling is flexible. Students have time to engage in active learning, problem solving, hands-on activities, and resource-based learning.

Ability grouping and tracking have been replaced with heterogeneous grouping, and much of students' classroom time is taken up with cooperative or collaborative work. Teachers at Promise Street spend little time in lecture and more time engaging students in active discussion about subject matter. Students have easy access to advanced learning technologies (including personal computers and appropriate software, electronic networking and search facilities, and calculators). A rich library collection of books, videotapes, audiotapes, and other information resources is also available. Science laboratories are well equipped and staffed by knowledgeable faculty.

Promise Street students have acquired and regularly use the skills of independent inquiry and original research. They read regularly, write often, engage in artistic performance and expression, and use mathematics for recognizing patterns and solving real-world problems. Interdisciplinary work is encouraged and facilitated by teams of administrators, teachers, a library media specialist, and other professional staff. Student assessment is designed to further student learning, not to screen students out of more challenging educational experiences. Teachers have devised and regularly use a wide range of classroom assessment techniques and rely upon student portfolios, projects, performances, and other strategies to provide a timely and accurate picture of student understanding. The curriculum respects students' racial, ethnic, and linguistic background and views this diversity as a source of strength in the academic program. Our mission in MCS is to deliver on this "promise" to our children.

The Strategic Plan

The process of developing strategic goals for the Memphis City Schools took place between January and May 1993. A broad-based group of 64 members, representing a cross-section of community, religious, educational, business, and parental leadership, was asked to serve on the Steering Committee. The participants were divided into seven task groups. The subject matter studied by these groups paralleled the Statement of Beliefs developed and adopted by the Board in September 1992. Each task group added additional individuals to gain expertise or experience. The Steering Committee and task forces eventually had a total of 106 members. An executive-on-loan from Memphis Light, Gas and Water coordinated the strategic planning process.

In arriving at goal statements, each task group utilized a series of steps which included a review of the assigned belief statement to ensure a thorough understanding by all members, suggestions for attaining these beliefs, and a review of existing reports by Memphis 2000 and Shelby County Interfaith (SCI) and the current Memphis City Schools' five-year plan. Finally, it was stressed that each group was to develop goal statements rather than objectives. The latter were to be developed by the Superintendent and Memphis City Schools staff based on the task groups' goals.

Themes which emerged or were repeated most often from task group recommendations included more emphasis on human resource development and training, participatory decision making, focus on students as customers, accountability, and development of multiple measurements of student success. Further, concepts developed by SCI in its report, such as school-based governance, accountability, and schools as the center of community life, are also repeated in goal statements developed by the Strategic Planning Task Groups. Thus, what has emerged can most definitely be termed a community-wide consensus of recommended strategic directions from which the Board and superintendent can chart the course for attaining the mission of the Memphis City Schools.

The following is a brief outline of the district's strategic plan.

The Mission

The mission of the Memphis City Schools is to prepare all children to be successful citizens and workers in the twenty-first century. This will include educating them to read with comprehension, write clearly, compute accurately, think, reason, and use information to solve problems.

Guiding Principles

1. Students, the quality of work provided to students, and the needs of students will be central concerns in all decisions made in the school district.
2. Fairness, honesty, responsiveness, and openness are core values in the district.
3. Decisions should be made as close to the point of implementation as possible.
4. The schools belong to the community and the community's opinions and partnerships are essential to effectively meet the needs of students.

Goals

Goal 1. To create a challenging, supportive educational environment that results in higher levels of achievement for all students

Goal 2. To provide leadership to agencies that serve youth and families to ensure that families have the necessary support to actively work to help achieve academic success for their children

Goal 3. To help all employees become educational leaders responsible for providing quality leadership at all levels and to all publics, internal and external, to achieve quality instruction for students

Goal 4. To hold everyone in the organization accountable for contributing to the educational bottom line: student achievement

Goal 5. To create an organizational culture that treats its people as its most valuable resource, invests in their growth and development, and encourages risk taking consistent with the organization's mission and beliefs

Goal 6. To create within the total community a sense of ownership of the schools and a belief that a quality public school system is an investment in the continued growth and prosperity of the city

The Restructuring Initiatives

Streamlining the Central Office

Memphis City Schools has undergone a massive reorganization to improve the education for the district's more than 106,000 students. A key focus of this effort has been the central office. The major goal of the central office reorganization is to improve and enhance learning opportunities for students and to decentralize authority and decision making.

The top-level redesign was planned to accomplish the following organizational objectives:

1. To make teaching and learning the central focus of the organization's structure
2. To bring the superintendent closer to schools by eliminating layers between the superintendent and principals
3. To flatten the organization by removing layers of the bureaucracy so that ideas and concerns can flow more easily up and down the organization
4. To promote horizontal work groups across departments so that problems are more easily solved.
5. To bring together major functions of the organization that logically fit together so that better coordination of services can occur

6. To shift responsibilities of administrators from traditional telling, monitoring, supervising, and "paper pushing" activities to direct delivery of services to schools based on the needs of students
7. To clarify who is accountable for what and to ensure that they are accountable
8. To establish a dynamic organizational structure that nurtures and supports school-by-school restructuring, professional development, new standards for student learning, and improved forms of assessment

In the new organization, the superintendent is linked directly to the planning and change process, with two associate superintendents assuming greater responsibility for day-to-day operations. One associate is in charge of programs and services and the other is in charge of business operations. Critical goals of restructuring are to place a greater focus on standards for what students should know and be able to do, to develop frameworks and guidelines to link curricula to the new standards, and to develop assessments that are tied to the new standards and which reinforce the curricula. In the reorganization, there is a division, headed by an executive director, whose role is to define standards and to ensure accountability.

The organization also places a high priority on professional staff development. Thus, a division has been created to help teachers and principals understand the demands of restructuring and improve their ability to teach and lead in new ways that will be measured by new standards. The Division of School Redesign and Training/Development, headed by an executive director, is responsible for directly supporting schools in the school-by-school restructuring and the training/development that will take place. Additionally, an Academy for Teaching and Learning is being established and will function as a coordinating center for all the training and development activities in the district.

The new structure eliminates some of the layers between the superintendent and the schools. Twelve cluster leaders who are practicing principals serve on the superintendent's leadership team, and principals are directly accountable to the superintendent. With the elimination of some administrative positions and the revamping of others, much of the decision making which affects the operation of the schools has been moved to the school level. The flattened organizational structure eliminates much of the red tape teachers and principals have long complained about.

Communications and public relations are critical components of any school system, particularly large districts. The reorganization recognizes this by the creation of a division for this function, headed by a director who reports directly to the superintendent. Other functions relating to communications, school/business coalitions, and public information, which are presently assigned to several other departments, are coordinated in this division.

The following changes occurred in top leadership as a result of the reorganization:

- There are no deputy superintendents.
- The four assistant superintendent positions were abolished. Two associate superintendents were employed.
- The three area offices, which include a director, administrative assistant, and support staff, were abolished.
- The curriculum and instruction division was restructured into two divisions: a division for standards and accountability and a division for school redesign and training.

Moving Toward Site-Based Management

After a year of planning and training, the first group of schools in the district was ready to launch the site-based decision-making model for school leadership and reform. As a result of a week-long training program, cluster leaders identified the following seven goals for the site-based decision-making process:

- To focus on school improvement
- To develop ownership in the school
- To help parents feel their contributions are worthwhile by involving them in significant decisions about school improvement
- To involve the broader community, particularly business/ corporate members, in supporting the school

- To improve the marketing of the school's program by increasing the number of persons who are knowledgeable about the school
- To demonstrate that participatory decision making can work effectively
- To improve the quality of decisions made with regard to school improvement issues

Twenty-six schools are involved in the first phase of site-based management. In 1995–96, all schools will be site-based managed.

School Leadership Councils

Each school participating in site-based management formed a School Leadership Council composed of parents, teaching and nonteaching staff, the principal, community members, and secondary students. Parents were elected by parents, and teachers and support staff representatives and students were elected by their peers. Community members were appointed by the council. The numbers of parents and staff (minus the principal) had to be equal. Parent representatives had to have children in the school. The principal, a representative from the parent group, and a staff member decided the size of the first council. Once the first council was elected, it decided on the size of future councils. Informational sessions to explain the purpose, goals/objectives, roles/responsibilities, qualifications, and selection process were held prior to the election for all persons interested in serving on the council.

Training was mandatory for all council representatives. The first councils received ten hours of mandatory training, which was held on Saturdays. Training will be an ongoing process for all council members.

Selection Process for Representatives

The established parent organization at the school was responsible for developing procedures for the parent election according to the following ground rules:

- All parents at the school had to have the opportunity to participate in the process.
- Provisions had to be made for the election of a diverse group, reflective of the school's diversity (racial, ethnic, and geographic, and so on).
- The election had to be conducted in a fair and defensible manner. The parent group needed to determine the balloting process, when and where the election occurred, and who would count the votes.

A similar process, using peer group elections, was used to determine staff and student representatives.

Clustering of Schools

As part of a comprehensive three-year plan to improve services to schools and reduce the bureaucracy, the district's 155 schools were divided into twelve clusters. Practicing principals were selected by their peers to serve as leaders for each of the clusters. The cluster leaders are expected "to work on" and to "work in" the school system while they are working to restructure their own schools as models for their colleagues to adopt and replicate. They are also expected to work with the superintendent's executive staff to identify policies, procedures, and practices that impede change. Cluster leaders meet with the executive staff twice a month to present, discuss, and create solutions to problems. The objectives of the cluster plan are to

- Allow for closer contact between the superintendent and the principals
- Provide for greater cooperation and support among principals themselves
- Assist in implementing the restructuring process
- Set up a peer-oriented accountability system

Cluster leaders have been defined as "first among equals" and charged with the following responsibilities:

- To continue to carry out the duties of a building principal in the building to which he or she is assigned according to the job description for principals
- To provide leadership to the other principals in their assigned cluster and to create a collegial atmosphere among the principals that fosters shared decision making and encourages clusters to function as self-regulating work teams
- To systematically pursue a course of action that ensures that the building headed by the cluster leader exemplifies the qualities desired in all schools in Memphis
- To work with the superintendent and other designated staff to develop and implement policies, programs, procedures, and practices that are more clearly focused on the needs of students

From the cluster schools should come twelve models of exemplary schools that embody the beliefs, vision, and goals of the Memphis City Schools.

School Incentive Grants

Teachers and principals who want to try new ways to improve student success are getting a boost from the district's newly created incentive grant program. The first year, twenty schools received $5,000 grants to encourage and support innovation, creation, and collaboration at the school site. Funds cannot be used to purchase the equipment and supplies unless they can be linked directly to the project.

All applications were reviewed and rated by a panel of teachers and administrators based on the following criteria. Projects had to

- Relate to a goal or objective in the school's long-range improvement plan or be an innovative step toward school restructuring.
- Be creative and innovative. They could not be based on the maintenance of an existing practice or be an initiative that had not been successful in the past.
- Be school-based and developed through a collaborative approach with teachers and administrators. Grants were awarded

to the school based on school-wide initiatives, rather than to individual teachers.

Applications had to include the following information:

- A detailed description of the project
- A rationale for how the project relates to a long-range school improvement goal or is an innovative step toward school restructuring
- The implementation schedule for the project
- A statement of who was involved in the development of the project and how the process took place
- A detailed budget
- A statement of how the project would be evaluated
- A statement on how the program would be maintained if it is successful

This is definitely a risk-taking venture. Teachers and administrators need support as they question the old ways and try new approaches.

Standards and Assessment

As Memphis City Schools moves forward with its mission to prepare students for the twenty-first century, we must look first and most carefully at the classroom, at what we teach and how we teach. We must continually ask ourselves: *Will this give our children what they need to succeed in the coming decades?* This careful systemic look at teaching and learning is getting under way with the creation of educational standards. Learning in today's classrooms is too often fragmented into isolated skills and bits of information that have no cohesiveness. MCS is laying the groundwork to improve learning by implementing performance standards to measure not only what students know but what they can do.

Just what are standards, and more importantly, what do they have to do with teaching the district's 106,000 students? Standards are the combination of knowledge, skills, and abilities needed to succeed in life. And once they're defined and established in city schools, they will have plenty to do with preparing students to

succeed in the twenty-first century. The use of standards will bring
about positive changes in what we teach, how we teach, and how
we assess student progress. For example, rather than always being
treated as passive recipients of information taught only through
lectures, students will spend more time actively engaged in the
learning process.

The standards to be developed for city schools will rely on expanding the "basics" of education: reading, writing, and arithmetic.
The basics will remain in place, but they will be enhanced by the
addition of creative thinking skills, problem-solving abilities, interpersonal skills, goal-setting abilities, teamwork skills, and a lifelong
desire to learn. Without standards, there is potential for disagreement about what our children should learn, and each part of the
educational system is free to purchase different, and sometimes
contradictory, goals. Standards will help us develop an integrated
focus across the curriculum [see Figure A.1].

MCS presently emphasizes curriculum objectives, not performance standards. Instead of just being taught isolated skills with
bits and pieces of factual information, students should be learning
how to put it all together, so they can do research and develop
compelling arguments, or plan and execute projects, or perhaps
draw conclusions from different kinds of data, and be able to think
critically. What will it take to develop these performance standards
and implement them district-wide?

First, community input is essential in developing standards for
MCS. A steering committee, composed of a cross-section of community members, has been formed to determine what the community expects of MCS students. Its mission is to define what
students should know and be able to do in the real world. Members include area employers, college admissions officers, educators, parents, students, service agencies, government officials, and
Board of Education representatives. Data collected by the community steering committee will be studied by school personnel and
used to develop content and performance standards through
grade-level study teams. These teams will include teachers, curriculum specialists, principals, and administrators.

An improved curriculum and assessment system must also be
developed to allow teachers to accurately measure not only what
students know but what they can do. The development of standards for educational performance will prepare our students for

Figure A.1.

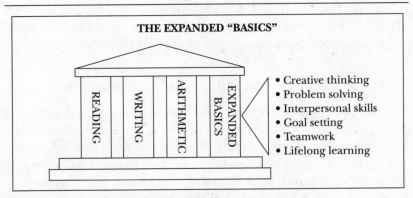

New standards must include the "New Basics."

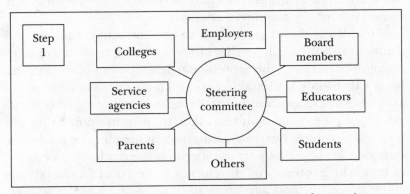

Many sectors of the community will be involved in the development of community standards.

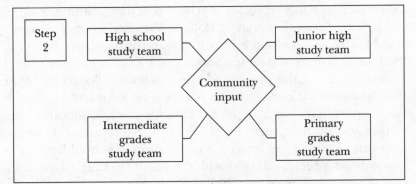

Community standards will provide the basis from which educational teams will develop content standards.

the rigors they will face in life. Teachers will use these standards to guide their instruction. Principals will use them to develop their school improvement plans. Parents will use them to understand the content and purpose of their children's schooling.

Professional Development and Training Academy

The Plough Foundation Board of Trustees has approved a grant of $1.25 million to provide start-up funds for the establishment of a teaching and learning academy. Staff will receive high-quality training, technical assistance, consultation, and opportunities for professional development through the academy. The Partners in Public Education Foundation (PIPE) has also pledged to provide the more than $1 million needed to renovate the recently purchased site for the training academy.

One of the major goals of this academy is to create an environment in which teachers feel they are being treated as professionals. For too long, the professional development of teachers has been a third-rate undertaking conducted under conditions that are not only uninspiring but sometimes humiliating. If teachers are expected to treat children as the important people they are, then teachers must be treated as important people. The academy is intended to serve that purpose. Because the academy is designed to meet the professional development needs of teachers, they, along with principals and other staff, will be part of the advisory team to help get the academy up and running.

One of the first tasks in establishing the academy is to employ a top-notch executive director of school redesign, training, and development. Plough Foundation dollars were used to pay for the executive director's position for the first year. During the second year, the foundation funds will support about half of the salary. Use of private money for this purpose will free up budget dollars for other staff development needs such as release time for teachers. Plough Foundation funds will also pay for books, materials, supplies, consulting and training services, release time, stipends, and conferences and travel. The Center for Leadership in School Reform in Louisville, Kentucky, will work with the district to start up the academy. The center's president, Phillip Schlechty, coordinated the establishment of the nationally recognized Gheens Professional Development Academy in Louisville.

Positions to staff the academy will result from the district's over-all restructuring efforts. Some central staff who have been providing development services to schools will become a part of the academy. In addition, the school district is expected to support the training costs. Presently, the district has a $400,000 budget for staff development. There are also a few other staff development funds in the budget, which will eventually be coordinated through the academy. The Plough Foundation grant also requires the district to house the academy. Plans to identify and equip an appropriate facility are already under way, with support from the recently organized public school foundation, Partners in Public Education. It will take two to three years for the academy to become fully operational.

Urban Systemic Initiative

Memphis City Schools is one of only twenty-five urban school districts nation-wide eligible for a $15 million Urban Systemic Initiative (USI) in Science, Mathematics and Technology Education grant to be awarded by the National Science Foundation. The National Science Foundation established the USI to challenge urban school districts to make a commitment to sustain school reform. Eligibility is limited to the twenty-five cities with the largest number of school-aged children living in economic poverty as determined by the 1990 U.S. census.

Memphis City Schools already has been awarded a $100,000 planning grant to develop a proposal for awards of up to $15 million over a five-year period. The goals of the USI are to

- Improve the scientific and mathematical literacy of all students in urban communities
- Provide the mathematics and science fundamentals that will permit all students to participate fully in a technological society
- Enable a significantly greater number of these students to pursue careers in mathematics, science, engineering, and technology

We're working with the foundation to achieve these goals and develop a proposal that will examine, analyze, and redesign our existing educational system so that all children have equal access to quality science, math, and technology education. This is not an appendage to what we're already doing in these areas. We plan to use this initiative as a hub of reform.

Success for All Children

Memphis City Schools is one of eight school districts in the nation participating in a five-year "Success for All Children" project sponsored by the Danforth Foundation to ensure that young children reach school ready to learn. There is no doubt that the needs of young children must be a priority of this community if we are to increase the academic success of all children. Memphis City Schools became involved in the project after Superintendent Gerry House was selected to the Danforth Foundation's Forum on the American School Superintendent. Fifty school districts were invited to participate, and eight of the twenty-one districts whose superintendents submitted applications were accepted.

A primary purpose of the forum is to enhance the professional development of the superintendents by providing opportunities for them to identify and discuss common problems, hear about pertinent issues from leading experts, develop plans for tackling problems, and establish professional networks. Another goal of the forum is to provide support and resources to school districts in identifying and responding to issues which impact the educational success of children. "Success for All Children" is the forum's first project initiated to fulfill that goal.

The Danforth Foundation has outlined specific program objectives to help superintendents to

- Develop early childhood initiatives that encourage community-wide support for learning
- Become stronger advocates for children
- Develop and strengthen programs to ensure that all children reach school ready to learn, and
- Develop skills needed to collaborate with other service providers

Other foundation contributions include paying up to $2,000 per year for services of a project documenter, assistance from a member of the project advisory board to help develop an early childhood program implementation plan, and a directory of experts who can be contacted for consultation. Community support for the project will be critical but is already evident through initiatives like Memphis 2000, which, in part, hopes to address the educational and health needs of preschool children. One of the Board of Education's goals is to provide leadership to agencies that serve youth and families to ensure that families have the necessary support to actively work to help achieve academic success for their children. These goals suggest that the community understands the seriousness of the problem and is committed to addressing the identified needs.

Finally, the foundation is providing up to $5,000 during the first year to each of the eight participating school districts to support planning activities and will offer districts an opportunity to apply for a foundation grant to help implement the team's early childhood program implementation plan in its community.

Phillipsburg School District, Phillipsburg, New Jersey

School District Profile Team Report

During the winter and spring of 1995, a fifty-member District Profile Team of teachers, administrators, parents, students, and citizens gathered information and ideas about the current state and future needs of the Phillipsburg School District. Ten subteams convened focus group sessions, conducted interviews, and reviewed documents in order to develop a "profile" of the district—a picture of our capacity to begin and maintain a long-term change process.

The subteams held 107 group sessions, conducted 301 interviews, and engaged 1,628 individuals in the process—including staff, students, parents, and citizens. Each subteam's data gathering was organized around one of ten areas of *capacity* for strategic action. Each subteam was responsible for creating a preliminary report detailing *findings* about factors likely either to *support* or *inhibit* the district's capacity to pursue the change process successfully. Each subteam was also responsible for developing a set of *recommendations* for strategic action as an outgrowth of its findings.

On May 1, the full District Profile Team met to share the findings and recommendations for each of the ten subteams. Seven themes emerged from this meeting—cross-cutting themes which we feel must be addressed by those who develop policies for the

Thomas L. Seidenberger is superintendent of the Phillipsburg School District. This report was written in 1995. I would like to thank Dr. Seidenberger for permission to publish this document.

district, who manage programs, who teach in classrooms, who work in and around the schools, and who provide support to students—as parents and as citizens. The first section of this report is organized around the seven themes, now presented as *strategic goals,* and includes the action recommendations proposed in the subteams' preliminary reports. The second section of the report presents the subteams' findings concerning factors that support or inhibit the ability of the system to support change.

We are confident that the many perspectives we encountered are thoughtfully represented in this District Profile, and we believe that our recommendations can be helpful to all those involved in the continuous improvement of the Phillipsburg School District. We trust that the details of the findings and recommendations of the subteams will be broadly read, discussed, weighed, and acted on. As a first step, we offer our thinking to the Superintendent of Schools and the Board of Education in hopes that this District Profile will initiate strategic planning for the district and provide suggestions of specific activities to help us achieve what we envision for our children and our communities.

Assuming that these recommendations are accepted by the Board and the Superintendent as a basis for action, the next step will be to develop concrete steps to move in the directions our findings suggest to be appropriate. It is our hope that in developing these plans and in monitoring progress in responding to these recommendations, members of the District Profile Team will be called on to play active roles. We believe, however, that the planning and implementation stages will require the active participation of many persons beyond those who participated in this initial study. Indeed, a core recommendation of the District Profile Team is that the contents of this report be widely disseminated in the community, and that care be given to ensure that the intent of these recommendations is understood by the widest possible audience.

Finally, we wish to say that we found a great deal to be proud of in Phillipsburg and the Phillipsburg School District. We want to ensure that the positive qualities and practices we found are not lost in the process of change. As we discussed the recommendations and the Profile, we found ourselves feeling that it is "a human document" and "uniquely Phillipsburg." It attempts to be descriptive, not judgmental, and it is written in the language of hopes and aspirations. These are our schools and our communities, and their development is in our own hands. We trust that all who read this document and act on its suggestions will share our spirit as well.

The seven strategic goals we recommend are

Goal 1. Broaden the involvement of staff, students, and the community in understanding the need for change—and in taking part in the change process.

Goal 2. Promote innovation and risk taking at the district, building, and classroom levels by providing recognition, support, and information sharing.

Goal 3. Make "the big picture" visible to all—articulate the ways that components of the system fit together to serve the needs of students.

Goal 4. Vary learning opportunities to better meet the varied learning needs of students—provide high-quality, long-term staff development opportunities for staff to achieve this end.

Goal 5. Ensure the availability of adequate resources to support quality learning opportunities for all students—and quality environments for all district activities.

Goal 6. Broaden public understanding of—and participation in—the life of the schools.

Goal 7. Establish consistent decision-making processes across the district—focus attention on assessment of results.

Strategic Goals and Recommendations for Action

Goal 1. Broaden the involvement of staff, students, and the community in understanding the need for change and in taking part in the change process.

1. Improved rapport should be established between the school district and the municipal governing bodies (that is, Phillipsburg and sending districts). A good working relationship is needed to communicate the problems our student body is experiencing in the community. Just as it is the obligation of the school district to maintain a safe environment within the school facility, it is also the

obligation of the governing bodies to maintain a safe
community environment for its citizens. Our students
relayed the feelings that they do not always feel safe in
the community.
2. Programs that inform and educate the faculty about the
problems of the community are encouraged. If teachers
understand the unique problems of the community, they
will be able to better serve children.
3. The district needs to be proactive in changing the cultural
climate of the community to be more supportive of academics and the arts.
4. A centralized system needs to be developed so that all
members of the educational community are cognizant
of systemic changes that are taking place.
5. There should be ongoing assessment of district-level and
building-level needs to ensure that problems are identified and rectified before they are magnified.
6. There needs to be an increased commitment to diversify
the representative body that serves on various educational
committees.

Goal 2. Promote innovation and risk taking at the district,
building, and classroom levels by providing recognition, support, and information sharing.
1. Prior to implementation of an innovation, adequate training is needed to prepare staff. Goals, objectives, methods
of evaluation, and curricular integration must be a part of
the training process.
2. Teaming should continue in the middle grades and
should be investigated for the upper grades.
3. The district should search for and encourage creative
and new in-service programs that "push the envelope" and
"break the mold."
4. A district policy needs to be created in which procedures
to implement an idea or innovation are clearly defined.
This could include school site-based team input and review by the Education Council (to check impact on other
schools). This process should apply to administration,
staff, parents, and students.

5. Equivalency and waiver processes should be examined as methods of making curriculum more flexible and alleviating the rigidity of state mandates.
6. More interaction should be promoted among staff. Attention to staff morale through celebrations and "paying attention to the little things" should be among the priorities. Building-level action plans in this area are suggested.
7. Innovative programs should be evaluated in a consistent and timely manner, and evaluation results should be disseminated throughout the district. We should not be reluctant to abandon ineffective programs.
8. At the building level, recognition of educational innovation and risk taking by staff needs to be both encouraged and acknowledged. Development of a presentation format in order to share these ideas is suggested.
9. Reasonable risk taking should be encouraged at all levels.
10. Meaningful dialogue should be promoted between the Phillipsburg School District and the Department of Education to engender a collaborative and supportive relationship regarding regulatory requirements.

Goal 3. Make "the big picture" visible to all—and articulate the ways that components of the system fit together to serve the needs of students.
1. The district should continue and expand "cluster articulation" with the five sending districts. Curriculum issues should be at the forefront of these discussions, but all areas should be encompassed. This process could be enhanced through the utilization of exchange days, visitations, and articulation committees with all schools involved.
2. District educators need opportunities for classroom visitations within our own district. Swap days between staff should be a consideration; this would serve to broaden a teacher's perspective of the district's educational endeavor, as well as strengthen collegiality.
3. The district should continue publicity and financial support for innovations.
4. Curricula on every level need to be comprehensively mapped, vertically and horizontally, to eliminate overlaps

and highlight gaps. This will help avoid redundancy and will provide an indication of the time and space available for opportunities such as interdisciplinary units and new courses.

5. The question of possible regionalization must be settled, as it will have a profound effect on all aspects of strategic planning.

6. Issues and ideas concerning flexibility should be articulated among grade-level site-based teams.

7. The community as a whole should be considered a learning resource. Programs like "shadowing" should be encouraged to develop partnerships among the schools, businesses, and the community.

8. Management and decision making at the building level should reflect the district vision and the consensus of all those involved. Programs, practices, and procedures should be frequently evaluated in terms of their effectiveness in producing successful learning and quality work.

9. Interactive in-service programs should be developed to expand staff contact among district buildings. Teachers should be aware of each school's curriculum and programs.

Goal 4. Vary learning opportunities to better meet the varied learning needs of students—provide high-quality, long-term staff development opportunities for staff to achieve this end.

1. Curricula need to be integrated to allow students to see the intrinsic, natural connections between subject areas.

2. Instructional techniques that emphasize hands-on involvement of students should be implemented in every building at every grade level.

3. Different scheduling patterns need to be investigated, studied, and either implemented or adapted. Schedules should be implemented to eliminate the current arbitrary seven/eight-period day and allow the individual schools flexible schedules—to meet student learning needs as opposed to administrative convenience. Restructuring the schedule might provide teachers with fewer students but more intensive student contact.

4. Instructional concepts like cooperative learning, multiple intelligences, and teaming should be integrated into the district's curriculum. Students are very complex, and a "one size fits all" approach does not work. Varied programs are needed to meet the uniqueness of the students.
5. The district needs to investigate alternative staffing patterns that correspond with flexible time scheduling patterns.
6. The district should develop creative ways to meet state mandates in the area of staff development.
7. The district should develop and institute a coordinated and organized staff development program that will encompass the following:
   - Determine a specific number of sessions for each staff member (including administrators) each year to encourage professional growth
   - Develop guidelines for procedures that will ensure common interpretation among staff and provide equal opportunities for all
   - Provide timely notification of available training programs that are relevant, practical, and whenever possible, hands-on
   - Develop and sustain a professional climate that will support risk taking and encourage and acknowledge innovation
   - Provide for communication and sharing opportunities between grade levels and among school buildings
   - Guarantee adequate training prior to the implementation of new programs
   - Guarantee continuity and ongoing training for programs already in place
   - Maintain a clear record-keeping system that will accurately reflect the scope of the program (that is, staff development opportunities, assessment of those opportunities, staff surveys for suggestions for future sessions, program costs)
   - Encourage creative and flexible scheduling for staff development programs and alternative means for reimbursement for training beyond the school day

- Develop criteria so that we may establish a definitive return on our investment

8. Consideration should be given to reinstating a regional
in-service day . . . in order to address the varied needs of
staff members.

9. District support for staff development should be maintained, such as the current board policies outlined in
sections 4131–4131.4 [of the school district policy
manual] addressing credit reimbursement, sabbaticals,
conferences, and the NJEA [New Jersey Educational
Association] Convention.

10. The use of multiple indicators of student achievement,
including portfolios, should be expanded and explored
further.

11. The district should seek ways and means to prevent
staff burnout and to take opportunities to celebrate
accomplishments.

12. The teacher evaluation process, including the forms,
should be revised to emphasize the appropriateness of
teaching decisions as they relate to the needs of the students and the goals of instruction.

13. Each building site team should develop a yearly staff
development plan to support teachers and aides in the
appropriate use of innovative and effective instructional
techniques.

14. Programs emphasizing life skills, job skills, parenting, and
career education should be integrated into the curriculum.

15. The schools should be open to the opinions and needs of
their students.

16. The staff should keep pace with educational and subject-
level academic research. Individuals' staff development
and academic pursuits should be encouraged.

Goal 5. Ensure the availability of adequate resources to support quality learning opportunities for all students—and quality environments for all district activities.

1. Schools need to expand their efforts to publicize and
exhibit quality work of students. Partnerships need to
be developed with businesses, as well as colleges and

universities, to utilize their expertise to challenge students and enhance student learning.

2. The district should begin now to look at options and alternatives for increasing district space. Involve parents, teachers, and administration in these investigations, and weigh the potential consequences of various courses of action.

3. The space needs of all sending districts should be considered. Continue investigation of regionalization or other alternatives.

4. The district should provide leadership and coordination to promote collaborative efforts between school and community services. Set aside district space, as appropriate, and emphasize newspaper, television, and radio communication about collaboration.

5. The district must address the needs and resources required for additional time and space to provide adequately for programs and activities.

6. Student involvement in building-level affairs should be addressed. Students are valuable resources for specific committees and roundtable discussions. Pictures of students and teachers involved in varied school activities should be highlighted in areas of public visibility. Bulletin boards for each school need to be provided.

7. Schools should continue to be safe places for students. The discipline should be strict, fair, and consistent.

8. The district should research and develop plans to expand facilities to enhance the educational opportunities of all students. Creative and more flexible scheduling alternatives and better student-teacher ratios should be investigated to meet the diverse needs and interests of students.

9. Alternate staffing patterns should be investigated to avoid fragmentation and to integrate curriculum, for example, through providing a full-time librarian; art, music, and physical education teachers; and a guidance counselor in each elementary building.

10. Schools need to be more user-friendly, particularly after school hours. The district should examine the potential of expanded building use by community groups.

11. Where certification allows, teachers should be encouraged to move around the district, in order to gain a fuller picture of the school district.
12. Building administrators should enhance positive interaction between Central Office and the buildings.
13. The district should examine "change of use" requests for noninstructional areas.

Goal 6. Broaden public understanding of—and participation in—the life of the schools.

1. The school district should not be an isolated entity. Instead, it should share itself with the community by allowing representatives from the faculty to participate in the activities of civic groups such as Rotary. This would enable the community to see the educational institution not as an isolated facility that houses students from eight to three, but as an institution that is intricately part of the community.
2. Classes for parents or guardians unfamiliar with contemporary methodology should be offered through such vehicles as the Parent Academy.
3. Reaching out to the community needs to be a district priority. Advisory panels could be established for additional input into our educational decisions. "Coffee hours" that include varied community members should be established, both to provide input from the community and to publicize our district accomplishments.
4. Schools should be academic and cultural centers for the community—and should provide opportunities for children and families to learn together.
5. New vehicles for encouraging parent/guardian involvement in the education of their children should be developed and implemented on the building level—for example, Booklinks.
6. Current programs that encourage school/community interaction should be continued and the involvement of members of the community in these programs should be expanded ([programs such as] Renaissance Program, Career Day, PIE (Parents in Education), parent volunteering, and so on).

7. The district newsletter should be published on a monthly basis and its circulation should be increased. Issues should include information about staff development as well as news from each school building. The publication should be used to celebrate and proclaim the accomplishments of the students and the district in general. Additionally, it should serve as an *invitation* to parents, as well as the broader community, to attend staff development and other events and to become involved in the education of our youth.

8. The district should provide opportunities for community members to take part in staff development sessions whenever possible.

9. Local media should be enlisted in pursuing a public education campaign to inform parents and the broader community of the specific purposes of staff development programs.

10. Parents, as the first teachers, should be supported and aided by the faculty.

11. As at the elementary and middle school levels, afternoon and evening conferences should be instituted in the high school to increase parent-teacher contact.

12. The Superintendent of Schools and the Board of Education should develop more proactive means to enhance communication within the district and with the community.

13. The district should develop a comprehensive collaboration policy with youth-serving agencies and other community agencies.

14. A plan for coordinating school and nonschool sports and cocurricular activities should be developed to keep personnel in touch with students' problems and concerns.

15. The district should strive to communicate more effectively its programs, goals, and evaluation processes among its staff, parents, and community.

Goal 7. Establish consistent decision-making processes across the district—focus attention on assessment of results.

1. In order to encourage collaborative decision making and to ensure staff involvement and support in the planning and implementation of training programs, site-based

management teams should be provided ongoing developmental support. Training for site-based teams should include different ways to evaluate the site-based process and educational programs.

2. There needs to be an evaluation within a year to determine if the Phillipsburg community has increased its awareness of and involvement in the decision-making processes of the district.

3. There needs to be a consistent effort from all levels of the educational system to solicit district-wide input concerning problems before, not after, decisions have been made.

4. After a program has been implemented, an evaluation process should be part of the program format to ensure its continuity and viability in terms of original goals and objectives.

5. Awareness concerning the decision-making process needs to be real, authentic, and not just a formality.

6. Decisions that are made concerning curriculum, instruction, and leadership need to be formally evaluated for their effectiveness.

7. Discipline policies and procedures should be reexamined annually by site-based committees of administrators, teachers, parents, and students; this annual examination needs to focus on the goal of discipline as student growth.

8. School policies should be consistent throughout the district. Once policies are established, Central Office should support and not interfere with implementation at the building level.

9. District- and building-level goals should be clearly established to reflect and measure quality work that is student centered. Policies and procedures to support such goals need input and participation from all levels: business, community, parents, teachers, and students.

Team Findings: Supporting and Inhibiting Factors Concerning District Capacities for Change

Capacity 1. To develop, among those who will be called on to lead the reform effort and those whose support must be

garnered if the reform is to be sustained, a shared understanding of the nature of the problems that give rise to the
need for fundamental reform in our schools

1. Supporting factors
   - District educational improvement plans indicate an
     understanding of the need to research current trends.
   - Partnership with CLSR [Center for Leadership in School
     Reform] reflects a district commitment toward reform.
   - District-wide initiative on increasing technological
     activities in all areas of the curriculum is evident.
   - Parents and students desire reform.
   - Parent organizations are in place at all building levels.
   - EIP [Educational Improvement Plan] driven goals fos-
     ter increased parental involvement.
   - Staff development through workshops and visitations is
     encouraged.

2. Inhibiting factors
   - Mutual professional trust is not consistent at all levels.
   - Parents, students, and teachers feel respect is not always
     apparent or practiced.
   - Communication is lacking within schools, between
     schools, and between schools and community.
   - Risk taking is not always encouraged.
   - Limited horizontal articulation is practiced. Vertical
     articulation and articulation with the sending districts
     is virtually nonexistent.
   - Facilities and space are lacking.
   - District has a reputation for lack of closure on many
     previous innovations.
   - Because seemingly "little concerns" of students and
     staff are not always considered worthy of action, the
     likelihood of major changes is questioned by many.
   - The community's understanding of the policies and
     practices of the school district are very limited.

Capacity 2. To develop within the local context a compelling vision of what schools can be and how schools should
be related to the community—a vision capable of earning
wide support in the school district and the community and

consistent with a set of well-articulated beliefs regarding the
nature of schools and the schooling enterprise

1. Supporting factors
   - The teaching staff is aware that new teaching models
     are needed to address a changing society. They are
     acutely cognizant that the structures of society, like the
     family, are under attack. Therefore, new models of
     teaching, which allow greater teacher-student contact,
     are needed to meet these situations.
   - The teaching staff is eager to assume shared responsi-
     bilities with the administration to restructure the school
     district. This has begun with the establishment of site-
     based teams.
   - Staff development is ongoing. Members from all
     levels of the school district have attended conferences
     and seminars to investigate the changing models of
     education.
   - Educational models have changed at the middle school
     level with teaming.
   - Since Phillipsburg was classified a "Special Needs" dis-
     trict, state aid has increased.
   - The Phillipsburg school district has invested in tech-
     nology and related staff development. Therefore,
     Phillipsburg has made great strides in technology in
     all levels of the district.
   - Phillipsburg High School has adapted the state-
     mandated proficiencies. Based on this application,
     new teaching models and assessment procedures have
     been integrated into the curriculum.

2. Inhibiting factors
   - The district is often misperceived by the public.
   - There is a lack of communication between and among
     the district, the parents, and the public.
   - The district budget is usually voted down in the school
     board elections.
   - The physical facilities throughout the district are
     inadequate.
   - The anticipated growth rate is exceeding our facilities.
   - The status of regionalization is uncertain.

- The faculty and public do not believe that the school district has a clear vision for the future.
- Some students believe the faculty does not respect them.
- State mandates that are counterproductive to our district cause undue problems. Waivers are needed to allow the district to experiment with new programs.
- Educational programs do not reflect the "real world."
- There is lack of parent-teacher contact in the high school.
- Hiring practices are often narrow and parochial.
- There is a "silent majority" of teachers whose opinions are never "tapped"—they have concluded that the only opinions wanted are from the favored members of the faculty.
- Some students complained that favoritism exists—that special treatment is given to a select "few." Therefore, they feel isolated from the mainstream of the school.
- It is the perception of many teachers that favoritism exists. Therefore, it is believed that the administration operates on a "we" and "they" level.

Capacity 3. To develop throughout the system a clear focus on the student as the primary customer of the work of the school and on the needs and expectations of those whose support is needed if students are to be served effectively

1. Supporting factors
   - Most members of the school community seem to hold the vision that students (and their parents) are the appropriate focus of the school system, as opposed, for example, to political or budgetary concerns.
   - There are currently programs at all levels that focus on students—for example, OP [Opportunity Period], Barber Shop, TAG [Talented and Gifted], AAG [Almost Anything Goes].
   - Formal procedures in the schools encourage parental involvement on a minimal level—such as progress reports, conferences, newsletters, American Education Week visits.
   - In some schools in the district, depending on the attitudes of the administrators and the staff, the atmosphere is conducive to parental involvement.

- The requirement that site-based teams include parental representation is conducive to involvement, but only for a few parents.
- In some district schools and some classrooms, teachers use a wide variety of instructional techniques; these more contemporary techniques have a good chance of "hooking" more students.

2. Inhibiting factors
   - This vision of students as the appropriate focus of the school system isn't necessarily shared or unified across the district.
   - This vision isn't reflected in some of the most influential practices of the system—for example, scheduling, parental involvement, and the system of tracking.
   - Classroom instruction—especially in the upper grades— seems to be focused on the coverage of material and on adherence to rules and regulations, rather than on problem-solving techniques and creative thinking.
   - Too much classroom instruction is teacher-centered and traditional, focused on teacher lectures and skill-and-drill student activities.
   - Student discipline policies and procedures are focused on punishment rather than on student growth.
   - The overcrowded curriculum fragments knowledge; the lack of curricular integration fosters needless repetition and precludes time being spent on more important topics.
   - The emphasis on sports as opposed to academics is clearly out of proportion to the value of athletics in the life of students.
   - Somewhere around grade six, kids begin to lose enthusiasm for learning; moreover, the "silent majority" are often overlooked by teachers who are focused on the disruptive student(s).

Capacity 4. To develop a results-oriented management system and a quality-focused decision-making process that are consistent with the beliefs that guide the system and that ensure that the measures of quality conform with the requirements of those who provide support to the customers of the schools

1. Supporting factors
   - Student-centered quality work is becoming more prevalent throughout the district. High scores on national and state assessments (SAT [Scholastic Aptitude Test], CTBS [Comprehensive Test of Basic Skills], EWT [Early Warning Test], and HSPT [High School Proficiency Test]) have typically and consistently exemplified student achievement. However, special programs such as PIE, TAG, OP, Developmentally Appropriate Practices, In-Class Support, Teaming, and Accelerated Reader are being implemented to support quality work in schools by focusing on meaningful, relevant, and engaging learning experiences.
   - Teachers are beginning to rethink what students should know and what they should be able to do in order to demonstrate the depth of their learning. Portfolios and multiple indicators of student achievement are being increasingly utilized to demonstrate the acquisition of information and knowledge.
   - Exhibitions and displays of student work within the schools and community illustrate the efforts of teachers to focus on quality work.
   - An increase in the student use of technology has been enhanced through staff development opportunities and continued support in the classroom.
   - Building-level site-based teams have worked to promote quality schoolwork through their EIP objectives.
   - There have been increased initiatives through building-level objectives to involve parents as partners in their children's learning (PIE [Parents in Education], PAT [Parents as Teachers], Learning Thru Play, and Parent Academy).
   - There is a growing recognition of the need to develop partnerships with social and community agencies to support students in crisis, at risk, and in need.
2. Inhibiting factors
   - The existence of district policies and procedures is not enough to ensure quality schoolwork. The lack of consistency and follow-through in implementing policies

and procedures has inhibited the efforts of teachers
to rethink their own practice and to construct new classroom roles and expectations about student outcomes.
There has been minimal teacher input regarding student expectations.

- State mandates are restrictive and inhibit efforts to
change teaching practices.
- Not all staff members feel that they have the professional training and administrative support to implement
educational initiatives. Current teacher evaluation
forms focus on teaching for transmission rather than
teaching for understanding and the professional development it requires.
- The changing roles of parents, the community, and social
agencies in building partnerships to promote high standards of achievement have not been fully recognized.
The cultural climate of the community is more supportive of athletics than academics and the arts. Community
members are more aware of quality work in the form of
athletic achievement and test score results than other
forms of assessment. Parents often identify student
achievement with what they experienced in school.
- A lack of facilities, time restraints in scheduling, and
large class sizes with fewer aides inhibit the ability of
teachers to implement new perspectives of teaching and
learning.
- Expectations for student achievement vary from teacher
to teacher. Clear guidelines are not always established
for students. There is a lack of high expectations for all
students. Students often find work is not relevant, with
too much review of previously learned material (lecture,
worksheets).

Capacity 5. To develop a pattern of leadership and decision
making within the school district and between the school district and other youth-serving agencies that is consistent with
the assumption that teachers are leaders, that principals are
leaders of leaders, and that the community must guarantee
each child the support needed to ensure success in school

1. Supporting factors
   - Site-based teams provide an apparatus for members of the Phillipsburg School District to share in the decision-making process, voice concerns, disseminate information, and develop building-level goals. They have changed the design of leadership, leading in the direction from the vertical to the horizontal.
   - There is an increasing commitment to the in-service process, enabling staff to become informed consumers of knowledge and to enhance their ability to participate in the leadership process.
   - The PEA continues to play an active role in the decision-making process. There is an improved climate of cooperation among the Board, Central Office staff, and PEA.
   - There are a multitude of committees focusing on issues affecting decision-making processes in the district.
2. Inhibiting factors
   - There is no centralized system for disseminating information concerning the decision-making process that is accurate at the various committee levels.
   - While there has been an increased focus on in-service training, there is minimal follow-up and evaluation of results based on in-service and other formats of service delivery.
   - There is a focus is on reactive rather than proactive problem solving and decision making.
   - While there has been an emphasis on less centralized decision making, there is still a strong consensus that decisions are often made and then feedback concerning the decision is solicited.
   - While members of the educational community are optimistic concerning the change in dialogue that is occurring, there is a perception that a select few are truly involved in decision making.

Capacity 6. To develop a policy environment and a management system that foster flexibility and rapid response; that encourage innovative use of time, technology, and space; that encourage novel and improved staffing patterns; and that create forms of curriculum organization that are responsive to the needs of children and youth

1. Supporting factors
   - There are several programs throughout the district that support flexibility—OP period at the high school, In-Class Support, Parents in Education, Barber Shop, PEP, 9th Grade Algebra Program, Advanced Placement Program, and Basic Skills Program.
   - Some school administrators encourage risk-free environments to implement new ideas such as integrated computer technology, team teaching and pod planning, cooperative learning centers and projects, and the development of a six-day schedule at the middle school.
   - Personnel have developed a support system for one another based on mutual trust and respect.
   - Articulation among cluster districts has been initiated to foster such programs as the 8th Grade Algebra Program.
2. Inhibiting factors
   - Differing educational philosophies among school administrators inhibit risk-free environments in some schools (that is, observation policies, opposition to team teaching, rigid schedules, lack of consistent discipline policy throughout elementary, conflict between site-based philosophy and top-down matrix).
   - Required state mandates inhibit flexibility within the educational system.
   - Required state mandates lead to an overcrowded, restricted curriculum, the end result being a content-driven curriculum rather than a student-centered one.
   - Limited space and staff resources result in fragmented programs and fewer opportunities for developing a flexible educational system.
   - The old school philosophy "we have never done it that way before" still exists among some people and inhibits the district ability to change: defeated school budgets, priority for athletics, inflexible schedules, and tracking.

Capacity 7. To develop and maintain systems and programs that encourage systemic innovation and the assessment of innovation within the context of a Total Quality Management framework

1. Supporting factors
   - There is an openness within the district that allows for and supports innovation.
   - There have been successful innovative programs recently implemented (Barber Shop, OP, and Renaissance Program).
   - More money has been devoted to innovations—as in technology.
   - Staff members have been encouraged to make visitations and go to conferences and conventions.
2. Inhibiting factors
   - The district appears to lack a district-wide goal or vision. Each site implements innovations in its own way with little or no overall direction, plan, or curriculum. Consequently, innovations are not uniform in same-level schools.
   - Personnel do not feel they are adequately trained for the innovations (technology, methodology, and In-Class Support).
   - It appears that the district does not have a procedure to evaluate innovations.
   - The innovations appear to be handed down from administration to the teachers, as opposed to ideas coming from the teachers and given to the Central Office/ administration.
   - The district appears to lack a procedure for teachers to share or implement an innovative idea that they may have.
   - There is not enough time or space to accommodate innovations.

Capacity 8. To encourage and support the creation of new relationships between and among those agencies and groups that provide service to children and youth, in order to ensure that each child has the support needed to succeed in school and in the community

1. Supporting factors
   - The district has a well-established alcohol/controlled dangerous substances abuse policy.
   - The district has a well-established student assistance program, called SHARP.
   - There are at least thirty-three programs/agencies that have been identified to serve the needs of the students.
   - In addition, teachers have been identified as a wonderful source for student information.
   - Teachers show a strong interest in being involved with their students. At present some teachers are actively participating in collaborative programs that benefit the students.

2. Inhibiting factors
   - There is no policy about collaboration among these agencies. In addition, people are not aware of their program/policy guidelines and responsibilities.
   - Although there are thirty-three known programs/agencies, many are "building or community specific."
   - In some cases communication of information is prevented by State law. Incomplete information could be detrimental to student/teacher relationships. This can also cause mistrust among agencies.
   - There is lack of coordination of student services/programs.
   - Agencies and schools are not working together as a team for the benefit of the student.
   - Burnout develops among concerned individuals.
   - Space is needed for agencies within buildings.

Capacity 9. To ensure continued support for innovative efforts after initial enthusiasms wane, so long as the efforts continue to produce desired results

1. Supporting factors
   - Excellent programs are available on all levels with key people in charge.

- Business sector is willing to offer assistance to become involved.
2. Inhibiting factors
   - There is a lack of communication among staff at grade levels, in the schools, among parents, and among members of the community.
   - The local media is not educationally oriented, but focuses on the athletics of the schools.
   - Once a key person who was an integral part of a program leaves, there is no guarantee that the program will continue.
   - Evaluation procedures are not built into programs to measure effectiveness.
   - There is minimal staff involvement in community service organizations.
   - There are no policies in place to ensure the continuance of student-oriented programs.

Capacity 10. To provide systems of training, incentives, and social and political support for those who are committed to the objectives outlined herein and to widen the support for the pursuit of these objectives among all members of the community
   1. Supporting factors
      - District newsletter—parents indicated that they read it "cover to cover." (They would like to see it published more frequently.)
      - General feeling among members that teachers should keep up with current trends.
      - Credit reimbursement for graduate work.
      - Building and district site-based decision-making teams/EIPs' allocation of funds for staff development.
      - Recent staff development programs that were relevant and hands-on (computer training) and the use of talented district staff as presenters.
      - Availability of funds to support training/staff development.

- Current programs that encourage school/community interaction (Renaissance Program, Career Day, PIE, parent volunteers in classroom).
- Eagerness on the part of community organizations to participate.
- District staff development policies (4131–4131.4):
  a. Credit reimbursement—twelve credits per year ($26,000 in the 1994–95 school year—twenty people)
  b. Visitations and conferences in 1994–95—$28,000 in costs for substitutes
  c. School closed for NJEA Convention
- Parental feeling that incentives (grants) should be given to teachers who try innovative programs.
- Superintendent and Board support for staff development.

2. Inhibiting factors
- Need to be informed—parents felt that they were uninformed about staff development programs and the reasoning behind them.
- Need for more positive public relations activities.
- Need for ongoing training for administrators, including the areas of interpersonal relations and flexibility.
- Need for training before and during implementation of new programs (SHARP, In-Class Support, Crisis Intervention).
- Need for a more coordinated and organized staff development process, a common interpretation of guidelines on the part of administrators, and timely notification about events to ensure that people are informed and have the opportunity to attend.
- Need for better communication between grade levels in buildings and between schools.
- Need for more sharing opportunities within and between grade levels and schools.
- Need for continuity, follow-through, ongoing training, and assessment of programs already in place.
- Sentiment that length of the school day is too short to implement programs effectively.
- Need for more programs and Career Days with hands-on community involvement—community is not asked to participate often enough.

- Perception of members of the public that they are unwelcome in schools.
- Public perception that half days are a waste of time for teachers and students. The half days also create child-care problems.
- No minimum requirement for training.
- Need for clear record-keeping in the area of staff development.
- State mandates steal time from more relevant programs.
- Need for reinstatement of regional in-service day and the ability to address the needs of all staff members.
- Need for more creative and flexible scheduling for in-service.
- Need for teacher surveys and the opportunity to evaluate and comment.
- Teacher sentiment that programs are often discontinued in a few years. Teachers are hesitant to become involved.

References

Bellah, R., and others. *The Good Society*. New York: Knopf, 1991.

Berliner, D. "Executive Functions of Teaching." *Instructor,* Sept. 1983.

Berliner, D. C., and Biddle, B. *The Manufactured Crisis: Myths, Fraud, and the Attack on America's Public Schools*. Reading, Mass.: Addison-Wesley, 1995.

Bestor, A. E. *Educational Wastelands: The Retreat from Learning in Our Public Schools*. Urbana: University of Illinois Press, 1953.

Bracey, G. W. "The Condition of Public Education." *Phi Delta Kappan,* Oct. 1992, 1993, 1994, 1995. (Article published annually.)

Bruner, J. S. *Toward a Theory of Instruction*. Cambridge, Mass.: Harvard University Press, Belknap Press, 1966.

Burns, J. M. *Leadership*. New York: HarperCollins, 1978.

Chubb, J. E., and Moe, T. M. *Politics, Markets, and America's Schools*. Washington, D.C.: Brookings Institution, 1990.

Corwin, R. *A Sociology of Education*. New York: Meredith, 1965.

Cremin, L. *The Transformation of the School*. New York: Knopf, 1961.

Crosby, P. B. *Quality Is Free: The Art of Making Quality Certain*. New York: McGraw-Hill, 1979.

Cuban, L. "What Happens to Reforms That Last? The Case of the Junior High School." *American Educational Research Journal,* Summer 1992, pp. 227–251.

Cuber, J. F., with Harroff, P. B. *Sex and the Significant Americans: A Study of Sexual Behavior Among the Affluent*. New York: Penguin Books, 1965.

Deal, T., and Kennedy, A. *Corporate Cultures: The Rites and Rituals of Corporate Life*. Reading, Mass.: Addison-Wesley, 1982.

Deming, W. E. *Out of the Crisis*. Cambridge, Mass.: MIT Center for Advanced Engineering Study, 1986.

Dewey, J. *The School and Society*. Chicago: University of Chicago Press, 1899.

Dewey, J. *The Inglis Lecture: The Way out of Educational Confusion*. Cambridge, Mass.: Harvard University Press, 1931.

Dreeben, R. S. *On What Is Learned in School*. Reading, Mass.: Addison-Wesley, 1968.

Dreeben, R. S. *The Nature of Teaching: Schools and the Work of Teachers.* Glenview, Ill.: Scott, Foresman, 1970.

Drucker, P. F. *Management: Tasks, Practices, Responsibilities.* New York: HarperCollins, 1974.

Drucker, P. F. *Managing in Turbulent Times.* New York: HarperCollins, 1980.

Drucker, P. F. *Innovation and Entrepreneurship.* New York: HarperCollins, 1985.

Durkheim, E. *Education and Sociology.* (S. D. Fox, trans.) New York: Free Press, 1956.

Durkheim, E. *The Rules of Sociological Method.* New York: Free Press, 1966. (Originally published 1895.)

Elam, S. M., and Rose, L. C. "The 27th Annual Phi Delta Kappa/Gallup Poll of the Public's Attitudes Toward the Public Schools." *Phi Delta Kappan,* Sept. 1995.

Etzioni, A. *A Comparative Analysis of Complex Organizations: On Power, Involvement, and Their Correlates.* New York: Free Press, 1961.

Farkas, S., and Johnson, J. *Given the Circumstances: Teachers Talk About Public Education Today. A Report from Public Agenda.* 1996.

The Federalist Papers. Alexander Hamilton, James Madison, and John Jay. New York: The New American Library, 1961. (Originally published 1787–1788.)

Fiske, E. *Smart Schools, Smart Kids: Why Do Some Schools Work?* New York: Simon & Schuster, 1991.

Fullan, M. G. *The New Meaning of Educational Change.* (2nd ed.) New York: Teachers College Press, 1991.

Glasser, W. *Control Theory in the Classroom.* New York: Perennial Library, 1986.

Glasser, W. *The Quality School: Managing Students Without Coercion.* New York: HarperCollins, 1990.

Handlin, O. *John Dewey's Challenge to Education: Historical Perspectives on the Cultural Context.* New York: HarperCollins, 1959.

Hofstadter, R. *Anti-Intellectualism in American Life.* New York: Knopf, 1963.

House, E. *Evaluating with Validity.* Thousand Oaks, Calif.: Sage, 1980.

Hullfish, H., and Smith, P. *Reflective Thinking: The Method of Education.* New York: Dodd, Mead, 1961.

"If Japan Can . . . Why Can't We?" Television documentary. NBC News, June 24, 1980.

Illich, I. *Deschooling Society.* New York: HarperCollins, 1971.

Joyce, B., and Showers, B. "Synthesis of Research on Staff Development: A Framework for Future Study and a State-of-the Art Analysis." *Education Leadership,* Nov. 1987, *45*(3).

Koerner, J. *The Miseducation of American Teachers.* Boston: Houghton Mifflin, 1963.

Kozol, J. *Savage Inequalities: Children in America's Schools.* New York: Crown, 1991.

Levin, H. M. "Accelerated Schools for Disadvantaged Students." *Education Leadership,* Mar. 1987, *44*(6), 19–21.

Lortie, D. *Schoolteacher: A Sociological Study.* Chicago: University of Chicago Press, 1975.

Lynd, A. *Quackery in the Public Schools.* New York: Little, Brown, 1953.

Miller, L. "Colo. Bill Would Kill Compulsory Age for School." *Education Week,* Nov. 15, 1995, *15*(11).

Mills, C. W. *The Sociological Imagination.* New York: Oxford University Press, 1959.

National Commission on Excellence in Education. *A Nation at Risk.* Washington, D.C.: National Commission on Excellence in Education, 1983.

National Education Commission on Time and Learning. *Prisoners of Time: Report of the National Education Commission on Time and Learning.* Washington, D.C.: National Education Commission on Time and Learning, 1994.

"Numbers Game at Bausch & Lomb?" *Business Week,* Dec. 19, 1994, pp. 108–110.

Ouchi, W. *Theory Z: How American Business Can Meet the Japanese Challenge.* Reading, Mass.: Addison-Wesley, 1981.

Pascale, R., and Athos, A. *The Art of Japanese Management: Applications for American Executives.* New York: Simon & Schuster, 1981.

Patton, F. G. *Good Morning, Miss Dove.* New York: Dodd, Mead, 1954.

Perelman, L. J. *School's Out.* New York: Avon, 1992.

Perrow, C. *Complex Organizations: A Critical Essay.* Glenview, Ill.: Scott, Foresman, 1972.

Peters, T. J., and Waterman, R. H., Jr. *In Search of Excellence: Lessons from America's Best-Run Companies.* New York: HarperCollins, 1982.

Phelps, W. F. *NEA Proceedings,* 1870.

Rosenthal, R., and Jacobson, L. *Pygmalion in the Classroom.* Austin, Tex.: Holt, Rinehart and Winston, 1968.

Schlechty, P. C. *The Psychological Bias of American Educators.* Faculty Lecture Series. Muncie, Ind.: Ball State University, 1969.

Schlechty, P. C. *Teaching and Social Behavior: Toward an Organizational Theory of Instruction.* Needham Heights, Mass.: Allyn & Bacon, 1976.

Schlechty, P. C. *Schools for the 21st Century: Leadership Imperatives for Educational Reform.* San Francisco: Jossey-Bass, 1990.

Schlechty, P. C. "On the Frontier of School Reform with Trailblazers, Pioneers, and Settlers." *Journal of Staff Development,* Fall 1993, *14*(4), pp. 46–51.

Schlechty, P. C., & Whitford, B. L. "The Organizational Context of School Systems and the Functions of Staff Development." In G. A. Griffin (ed.), *Staff Development: Eighty-Second Yearbook of the National Society for the Study of Education*. Part II. Chicago: University of Chicago Press, 1983.

Secretary's Commission on Achieving Necessary Skills. A *SCANS Report for America 2000*. Washington, D.C.: Secretary's Commission on Achieving Necessary Skills, U.S. Department of Labor, 1992.

Senge, P. *The Fifth Discipline: The Art and Practice of the Learning Organization*. New York: Doubleday, 1990.

Sizer, T. *Horace's Compromise: The Dilemma of the American High School*. Boston: Houghton Mifflin, 1984.

Sizer, T. *Horace's School: Redesigning the American High School*. Boston: Houghton Mifflin, 1992.

Slavin, R. E. *Student Team Learning: A Practical Guide to Cooperative Learning*. Washington, D.C.: National Education Society Professional Library, National Education Association, 1991.

Smith, M. B. *And Madly Teach: A Layman Looks at Public School Education*. Washington, D.C.: Regnery, 1949.

Thornburg, D. *Education, Technology, and Paradigms of Change for the 21st Century*. Mountain View, Calif.: Starsong, 1989.

Urbanski, A. "Real Change Is Real Hard: Lessons Learned in Rochester." *Stanford Law & Policy Review*, Winter 1992–93, pp. 123–133.

Urbanski, A. Speech delivered in Hammond, Indiana, Jan. 9, 1996.

Valentine, *School and Society*, June 7, 1952, *75*, 354.

Waller, W. *The Sociology of Teaching*. New York: Wiley, 1967. (Originally published 1932.)

Walton, M. *The Deming Management Method*. New York: Putnam, 1986.

Williams, R. *American Society: A Sociological Interpretation*. New York: Knopf, 1960.

Index

Center for Leadership in School Reform: partnership with, 269; and personnel evaluation, 185n; and staff development, 252

Central Park East Secondary School: and district capacity, 77

Challenger disaster, 66n

Change: actors in, 210–219; aspects of process for, 204–221; capacities for, 83–85, 100–133, 268–281; common view for, 101–105; conclusion on, 131–133; at district level, 78, 80–82; maintaining, 84, 109–111; motivation for, 18, 216; parallel systems strategy for, 123–124; procedural, 204–205, 206–207; resistance and commitment to, 219–220; technological, 26–28, 205, 207–208; types of, 204–206. *See also* Systemic change

Charter school district: aspects of, 227–237; consequences of, 232–233; funding for, 231–232; initiating, 229; legislation enabling, 230–232; provisions for, 230–231

Chicago, site-based decision making in, 116

Chicago, University of, and Great Books, 34

Choice, in work, 155–156, 173–174

Chrysler Corporation, management of, 67

Chubb, J. E., 78, 168

Cincinnati, Ohio: personnel evaluation in, 185n; staff development in, 99n

Clinton, W. J., 10

Collaboration, need for, 126–128, 130–131

Colorado, compulsory schooling issue in, 191

Commitment: to change, 219–220; of time, 97–99; and values, 73–75

Community: and charter system, 228, 232; as customers, 143, 147;

and districts, 77–80; as guarantors, 128–131; needs of, 148; results for, 199–200

Concept development lessons, in system change, 209, 213

Constitutional Convention of 1787, 104–105

Continuity, ensuring, 119–120, 225, 234–235

Corwin, R. G., 165n

Crane, I., 48n

Crockett, D., 213–214

Crosby, P. B., 52, 56, 221

Cuban, L., 2

Cuber, J. F., 165

Culture: common, 79–80; defined, 41; of management, 53–54; and structure, 134–137, 165–166; and work, 180–181

Curriculum, reforms of, 166–169

Customers: beliefs about, 67–68; communities as, 143, 147; getting and keeping, 201–202; needs of, 140–142; wants of, 142–147

D

Dade County, Florida, and decentralization, 117

Danforth Foundation, 254

Dangerfield, R., 48

Deal, T., 54, 220

Decentralization: divestiture distinct from, 118–119; and leaders, 117

Decision making, site-based, 114–117, 245–246

Declaration of Independence, 107, 216

Deming, W. E., 52, 54–55, 140, 190, 221, 225

Demonstration lessons, in systemic change, 209, 213, 214

Development, need for, 123–126

Dewey, J., 4, 10, 79

Districts: aspects of capacity in, 77–99; assessment strategy for, 90–93; change at level of, 78,

Urban Systemic Initiative (USI) in Science, Mathematics and Technology Education, 253
Urbanski, A., 75, 157n

V

Valentine, 3
Value clarification lessons, in systemic change, 208–209, 210–212, 213, 214
Values, and commitments, 73–75
Vision: in action plan, 239–241; concept of, 62–63; conclusion on, 75–76; as goal, 86–87; mission linked to, 65–66; and strategic planning, 84; for systemic change, 70–73
Vouchers. *See* Privatization

W

Waller, W., 14, 47, 48n, 91, 127
Walton, M., 190

Waterman, R. H., Jr., 54, 220
Whitford, B. L., 84
Williams, R., 165
Winter, W., 10
Work: affiliation in group, 153–154, 173; analyzing, 171–175; aspects of working on, 170–185; attributes of, 151–159, 170–171; authenticity in, 156–157, 174; choice in, 155–156, 173–174; conclusion on, 185; culture and structure in, 180–181; designing, 145–146; dialogue on, 175–176; knowledge, 41–59; language of, 149–151; leadership for, 183–185; and learning, 42–44; novelty in, 154–155, 173; product focus of, 151, 171–172; quality of, 57–59, 168–169; resources for, 176–180; standards for, 151, 172; tacit understandings in, 181–183